Knowing Our Value and Our Values

Knowing Our Value and Our Values
Toward An Ethical Practice of Library Assessment

Scott W. H. Young

Library Juice Press
Sacramento, CA

Copyright 2024

Published in 2024 by Library Juice Press.

Litwin Books
PO Box 188784
Sacramento, CA 95818

http://litwinbooks.com/

This book is printed on acid-free paper.

Publisher's Cataloging in Publication
Names: Young, Scott W. H.
Title: Knowing our value and our values : toward an ethical practice of library assessment / Scott
    W. H. Young.
Description: Sacramento, CA : Library Juice Press, 2024. | Includes bibliographical references and
    index.
Identifiers: LCCN 2024941131 | ISBN 9781634001434 (acid-free paper)
Subjects: LCSH: Libraries – Evaluation – Moral and ethical aspects. | Librarians – Professional
    ethics. | Library administration – Decision making – Moral and ethical aspects.
Classification: LCC Z678.85.Y68 2024 | DDC 025.1--dc22
LC record available at https://lccn.loc.gov/2024941131

Contents

1	**Chapter 1** **Approaching Ethics and Values in Library Assessment**
19	**Chapter 2** **Locating the Values of Library and Information Science**
61	**Chapter 3** **Sites of Tension for Ethical Decision-Making**
115	**Chapter 4** **Characteristics of Ethical Assessment Practice**
157	**Chapter 5** **New Insights into Library Assessment: Surveying the Field**
197	**Chapter 6** **A Classification of Values and a Practical Toolkit for Ethical Library Assessment**
227	**Chapter 7** **Contributions and Future Directions**
247	**Index**

Chapter 1
Approaching Ethics and Values in Library Assessment

Overview

Assessment librarians make decisions every day about what data to collect, how to collect it, who to involve in the assessment, how to engage library users, how to account for social impacts, how to communicate results, and how to align with parent-entity expectations. Assessment is a research-based practice that involves applying the right research method at the right time to collect and analyze data in support of better understanding the library and its community. Assessment decisions are made in complex, multi-stakeholder environments, and often involve dilemmas or tensions among competing viewpoints and values. In particular, tensions arise when demonstrating library value conflicts with adhering to library values. Further tensions arise when values conflict.

This book is based around a central question: *how can library assessment be practiced ethically*? To answer this question, the book features original research that investigates 1) the values that are relevant to assessment decision-making, and 2) how practitioners can put those values into practice to make ethical decisions about assessment. The research findings indicate that library assessment practitioners seek an ethical practice, but are challenged by a wide-ranging and decentralized values landscape that offers many choices for identifying and implementing values. Values can be derived from sources as wide-ranging as national professional organizations to closely-held personal values. Local settings offer distinct contextual priorities and pressures that further complicate ethical decision-making. Within library assessment, our specialty lacks a distinct set of values that speak to our work—a set of values that can complement and integrate with existing values sets such as the ALA Core Values, or local value statements of individual universities, libraries, or assessment departments.

In response to these challenges, this book posits that practitioners can practice ethical assessment by articulating and applying the values that are relevant in their local contexts. This book then offers two new contributions to the practice and scholarship of library assessment: the *Values Classification for Library Assessment* and the *Values-Sensitive Library Assessment Toolkit*. The *Values Classification* articulates 10 values that are relevant to the practice of library assessment. The toolkit is an accompanying ethical aid for working with the values. In summary, this book presents values relevant for library assessment, and a new toolkit for enacting those values in practice.

This introductory chapter provides a brief background to the topic of ethics in library assessment, a note on my positionality and my way into the research, and an overview of the structure of the book.

Motivation and Background

My motivation for examining ethics and values in library assessment can be traced back to a conversation with a colleague in 2017. A fellow assessment practitioner and I were discussing the emerging practices of learning analytics and data warehousing, whereby student behavior activity is tracked, with the resulting data stored and analyzed in a centralized university data repository. My colleague shared that their institution had requested that the library conduct assessment that would produce student activity data to support the university's learning analytics program. I posed a question related to professional library values, asking whether such a practice potentially threatens user privacy and the library's relationship with the student body. In response, my colleague commented that it was not the profession that hired them, but rather their institution. The library was in a position to demonstrate its value to the university by showing the impact of student library usage—that opportunity to convey value would take priority over values-related concerns like privacy. In this instance, my colleague made an ethical decision to prioritize institutional values over professional values. This tension among competing values struck me as a deeply compelling problem that held promise as a question of importance to the Library and Information Science (LIS) field. I had sensed that other practitioners were similarly grappling with values-in-conflict and would benefit from a close examination of ethics and values in library assessment.

Library values are articulated through professional organizations such as the ALA Code of Ethics and the IFLA Statement on Privacy in the Library Environment. Despite these guiding documents, however, library values represent contested ground vis-à-vis library value, because assessment is often focused on demonstrating value and impact to external audiences.[1] As a result, library assessment can tend to take on the values of external audiences. Long-held library values are then less visible in library assessment discourse and practice. Sites of tension then emerge where different values come into conflict. When assessment is practiced at a site of tension, a practitioner is confronted with a decision about which values to prioritize. This decision about values represents an ethical dilemma. These can include pressures and decisions related to market forces and financial measures, third-party technologies, learning analytics, and parent-entity alignment. The chapters of this book will examine these and other topics, with the goal of producing something new to say and do regarding ethical dilemmas, ethical resolutions, and values-based practice in library assessment.

We can see from the LIS literature that tensions among values and competing priorities are not an isolated case, but rather encountered widely by practitioners. The literature also reveals conflicting responses in terms of library assessment practice. Some of the literature advances a paradigm of assessment that that prioritizes the pursuit of library value in such a way that potentially threatens library values, while others propose alternative models that foreground library values in the practice of library assessment. As a key example of the value-forward approach, Oakleaf presented a model of library assessment practice that has matured into a well-developed suite of practices that aim to demonstrate the value of the library to external stakeholders.[2] As this approach has gained prominence the field,

---

1   Oakleaf, "The Problems and Promise of Learning Analytics for Increasing and Demonstrating Library Value and Impact"; Urquhart, "Principles and Practice in Impact Assessment for Academic Libraries."

2   Oakleaf, "The Value of Academic Libraries."

it has given rise to alternatives that serve as a counter-balance, such as the work from Jones and Hinchliffe reasserting privacy as a professional value to be prioritized in library assessment.[3]

The tension between demonstrating value and upholding professional values is a central problem that this book seeks to address. In formulating a response, I am motivated by others who have underscored this tension as a problem that warrants attention. Bourg, for example, describes this tension between value and values: "recent trends towards measuring everything and relying on metrics (usually business metrics) to defend our value is actually likely to contribute to a further diminishing of our true value to our institutions and to society in the long-term."[4] Drabinski and Walter similarly assert that this problem is indeed important: "theory and practice should be mutually informative in our field, and inquiry into 'values' should occupy as privileged a place as inquiry into 'value.'"[5] We can hear calls from the professional community to address this question of value and values, and to generate a theory and a practice for equalizing the pursuit of value and values.

To date, however, a classification of values and an ethical tool for library assessment has been elusive. The path toward resolution is not clear. The field lacks a shared understanding as to which values are relevant to those decisions, and how conflicts among those values are resolved. Given the tensions between conducting assessment that demonstrates library value, and conducting assessment that adheres to library values—how can practitioners implement an assessment practice that speaks both to library values and library value? How can the assessment practitioner community find a coherent vision for values-based decision-making that supports an ethical practice of library assessment? These issues form the motivation and the background for investigating ethics and values in library assessment.

Main Problem to Address

The main problem that this book seeks to address can be summarized as follows. Professional ethics and values are key aspects of

---

3   Jones and Hinchliffe, "New Methods, New Needs."
4   Bourg, "Beyond Measure," para. 8.
5   Drabinski and Walter, "Asking Questions That Matter," 267.

assessment for practitioners to cultivate and strengthen.[6] But ethical decision-making is complex, and the academic library assessment community has not articulated the ethical principles that apply to assessment practice. As a result, library assessment values are not universally understood or applied within our professional community, nor are resolutions to ethical dilemmas and values-in-conflict clear or consistent.[7] Ethical practices are diverse and varied. Relevant values are highly contextual and sometimes contradictory. Different local contexts present each practitioner with idiosyncratic priorities and pressures that further complicate a shared sense of ethical decision-making. Assessment decisions often involve tensions among competing stakeholders and values. Library assessment practitioners can benefit from confronting and resolving these tensions so that our practice can accommodate both measuring library value and adhering to library values.

Main Outcomes

In response to this main problem, I sought to produce new research-based insights and tools that could add to our field's scholarship and practice around values, ethics, and assessment. In sum, my research process showed me that assessment can be practiced ethically by identifying relevant values and implementing them at the right times—applying values helps us to know what the right thing to do is. I expand on this central point through the course of the book, first by delving into the literature in this area, and then by presenting new survey and interview data related to library assessment values and ethics. Finally, I focus the research down into two main outcomes that support a values-based practice of library assessment:

1. *Values Classification for Library Assessment,* a set of ten values relevant for assessment practice in North American academic libraries. I derived these values through an analysis of the literature in LIS, and through survey and interview research involving practitioners working in our field today.

---

6   American Library Association, "ACRL Proficiencies for Assessment Librarians and Coordinators"; Association of Research Libraries, "ARL Assessment Program Visioning Task Force Recommendations"; Schwertfeger and Swaren, "So You Are a New Assessment Librarian—What Do You Need to Know?"; Kyrillidou, "Academic Library Assessment."

7   Kendrick and Leaver, "Impact of the Code of Ethics on Workplace Behavior in Academic Libraries"; Horst and Prendergast, "The Assessment Skills Framework."

2. *Values-Sensitive Library Assessment Toolkit.* The toolkit illustrates the *Values Classification* in a card-based format, and provides a sequence of participatory design exercises for working with the values. The toolkit is an ethical aid for cultivating a values-based practice. The values apply in different ways at different times, according to different contextual factors. The toolkit helps practitioners interpret and apply the values in their own local settings.

The *Values Classification* and the toolkit work together to support a values-based, ethical practice: the classification presents a universe of values relevant for library assessment practice, and the toolkit functions as a practical guide for interpreting and implementing the values in a variety of local settings. On its own, the *Values Classification* is a fixed set of values that can speak to the practice of library assessment. The toolkit is expandable and flexible in use, transforming the *Values Classification* into an adaptable model that can suit changing local conditions. The classification and the toolkit help answer key questions for ethical assessment: What are our assessment values? How do we prioritize them, and when do we apply them? The answers will change according to the unique conditions of each individual practitioner—but if we all ask these questions together, our community can expand and refine our shared vision of ethical library assessment.

The Values Classification for Library Assessment

To provide an introductory frame for the book, I would like to share the end results here—first, the *Values Classification for Library Assessment*. The classification includes ten values relevant to library assessment practice, and the values have been developed from original research data that captured the viewpoints of practitioners working in our field of library assessment. The classification is presented fully in Chapter 6, along with the toolkit. But here in this first chapter, I include the values to give a sense of where we're going in the book.

1. **Alignment**
   Connecting assessment work to existing plans or statements, including organizational mission statements, strategic priorities, or professional values

2. **Care**
   Maximizing well-being, while minimizing harm

3. **Collaboration**
   Building and sustaining mutually beneficial relationships

4. **Communication**
   "Closing the loop" of assessment by communicating an assessment and its results to relevant audiences

5. **Imagining Otherwise**
   Imagining and embracing different approaches to assessment, and ensuring that results support change

6. **Justice**
   Diversity, inclusion, equity, and allyship

7. **Positionality**
   Acknowledging perspectives, positions, and power

8. **Stewardship**
   Ensuring that an assessment reflects organizational capacities—including staffing models, budgetary considerations, and data management and retention

9. **Transparency**
   Clear communication to participants about how data is collected, analyzed, and applied, with choices for participation

10. **Validity**
    Ensuring that an assessment is valid, especially focusing on a right fit between research question and research method

The Values-Sensitive Library Assessment Toolkit

The *Values Classification* then comes to life through the accompanying *Values-Sensitive Library Assessment Toolkit*, an ethical aid that includes exercises and instructions for applying the values in practice.

The *Values-Sensitive Library Assessment Toolkit* is available at the following URL: **doi.org/10.17605/OSF.IO/ZS5C8**

In the next section, I discuss the research approach that I followed to produce the *Values Classification* and the toolkit.

Main Approach: Practical Ethics and Constructivist Grounded Theory

Practical Ethics

Practical ethics forms the main scope of investigation for the research presented in this book. Practical ethics is the predominant approach for ethical decision-making in Library and Information Studies.[8] Practical ethics is concerned with the application of abstract values to real-world scenarios such that a decision can be made when confronted with conflicting paths forward.[9] Practical ethics prompts a process of principled reflection which leads to the clarification of assumptions, alternatives, and action.[10] Essentially, practical ethics poses the question, "what is the right thing to do?" Practical ethics examines the principles or values that are relevant to a decision, and attempts to elucidate ethical decision-making. For LIS professionals, "Values are strongly held beliefs that serve to guide our actions."[11] Further, "Understanding these values improves our ability to recognize ethical situations and to make ethical decisions and balance the competing organizational factors."[12] As a practiced-based profession with a long-standing sense of values, "the heart of a librarian's professionalism... lies in putting these values into practice."[13]

In the context of library assessment, values are relevant because they can also function as standards of goal-setting and aid in decision-making.[14] The practical purpose of professional values is summarized by Peterson: "It is clear that ethical principles and professional

---

8   Budd, "Toward a Practical and Normative Ethics for Librarianship"; Budd, "What's the Right Thing to Do?"

9   Singer, *Practical Ethics*; Buchanan and Henderson, *Case Studies in Library and Information Science Ethics*.

10 Smith, "Infoethics for Leaders."

11 Rubin, "The Values and Ethics of Library and Information Science," 534.

12 Rubin and Froehlich, "Ethical Aspects of Library and Information Science," 1750.

13 Buschman, Rosenzweig, and Harger, "On My Mind," 575.

14 Budd, "Place and Identity."

values are indispensable both in defining long-range goals and objectives on one hand, and in setting policies and determining procedures on the other."[15] Ethics is a system of determining the right thing to do; values are seen as a key component in this system by serving as the basis of deliberation and decision-making.[16] Ethics and values are interrelated elements that guide professional conduct. Attending to values in a process of ethical decision-making is an important element of professional practice: "For librarians, the heart of good practice lies in maintaining the core values of librarianship while adapting to continually changing information environments."[17] Shared values then become the operational principles of an ethical practice, and a standard that can aid LIS professionals in resolving dilemmas and measuring professional success. Then to understand the ethical operations of library assessment, librarians can develop an understanding of 1) the specific decision-points that prompt ethical reflection, and 2) the specific values that are relevant to those ethical decisions.

Constructivist Grounded Theory

The main methodological approach of this book involves applying grounded theory. Grounded theory offers a useful methodological framework of analysis for understanding library assessment. As a research methodology, grounded theory aims to generate or discover a theory for a process as shaped by research participants engaged in that process.[18] The purpose of grounded theory is to "inductively generate theory that is grounded in, or emerges from, the data," with the goal of "generat[ing] or discover[ing] a theory of a process, an action, or an interaction grounded in the views of the research participants."[19] Grounded theory is often characterized by the development of a framework or theory for further research or practice; the researcher integrates emergent categories of analysis into the framework in a way "that specifies causes, conditions, and consequences of

---

15 Peterson, "Ethics in Academic Librarianship," 137.

16 Koster, "Ethics in Reference Service"; Blake, "Ethics: The Other Dimension of Professionalism."

17 Diamond and Dragich, "Professionalism in Librarianship," 413.

18 Creswell, *Research Design*, 83.

19 Bloomberg and Volpe, *Completing Your Qualitative Dissertation*, 49–50.

the studied process."²⁰ In short, the grounded theory researcher develops a theory that is grounded in the data. In the case of this book, I am studying the ethical operations of library assessment. I collected research data from practitioners, and I analyzed that data to produce a theory about ethical library assessment. The theory that I developed features a new classification of values that are relevant to library assessment, along with a practical toolkit to guide the implementation of the values in support of an ethical practice.

I further integrated a constructivist grounded theory approach developed by Charmaz that critically engages notions of neutrality by acknowledging the context and perspectives both of the researcher and the research participants.²¹ As Charmaz instructs, the empirical world that is the subject of study does not exist in a fixed state apart from human experience; rather, we know the empirical world through the shifting contexts of language and action, thus: "No researcher is neutral because language confers form and meaning on observed realities. Specific use of language reflects views and values."²² The codes and themes produced by the researcher stem from an interpretive act that reflects the explicit and implicit assumptions of the researcher and the researched. Hence the grounded theorist does not construct an objective representation of reality so much as a subjective representation of the researcher's particular view of the data. This approach recognizes that the data does not speak for itself, but is given voice through the researcher. As this book is an inquiry into the values and viewpoints of library assessment practitioners, a constructivist grounded theory approach was particularly apt, as it explicitly acknowledges the subjective values and viewpoints of the researcher as integral components of the final research outputs. The *Values Classification* and the toolkit thus represent both my research participants' viewpoints and also my own viewpoints. I expand more on this point in the next section.

Positionality

Constructivist grounded theory involves a process of data analysis that centers subjectivity and complexity. It does not strive to present

---

20 Bloomberg and Volpe, 15.

21 Charmaz, *Constructing Grounded Theory*.

22 Charmaz, 46–47.

an objective or fixed view of the data. Rather, it acknowledges the role of interpretation and context, and strives instead to present a subjective and fluid view of the data. As a part of the interpretive process of data analysis, the constructivist approach underscores the researcher's position in creating their theory: "Constructivists acknowledge that their interpretation of the studied phenomenon is itself a construction."[23]

Following Charmaz, I wish to clearly mark out my perspective and my role in making sense of the data and constructing my theory of ethical library assessment. Charmaz develops this idea further: "Because constructivists see facts and values as linked, they acknowledge that what they see—and don't see—rests on values. Thus, constructivists attempt to become aware of their presuppositions and to grapple with how they affect the research."[24] This aspect of constructivist grounded theory—foregrounding the values of the researcher—is especially consonant with this book, as a focus on values is a centerpiece of the book. The presence of my own values necessarily affects my process of evaluating the values in the research data. As prompts for self-reflection, Charmaz offers: "Who defines this main concern? With which criteria? Whose definitions stick?"[25] Indeed, in the case of this book, I am defining the concerns, the criteria, and ultimately the definitions. Charmaz calls us to make our vantage point explicit. To make explicit my values: my approach to library assessment involves values of student participation, community involvement, social justice, and human-centered design. The system that I create will be inflected with these values.

My presence as the researcher reflects both the problem and the solution of my book. The main problem of the book can be summarized as follows: the library assessment community lacks a cohesive vision for ethical practice. Values and practices are diverse, varied, and sometimes positioned in conflict with one another. Moreover, local settings each offer distinct contextual priorities and pressures that complicate ethical decision-making. Likewise, my own perspective carries its own pressures, priorities, practices, and values. The kind of assessment that I wish to see in the library assessment community influences my

---

23   Charmaz, 187.

24   131.

25   180.

decisions in the process of data analysis. Following a constructivist approach, I recognize that the codes and the system that I produce is a construction that stems from and suits my particular interests. My unique perspective as the researcher-practitioner is therefore a representation of the problem of assessment ethics—I have my values and my context, while another practitioner will have their values and their context. In such an environment of competing priorities and multifaceted values, a unified ethics will remain elusive.

At the same time, my unique perspective as the researcher also presents itself as part of the solution. I bring my own views and values to the question of ethical library assessment and to the grounded theory analysis. In making sense of the data and developing a functional model of practice, I have attempted to smooth over the bumpy landscape of library assessment and bring a degree of coherence to the many values in play. In transforming, through grounded theory analysis, the research data into a model of practice, I am constructing one interpretive expression of a complex dataset. I present the *Values Classification for Library Assessment* not as an objective endpoint, but as a subjective contribution to what is already a continuing community effort. As a future direction, the library assessment community can continue to convene around the question of ethics, and to develop practical responses that can be implemented across the profession. The *Values Classification* presented here can be a point of reference or a prompt for our ongoing, community conversation related to ethics and values. This is ultimately the rationale for the *Values Classification*—as a model for what a values-based library assessment practice can be, either for an individual practitioner or the wider community.

In sum, there is currently a lack of clarity within the field of library assessment as to ethical practice. We know that assessment practitioners make decisions everyday about their work, but less clear is which values are relevant to those decisions, and how conflicts among those values are resolved. There are many values, practices, and contexts—how do we find coherence of vision and clarity of decision-making for ethical practice? This book asks, "How can library assessment be practiced ethically?" To practice ethical assessment, we must first know our values, and then we must know how to recognize and resolve tensions among those values in the course of our practice. The data analysis and the *Values Classification* presented in this book are a contribution to our community's ongoing conversation about ethics and values in assessment.

Structure of the Book

Research Questions, Research Goals, Research Methods

> The primary goal of this book is *to produce a practical tool to support ethical library assessment practice.*
>
> In support of that goal, the primary research question of this book is *how can library assessment be practiced ethically?*

As a researcher-practitioner, my approach to this project involves both research inquiries and practical considerations, with a strong focus on the *how* of the research question. I aim to produce a research contribution that adds to our field's understanding of this topic, while also developing a real product that can be used by everyday practitioners.

To answer this research question and to produce this new tool, I followed a three-step research design: a literature review, a survey, and interviews. The literature review focuses on the ethics, values, dilemmas, and practices of library assessment. A vignette-based survey then further investigated values and ethics in assessment. I analyzed the survey data through constructivist grounded theory. With the resulting insights from the research data, I propose a new classification of values relevant to the practice of library assessment. To make the values useful in actual practice, I developed a practical, creative toolkit that draws from the tradition of participatory design. As a final step of the research process, the toolkit was validated through interviews with assessment practitioners. This research design provides the structure of the book, as described in the sections below.

Chapters 2, 3, 4: Establishing the Values and Practices of Library Assessment

As step 1 of the research, we delve into the literature surrounding the research question. The landscape of ethical assessment comes in three parts: 1) situating ethics and values in the context of LIS, 2) common ethical dilemmas or values-in-conflict encountered by library assessment practitioners, and 3) the ethical practices that have already been developed by practitioners in response to common dilemmas. These areas are examined in Chapters 2, 3, and 4, respectively. The sequence of these chapters is structured in such a way as to establish a ground upon which to build further inquiry into ethical assessment practice: first we establish a theory of ethics in LIS and trace the history of professional values (Chapter 2), then we look at prominent examples of values-in-conflict—or ethical dilemmas—that library assessment practitioners encounter in their work, such as learning analytics, market forces, or online tracking (Chapter 3), and we examine responses that practitioners have developed for addressing the common dilemmas, including community-based assessment and care ethics (Chapter 4). Chapters 2, 3, 4 are meant to be read in a sequence. But these chapters also have a lot to say on their own about their areas, so they can also be read as stand-alone chapters.

Chapter 5: New Insights into Library Assessment

Chapter 5 presents the main research findings from the survey. Building on the literature review of Chapters 2, 3, and 4, this survey was administered to library assessment practitioners working in North American higher education, and it produced data related to the values and practices of library assessment. Chapter 5 provides an in-depth analysis of the data produced through this survey.

Chapter 6: A Classification of Values and Toolkit for Ethical Library Assessment

Chapter 6 contains the main contribution of this book, the new *Values Classification for Library Assessment*, and the accompanying toolkit for enacting values in practice, called the *Values-Sensitive Library Assessment Toolkit*. In this chapter, I discuss the process of translating the findings from the literature review and the survey into the values and the toolkit.

Chapter 7: Conclusion

In the concluding chapter, I offer wrap-up thoughts and potential future directions for continuing research and practice in the area of ethical library assessment.

Research Data

The full research dataset for this project is available via the Qualitative Data Repository with the following title and URL: *Practitioner*

Perspectives on the Values and Ethics of Library Assessment, https://doi.org/10.5064/F6ORSLQF.

Synopsis of the Book

This book is a research-based work with a practical outcome. As a contribution to the field, the book presents research that adds to our disciplinary understanding of professional values and ethical practices in the context of library assessment. In looking at library assessment through a lens of practical ethics, library assessment practitioners can conduct assessment ethically by articulating the values that matter and then enacting those values in practice. My ultimate goal is to aid practitioners in the process of articulating and enacting values. To accomplish this, I first conducted an extensive literature review and analysis to establish a view of the field. I then conducted original research via survey and interviews into library assessment ethics involving members of the library assessment community. Data analysis produced a new classification of values that are relevant for library assessment. These new values are given operational expression through the *Value-Sensitive Library Assessment Toolkit,* a new tool for supporting an ethical practice of library assessment.

Bibliography

American Library Association. "ACRL Proficiencies for Assessment Librarians and Coordinators: Approved by the ACRL Board of Directors at ALA Midwinter Meeting, January 2017." *College & Research Libraries News* 78, no. 3 (2017): 160–67. https://doi.org/10.5860/crln.78.3.9639.

Association of Research Libraries. "ARL Assessment Program Visioning Task Force Recommendations," December 4, 2017. https://www.arl.org/publications-resources/publications-ordering-information/4442-arl-assessment-program-visioning-task-force-recommendations.

Blake, Virgil L. P. "Ethics: The Other Dimension of Professionalism." *Public & Access Services Quarterly* 2, no. 1 (September 20, 1996): 13–39. https://doi.org/10.1300/J119v02n01_03.

Bloomberg, Linda Dale, and Marie F. Volpe. *Completing Your Qualitative Dissertation: A Road Map From Beginning to End.* Third edition. Los Angeles: SAGE Publications, Inc, 2015.

Bourg, Chris. "Beyond Measure: Valuing Libraries." *Feral Librarian* (blog), May 20, 2013. https://web.archive.org/web/20210427003926/https://chrisbourg.wordpress.com/2013/05/19/beyond-measure-valuing-libraries/.

Buchanan, Elizabeth A., and Kathrine A. Henderson. *Case Studies in Library and Information Science Ethics*. Jefferson, N.C: McFarland & Co, 2009.

Budd, John M. "Place and Identity." In *Self-Examination: The Present and Future of Librarianship*, by John M. Budd, 37–72. Westport, CT: Libraries Unlimited, 2008.

Budd, John M. "What's the Right Thing to Do?" In *Self-Examination: The Present and Future of Librarianship*, by John M. Budd, 111–46. Westport, CT: Libraries Unlimited, 2008.

Budd, John M. "Toward a Practical and Normative Ethics for Librarianship." *The Library Quarterly* 76, no. 3 (2006): 251–69. https://doi.org/10.1086/511140.

Buschman, John, Mark Rosenzweig, and Elaine Harger. "On My Mind: The Clear Imperative for Involvement: Librarians Must Address Social Issues." *American Libraries* 25, no. 6 (1994): 575–76.

Charmaz, Kathy. *Constructing Grounded Theory*. London: Sage, 2006.

Creswell, John W. *Research Design: Qualitative, Quantitative, and Mixed Methods Approaches, 3rd Ed*. Research Design: Qualitative, Quantitative, and Mixed Methods Approaches, 3rd Ed. Thousand Oaks, CA, US: Sage Publications, Inc, 2009.

Diamond, Randy, and Martha Dragich. "Professionalism in Librarianship: Shifting the Focus from Malpractice to Good Practice." *Library Trends* 49, no. 3 (2001): 395–414.

Drabinski, Emily, and Scott Walter. "Asking Questions That Matter." *College & Research Libraries* 77, no. 3 (2016). https://crl.acrl.org/index.php/crl/article/view/16508/17954.

Horst, S. Jeane, and Caroline O. Prendergast. "The Assessment Skills Framework: A Taxonomy of Assessment Knowledge." *Research & Practice in Assessment* 15, no. 1 (2020): 1–25.

Jones, Kyle M. L., and Lisa J. Hinchliffe. "New Methods, New Needs: Preparing Academic Library Practitioners to Address Ethical Issues Associated with Learning Analytics." In *Proceedings of the Annual Meeting of the Association for Library and Information Science Education (ALISE)*, 2020. https://scholarworks.iupui.edu/handle/1805/27643.

Kendrick, Kaetrena Davis, and Echo Leaver. "Impact of the Code of Ethics on Workplace Behavior in Academic Libraries." *Journal of Information Ethics* 20, no. 1 (Spring 2011): 86–112. http://dx.doi.org/10.3172/JIE.20.1.86.

Koster, Gregory E. "Ethics in Reference Service: Codes, Case Studies, or Values?" *Reference Services Review*, January 1, 1992. https://doi.org/10.1108/eb049148.

Kyrillidou, Martha. "Academic Library Assessment: Barriers and Enablers for Global Development and Implementation." *College & Research Libraries News* 79, no. 10 (2018): 566–70. https://doi.org/10.5860/crln.79.10.566.

Oakleaf, Megan. "The Problems and Promise of Learning Analytics for Increasing and Demonstrating Library Value and Impact." *Information and Learning Sciences* 119, no. 1/2 (January 5, 2018): 16–24. https://doi.org/10.1108/ILS-08-2017-0080.

Oakleaf, Megan. "The Value of Academic Libraries: A Comprehensive Research Review and Report." Chicago, IL: Association of College and Research Libraries, American Library Association, 2010.

Peterson, Kenneth G. "Ethics in Academic Librarianship: The Need for Values." *Journal of Academic Librarianship* 9, no. 3 (July 1983): 132–37.

Rubin, Richard. "The Values and Ethics of Library and Information Science." In *Foundations of Library and Information Science*, 533–79. Chicago: Neal-Schuman Publishers, 2016.

Rubin, Richard A., and Thomas J. Froehlich. "Ethical Aspects of Library and Information Science." In *Encyclopedia of Library and Information Sciences*. New York: Taylor and Francis, 2010.

Schwertfeger, Ron, and Chantelle Swaren. "So You Are a New Assessment Librarian—What Do You Need to Know?" Presented at the Southeastern Library Assessment Conference, Atlanta, GA, 2017. https://scholarworks.gsu.edu/southeasternlac/2017/2017/2.

Singer, Peter. *Practical Ethics*. Cambridge: Cambridge University Press, 1993.

Smith, Martha Montague. "Infoethics for Leaders: Models of Moral Agency in the Information Environment." *Library Trends* 40, no. 3 (1992): 553–70.

Urquhart, Christine. "Principles and Practice in Impact Assessment for Academic Libraries." *Information and Learning Sciences* 119, no. 1/2 (January 8, 2018): 121–34. https://doi.org/10.1108/ILS-06-2017-0053.

Chapter 2
Locating the Values of Library and Information Science

Overview

In this chapter, I discuss the development of ethics and values within LIS. I begin by tracing the outlines of professional identity as a way of staking out a claim to values. I then turn to the definition and purpose of values, before enumerating the main values present in the discourse of library and information studies. Finally, I present an overview of the contemporary conversation and practical applications related to values, focusing on the American Library Association (ALA) Core Values of Librarianship (2004). Altogether, I found that values and ethics has a deep history in LIS, with practical ethics and applied values being the most commonly-understood ethical lens through which practitioners view ethics in LIS. Many different values are potentially relevant for practitioners according to various contextual factors of different situations. A version of this chapter appeared in the Proceedings of the 2020–2021 Library Assessment Conference.[1]

Defining a Profession: Professional Ethics and Professional Identity

The ALA Glossary of Library and Information Science describes librarianship as "the profession devoted to applying theory and technology to the creation, selection, organization, management, preservation,

---

1 Young, "On Ethical Assessment."

dissemination, and utilization of collections of information in all formats."[2] Starting with this claim that library work is part of a profession, we can briefly examine the attributes that define a profession. To help illuminate these characteristics, we can look to the sociology literature, which provides five basic attributes of a profession: systematic theory, authority, community sanction, ethical codes, and a culture.[3] The analysis presented in this chapter will focus primarily on the ethical code as a professional attribute, as this book is focused on ethics and values. An ethical code is a guide to occupational behavior that carries an altruistic spirit and a public service-orientation.[4] An ethical code can be enforced formally by a professional association empowered to censure members, or informally via pressure exerted from one colleague to another. A code of ethics has traditionally been viewed as one of the basic elements of a profession, along with a professional association that can speak for the members of the profession.[5] A code of ethics or other mode of ethical self-regulation continues to be an important professional marker.[6] Values-based, ethical behavior generates trust both among professionals internally and also between professionals and external parties such as clients or community members who receive professional services. A shared set of values is commonly included in these discussions of professional characteristics.

The LIS literature includes its own discussions of professionalism, focusing on professional definitions and professional ethics. Ethical thought marks a profession, since professional ethics can help shape standards of professional conduct and set priorities when conflicts arise.[7] The boundaries of a profession, in essence, can be drawn by a self-defined standard of ethical behavior.[8] And the field of LIS has been interested in what these ethical boundaries look like—especially regarding shared professional values. As Hansson states, "As a special niche in this research [of library ethics] we find the quest for a shared

---

2   Levine-Clark and Dean, *ALA Glossary of Library and Information Science*.
3   Greenwood, "Attributes of a Profession."
4   Greenwood.
5   Larson, *The Rise of Professionalism*.
6   Roberts and Donahue, "Presidential Address."
7   Hansson, "On the Pre-History of Library Ethics: Documents and Legitimacy," 308.
8   Seminelli, "Librarian as Professional."

set of universal values for librarianship."[9] This niche represents a key aspect of the identity of LIS practitioners. Sager articulates the motivation for this search for shared values: "Without common values, we are not a profession."[10] This idea is echoed by Diamond and Dragich: "Professionalism in librarianship should also be defined largely in terms of values."[11] Connecting ethics with professional identity goes back decades, as demonstrated by Tyler, who in 1948 outlined an LIS professional boundary according to two primary characteristics, both rooted in ethical theory and practice: first, the presence of a recognized code of ethics or statement of principles; second, the use of professional techniques that are based less on routine action and more on the application and interpretation of principles.[12] This conversation reveals the definitional importance of ethics and values for the LIS profession.

Others, however, acknowledge the murkier boundaries of the LIS profession. Librarianship is sometimes referred to as a semi-profession because it lacks certain professional attributes—such as licensing bodies and fee-for-service models—that are present in law or medicine.[13] LIS professionals are neither purely consultants remunerated by individual clients nor purely scholars remunerated by professional organizing bodies.[14] Libraries are structured on an indirect fee-for-service model, in which a librarian is not directly compensated by a patron or a student for their services, but rather through public financing such as taxes or private financing such as university tuition. As a result, professional boundaries and expectations are less clear in librarianship. Librarians are members of the LIS profession and also typically employed by a library organization. Professionals therefore have commitments and responsibilities both to the profession and to their organization, and are influenced by the ethical guidelines of each entity.

---

9   Hansson, "Professional Value and Ethical Self-Regulation in the Development of Modern Librarianship," 1265.

10 Sager, "The Search for Librarianship's Core Values," 152.

11 Diamond and Dragich, "Professionalism in Librarianship."

12 Tyler, "Educational Problems in Other Professions."

13 Abbott, "Professionalism and the Future of Librarianship."

14 Hauptman, *Ethical Challenges in Librarianship*.

Professional ethical codes further demonstrate the nuanced professional status of information workers: Winter notes that ethical codes per se are not of high significance to the LIS profession because neither sanctions nor legal ramifications can be applied by a governing body, as can occur with, for example, disbarment in the legal profession.[15] As opposed to "structurally professionalized groups" such as law or medicine, Winter describes LIS workers as being members of a "normatively professionalized group," for whom an ethical code is not a binding or enforceable document, but for whom ethical issues are still of great importance and are investigated within the profession.[16] As a further example of this in-between professional status, the ALA offers accreditation for graduate education in library and information science, but does not offer accreditation, licensing, or ethical enforcement for library institutions or individual professionals. For reasons such as these, the LIS profession does not fit perfectly into established professional models.

But this question—how does LIS fit into established professional models—has drawn attention and criticism. Drabinksi notes, "In library discourses about professionalization, writers tend to begin with a discussion of what constitutes a profession and then describe the ways that librarianship does or does not 'measure up.'"[17] This attempt to measure up is related to status and compensation. Drabinski's critique of library professionalism and status is then turned inward by Moeller through a lens of exclusion, examining why some library professionals such as credentialed librarians are paid more than other library workers such as front-line staff who may lack high-status credentials.[18] But at this early point of the book, I want to spend this time looking at the professional identity of LIS, because it has ramifications for our collective sense of ethics and values.

While LIS doesn't fit neatly into other professional paradigms, our field shares an interest in ethics and values—and this interest functions as a key factor in our self-definition as profession. For LIS professionals, ethics and identity are closely interrelated. In an expansive work

---

15 Winter, "The Professionalization of Librarianship."

16 Winter, 37–38.

17 Drabinski, "Valuing Professionalism," 605.

18 Moeller, "Disability, Identity, and Professionalism."

on library ethics, Preer tells us, "I believe that a measure of a profession's development is its understanding of the values that govern its practice."[19] Rubin articulates a "value model" of LIS professionalism, whereby "the professional foundation of LIS is not its knowledge or techniques, but its fundamental values. The significance of LIS lies not in mastery of sources, organizational skills, or technological competence, but in *why* LIS professionals perform the functions they do."[20] The *why* of LIS work—rooted in shared values—is an essential attribute of the LIS profession. It's important here to position professional ethics and values as important to professional identity, as it demonstrates a factor that links individual practitioners within the LIS profession. With this connection in place, we can turn to the nuances of a value: definitions, purposes, and enumerations.

Defining a Value

From the LIS literature we can identify a working definition of a value. Our first definition states that values "provide premises for understanding and communication."[21] Values are also seen as "strongly held beliefs that serve to guide our actions."[22] The connection between values and beliefs is underscored elsewhere: "the values of a profession are the beliefs of the group."[23] These beliefs can shift and change over time, as professional values and their definitions are dependent on contextual factors such as political and social change.[24] Values are not fixed, but rather "continually produced and reproduced in the library discourse," and that professional values are "ideas to be struggled over in both discourse and practice."[25] From these sources, we can derive a working definition of a library value as a belief commonly-held and continually refined by members of the LIS profession that guides professional conduct. With this definition in mind, we turn next to the evident purpose of a value in the context of LIS practice.

---

19 Preer, *Library Ethics*, xiv.

20 Rubin, "Library and Information Science: An Evolving Profession," 283–284.

21 Yerkey, "Values of Library School Students, Faculty, and Librarians," 133.

22 Rubin, "The Values and Ethics of Library and Information Science," 534.

23 Seminelli, "Librarian as Professional," 64.

24 Koehler, *Ethics and Values in Librarianship*.

25 Drabinski, "Valuing Professionalism," 606.

Defining the Purpose of Values

In looking at the LIS literature that deals with professional values, we can see an ongoing interest in articulating the purpose of a value in the context of LIS practice. It will be helpful to first outline basic types of values: *regulatory* values that explicitly detail acceptable or unacceptable behavioral norms; *aspirational* values that are defined by abstract goals and represent a professional ideal; and *educational* values that provide specific instruction, guidance, and explanation.[26] These value categories are distinct but interrelated: "Regulatory values prescribe or proscribe behavior, aspirational values provide targets to quest toward, and educational values describe the reasons for prescriptions and proscriptions but also the map toward desired ends."[27] Within LIS, values do not appear as *regulatory*, since there is no explicit regulatory body to enforce norms or behaviors related to the values. Within our professional literature, values appear primarily as *aspirational*, with aspects of *educational*—values are typically presented as ideals of practice, and sometimes come along with instructions for how to enact the values in practice.

Let's take a closer look at the purpose of values in LIS. Sager helpfully outlines four applications of LIS values: 1) To aid [LIS professionals] in addressing the problems that we regularly confront, 2) To improve the preparation of those who are entering the profession, 3) To better articulate to our public and users the important role that libraries and librarians play in society, and 4) To build a bridge between the past and the future.[28] The first three of these applications can be brought together into a category of professional ethics. The fourth application is quite interesting and stands alone with its time-oriented aspect. In the sections below I further discuss these two main purposes for values in LIS: as a basis for professional ethics, and as a bridge through time.

Values as a Basis for Professional Ethics

When values are discussed in the LIS literature, the main focus is the influence of values on current practice. This represents the principal

---

26   Koehler, "Professional Values and Ethics as Defined by 'The LIS Discipline.'"

27   Koehler, 104.

28   Sager, "The Search for Librarianship's Core Values."

purpose of articulating a set of values for LIS—as a foundation for professional ethics. Values guide everyday action and decision-making for LIS professionals. Fister, for example, cites "our traditional values" as a way to guide the "practical steps" needed to build a more just world that LIS professionals wish to inhabit.[29] Weissinger argues that professional values rationalize collective action.[30] Our professional values can provide a framework for ethical conduct, policies, and services.[31] Preer recognizes that practical library operations "require not only professional competence but ethical judgment," and that professional values can help determine right or wrong conduct.[32] For Rubin, "'Ethical' considerations are those involved in deciding what is good or right in terms of the treatment of human beings, human actions and values."[33] This application of values presumes that people "want to do what is 'right.'"[34] LIS professionals have been shown to be committed to doing the "right thing", and see ethics as a key part of professional integrity.[35] For Gorman, "values can be of practical utility."[36] As professionals, "we must know, observe, and use ethical standards that embody our core values."[37] Values are additionally useful because they can also function as standards of goal-setting and assessment.[38] The practical purpose of professional values is summarized by Peterson: "It is clear that ethical principles and professional values are indispensable both in defining long-range goals and objectives on one hand, and in setting policies and determining procedures on the other."[39] The literature indicates that ethics and values are interrelated

---

29 Fister, "Librarians as Agents of Change," 6.

30 Weissinger, "Competing Models of Librarianship."

31 Preisig, Roesch, and Stückelberger, *Ethical Dilemmas in the Information Society: Codes of Ethics for Librarians and Archivists*; Wilkinson, "Principlism and the Ethics of Librarianship"; Koehler, *Ethics and Values in Librarianship*; Rubin, "The Values and Ethics of Library and Information Science"; Dressler, *Framing Privacy in Digital Collections with Ethical Decision Making*.

32 Preer, *Library Ethics*, xiii.

33 Rubin, "Ethical Issues in Library Personnel Management," 1.

34 Buchanan and Henderson, *Case Studies in Library and Information Science Ethics*, 9.

35 Ferguson, Thornley, and Gibb, "Beyond Codes of Ethics."

36 Gorman, *Our Enduring Values Revisited: Librarianship in an Ever-Changing World*, 2.

37 Gorman, *The Enduring Library*, 137.

38 Budd, "Place and Identity."

39 Peterson, "Ethics in Academic Librarianship," 137.

elements that guide professional conduct. Ethics is a system of determining the right thing to do; values are seen as a key component in this system by serving as the basis of deliberation and decision-making.[40]

In applying abstract and aspirational values to everyday scenarios, practical ethics is the main theoretical lens through which values are studied in the LIS literature. Practical ethics is defined as the application of ethical theory to real-world situations.[41] Practical ethics prompts the practitioner to ask how one should behave in a particular situation, with all of the attendant contextual factors and conflicts. Notably, practical ethics is not necessarily rooted in an existing code or a moral system, but rather serves to prompt a process of principled reflection that leads to the clarification of assumptions, alternatives, and action.[42] In the context of LIS practice, practical ethics is seen as vital.[43] Through this lens of practical ethics, the heart of library professional identity is putting values into practice.[44] A good practice is evident through the act of maintaining core values while adapting to continually changing information environments.[45] Understanding and applying values improves the professional ability to recognize ethical situations and to make ethical decisions that balance different competing factors.[46] In defining goals and setting policy, values can be indispensable.[47] Shared values then become the operational principles of an ethical practice, and a standard to which LIS professionals can resolve dilemmas and measure professional success.

In addition to signaling internally, professional values can also serve as a tool for coherent communication and engagement with those outside of the LIS profession. In this there is a secondary call to share our values to external stakeholders such as publics, campus entities, and

---

[40] Koster, "Ethics in Reference Service"; Blake, "Ethics: The Other Dimension of Professionalism."

[41] Singer, *Practical Ethics*; Buchanan and Henderson, *Case Studies in Library and Information Science Ethics*.

[42] Smith, "Infoethics for Leaders."

[43] Budd, "Toward a Practical and Normative Ethics for Librarianship"; Budd, "What's the Right Thing to Do?"

[44] Buschman, Rosenzweig, and Harger, "On My Mind," 575.

[45] Diamond and Dragich, "Professionalism in Librarianship," 413.

[46] Rubin and Froehlich, "Ethical Aspects of Library and Information Science," 1750.

[47] Peterson, "Ethics in Academic Librarianship," 137.

the wider community so as to communicate our traditional and lasting value as a profession and to build trust.[48] Sager's description of library values that can be used "to better articulate to our public and users the important role that libraries and librarians play in society"[49] is reinforced by Seminelli, who argues that LIS values themselves represent the value that libraries can bring to the community, and that librarians can focus on communicating values to our external communities as a bulwark against, for example, budget cuts.[50] Library values become a framework of communication for translating our work to external stakeholders and users.[51] By adhering to a set of traditional and aspirational values, LIS can gain a "greater understanding of our role in society, and society gains a clearer understanding of the importance of the library and information science profession."[52] In addition to providing standards for professionals to adhere to, values are important for communicating a professional identity with the wider world.[53]

Values as a Stabilizing Force through Times of Change

We've now seen how values can function as a guide for *current* practice. If we continue looking, the library literature reveals a further interest in examining values as influential for *past* and *future* practice. When looking to the past and into the future, values can function as a means of creating stability through time, especially in the face of change driven by technology or economic pressures. In short, enumerating and adhering to a set of professional values reflects a desire to root the unknown future of libraries in a knowable past. This concept of values as both the foundation and the future of ethical LIS practice is a concept that most clearly emerged toward the turn of the millennium.[54] While writers in LIS had shown some degree of interest

---

48 Finks, "Librarianship Needs a New Code of Professional Ethics"; Oppenheim and Pollecutt, "Professional Associations and Ethical Issues in LIS."

49 Sager, "The Search for Librarianship's Core Values," 149.

50 Seminelli, "Librarian as Professional."

51 Delaney and Bates, "Envisioning the Academic Library."

52 Sager et al., "A Question of Values," 218.

53 Foster and McMenemy, "Do Librarians Have a Shared Set of Values?"

54 Koehler, "Trends of Library Associations and Ethics in the US."

in values and ethics throughout the 20th century, that interest steadily increased as the year 2000 approached. This auspicious date prompted ethical reflection on the part of librarians, with the two decades leading up to the turn of the 21st century seeing "a dramatic increase in the number of articles dealing with ethics and librarianship"[55] Until this point, ethics had not been one of our "burning professional issues."[56] But engagement with ethics intensified as a surge of technology-driven change at the end of the 20th century generated new professional motivation toward values and ethics.

Information technologies looked poised to transform the information professions. Several writers draw attention to the rapid technological change of the coming 21st century, arguing that the LIS profession is being fundamentally redefined and restructured through technological, political, and social change.[57] With the introduction of modern information technologies, the production of information dramatically increased in both amount and type, presenting new challenges for LIS professionals in terms of collection development, reference services, online and in-person access, and preservation. Technologies that developed toward the turn of the 21st century promised a sea change, and so the decade of the 1990s was a time of concern for many LIS professionals related to the future of their practice.

The contemporary history of this era and the intensity of its concern is recounted by Sapp and Gilmour: "In librarianship, as indeed in almost all of modern society, the year 2000 was a numerically arbitrary but symbolically significant milestone…by 1995, librarians had been bombarded with a hailstorm of predictions about their future."[58] One such prediction comes from Abbot in a 1993 Plenary Lecture on the President's Program at the American Library Association: "To the profession as a whole, the central challenges lie in embracing the various information technologies of the future and the groups that service

---

55 Hauptman, *Ethics and Librarianship*, 2.

56 Lindsey and Prentice, *Professional Ethics and Librarians*, 19.

57 Christians, "Information Ethics in a Complicated Age"; Dougherty, "On My Mind"; Danner, "Redefining a Profession"; Symons and Stoffle, "When Values Conflict"; Koehler and Pemberton, "A Search for Core Values"; Dole and Hurych, "Values for Librarians in the Information Age"; Gorman, *The Enduring Library*.

58 Sapp and Gilmour, "A Brief History of the Future of Academic Libraries," 23.

them."[59] This was a central question for LIS professionals at this time: how best to understand and evolve with the rapid change brought on by information technologies.

A focus on professional values emerged as one path for addressing technology-driven change. Seeing that the rise of technology could alter the work of librarianship, members of the library profession issued appeals to define and emphasize values as markers of continuity.[60] Crowe and Anthes describe the expected impact of technology on ethical practice: "Academic librarians face a new working environment engendered by the rapid growth of information and advances in information technology…value conflicts and ethical dilemmas arise from the more active, substantive role required of the academic librarian by technological developments."[61] As practice in our field was being redefined by the computer and other networked technologies, values became a means of establishing stability through change. This is important to observe. LIS values are seen as a stabilizing force that can hold the profession together internally, as our practice undergoes significant change brought by external factors.

Through uncertain change, shared values can guide the profession into the future, serving as the foundation of professional activities and services.[62] In response to technology-driven change, Hauptman, for example, appeals to professional values as a guide: "Understanding foundational structures and principles in addition to technological gadgetry and at least attempting to foresee where we are heading will help information workers to serve their constituencies in a productive, legal, and ethical manner."[63] The foundational purpose of values in the face of professional uncertainty was further reflected through major organizing bodies, as evidenced by the then-President of the ALA Association of College and Research Libraries (ACRL) identifying the theme of 1997-1998 as *Facing the Millennium: Values for the*

---

59 Abbott, "Professionalism and the Future of Librarianship," 442.
60 Koehler, *Ethics and Values in Librarianship*.
61 Crowe and Anthes, "The Academic Librarian and Information Technology," 123.
62 Symons and Stoffle, "When Values Conflict."
63 Hauptman, *Ethics and Librarianship*, 14.

Electronic Information Age, and asserting that "traditional values are still relevant in the electronic information age."[64]

While technology was viewed as the primary driver of change in the 1990s, other forces such as market pressures and business logic have been viewed as a threat to alter LIS practice.[65] Budget reductions and resource scarcity, for example, prompted difficult decisions related to services and collections.[66] LIS professionals in the 1990s did not have an agreed-upon set of shared values. During this time of change, values were recognized as producing a steadying effect, so that practitioners would avoid making "different ethical considerations in hard times such as these when values and principles are harder to identify and prioritize."[67] Hauptman reiterates the call for a more values-based practice: "Ethics matters because it allows us to implement our divergent values," and that "if we adhere to traditional values, we will not be seduced into believing that when institutions change so must our commitments."[68] In times of perceived change such as with technology in the 1990s and political forces of the 2010s, LIS professionals seek to reclaim and reaffirm values in order to reestablish norms of professional practice and identity. Then-president of ALA Barbara J. Ford conveyed this idea directly in the president's message of 1998:

> Ethical principles and professional values guide the work of librarians. We have a special obligation to ensure the free flow of information and ideas now and to generations in the new millennium. In the emerging Digital Age, the identity and integrity of our profession are being challenged, and we must constantly reexamine our professional vision in order to seize every opportunity to put our values and ethics into practice.[69]

This call for a values-based practice is carried forward in 2014 by the then-President of the ALA's Reference and User Services Association, who—in an article titled "Continuity and Change, or, Will I Ever be

---

64 Hisle, "Values for the Electronic Information Age," 764.
65 Fister, "Librarians as Agents of Change"; Bourg, "Beyond Measure."
66 Bushing, "Acquisition Ethics."
67 Bushing, 52.
68 Hauptman, *Ethics and Librarianship*, 136–37.
69 Ford, "ALA President's Message," 54.

Prepared for What Comes Next?"—remarks, "The enduring principles that are the foundation of the library reassure me that libraries have a future, no matter the changes around us."[70] Through periods of professional uncertainty or difficulty, values are seen as a grounding element for the LIS professional.

Reflecting the aspirational purpose of values, Froehlich says that values represent an abstract, ideal professional, and that the habitual actions of librarians and library users are the measure of realizing values.[71] In this way, articulating and adhering to values is a means of connecting the past and the future together in the present. This approach seeks to establish a recognizable LIS professional through a continuum of practice, what Gorman calls a "golden thread" that defines librarianship as a profession no matter where it is practiced.[72] Sager et al. use additional metaphor to variously describe values as the "cement that holds the profession together," and "a global positioning system" that serve as "landmarks" directing LIS professions toward a shared future.[73] The quest for LIS values is motivated by a desire for stability, with a shared set of values functioning as a compass for current and future LIS professionals. Values then function to maintain a tradition of library practice into a future that is uncertain and quickly changing.

We have now established a sequence of points: LIS possesses certain key characteristics of a profession, notably an interest in ethics and set of shared values; values are defined as commonly-held beliefs of members of a profession; values function to guide ethical action during everyday situations, and to connect past and future practice. Now that we have discussed the role that values play in our profession, it will be helpful to ask—which values are we talking about exactly? This was a crucially important question in the LIS literature, especially around the turn of century as technology-related change began to affect the profession. Let us turn next to enumerating the common values.

---

70 Kern, "Continuity and Change, or, Will I Ever Be Prepared for What Comes Next?," 285.

71 "Intellectual Freedom, Ethical Deliberation and Codes of Ethics."

72 Gorman, *The Enduring Library*.

73 Sager et al., "A Question of Values."

Enumerating the Common Values

Value Studies in the 20th century: Toward Shared Values

The earliest published set of values for the LIS profession is most cited as Ranganthan's *Five Laws of Library Science*:

- Books Are For Use
- Every Reader His/Her Book
- Every Book Its Reader
- Save The Time Of The Reader
- The Library Is A Growing Organism[74]

Following Ranganathan, discussion of values appeared infrequently throughout the 20th century.[75] During these decades, a few LIS writers issued calls-to-action for other members of the profession to commit greater attention and resources toward the study of values and their applications. *Library Journal* editor Moon, for example, insisted that "the [LIS] profession does have ethical questions to grapple with and should find a way to formulate a position on some of them," offering a number of potential ethical questions for consideration, such as "automation and its potential for massive invasion of privacy."[76] To resolve our professional dilemmas, Moon proposes a renewed definition of the LIS ethos, a fresh ethical code, or some other mechanism that can help LIS professionals better enact a values-based practice. Cohen furthermore tells LIS professionals that "we would deal better with our daily tasks if we thought a little more often and a little harder about the principles and purposes that underlie our work."[77] Peterson notes a similar lack of professional consensus around the principles that define our practice: "Librarianship, claiming status among the professions, has struggled over the years to clarify and arrive at a set of ethical principles."[78] Indeed, the LIS profession did not demonstrate a wide-spread interest in articulating the underlying principles of the work until, as

---

[74] Ranganathan, *The Five Laws of Library Science*.

[75] McMullen, "Research in Backgrounds in Librarianship"; Benge, *Libraries and Cultural Change*; Atherton, *Putting Knowledge to Work*.

[76] Moon, "Ethical Bones," 131.

[77] Cohen, "President's Page," 1.

[78] Peterson, "Ethics in Academic Librarianship," 132.

discussed above, the fundamental change of automation and information technologies more fully developed as the century drew to a close.

At this time, it became vitally important to name our professional values. In a speech marking the 20th anniversary of OCLC, information school dean and then-President of ALA F. William Summers captures this motivation when he remarked on "the challenge that we face in trying to embrace technology without losing our basic values."[79] And what are those basic values? Summers offers five—individual autonomy, privacy, equality, freedom, and access—and closes with, "It is those values which we must seek to preserve in the years to come."[80] With this speech, Summers inaugurates the modern conversation around the enumeration of professional values. Summers' call is then picked up by Finks, who offers a "fresh look" at values by encouraging LIS professionals to "to call [values] to consciousness and criticize and question them, to apply them to our problems and quandaries, to invoke them as we plan and make decisions, and ultimately to cherish and celebrate them."[81] Finks searches for values that are the "essence of our calling," and "inherent in librarianship," and that "originate in the nature of our mission." The literature calls attention to a perceived need to articulate professional values in practice.[82]

The urgent question of values that are inherent, enduring, timeless, or core then becomes fertile ground for debate throughout the following decade leading up to the turn of the millennium.[83] Gorman is a prominent voice during this period; he attempts to speak for the profession in a series of publications. In *Our Singular Strengths*, Gorman offers 144 meditations on librarianship, including eight values and five updated laws to match Ranganathan's original set.[84] But Gorman's centerpiece contribution is *Our Enduring Values*, originally published in 2000 and updated in 2015. In this work, Gorman draws primarily on the

---

79 Summers, "A Vision of Librarianship," 26.

80 Summers, 30.

81 Finks, "What Do We Stand For?," 356.

82 Peterson, "Ethics in Academic Librarianship"; Baker, "Needed"; Johnson, "The Need for a Value-Based Reference Policy."

83 Buschman, Rosenzweig, and Harger, "On My Mind"; St. Clair, *Total Quality Management in Information Services*; Rodger, "Core Values"; Sager et al., "A Question of Values"; Froehlich, "Intellectual Freedom, Ethical Deliberation and Codes of Ethics."

84 Gorman, *Our Singular Strengths*.

work of Ranganathan,[85] Rothstein,[86] Shera,[87] and Finks[88] to propose 8 professional values for librarianship: stewardship, service, intellectual freedom, rationalism, literacy and learning, equity of access, privacy, and democracy. These 8 values constitute Gorman's enduring "golden thread" that ties together the LIS profession in timeless continuity. As motivation for developing these 8 values, Gorman invokes changes to the profession when positioning values as important both to the internal function and the external recognition of the LIS profession: "We need to examine and affirm the core values of our profession if we are to flourish in a time of change and maintain the ethic of service to individuals and society that distinguishes our profession."[89]

Gorman's enumeration has been recognized as the "most ambitious attempt to define a core set of values for the library profession since Ranganathan's Five Laws of Library Science."[90] This and other responses show that Gorman mostly hits the mark with this enumeration. Burd, for example, says that Gorman's values are "intrinsic to the profession."[91] Hauptman states that "Gorman's values are our values."[92] Follow-up research comparing Gorman's values to ethical codes and value statements across the world, however, shows the limits of Gorman's ability to identify values that are relevant to all information professionals. While there is some degree of broad consensus around a small core of values, Gorman's values reflect a particular American cultural perspective.[93] The small core of LIS values shared across the globe include service, privacy, and equity of access, while Gorman's American sensibility uniquely includes rationalism, democracy, and literacy and learning. This underscores an inherent challenge and necessary limitation to any pursuit of identifying core values across the profession.

---

85 Ranganathan, *The Five Laws of Library Science*.
86 Rothstein, "In Search of Ourselves."
87 Shera, *Sociological Foundations of Librarianship*.
88 Finks, "What Do We Stand For?"
89 Gorman, *The Enduring Library*, 80.
90 Foster and McMenemy, "Do Librarians Have a Shared Set of Values?," 251.
91 Burd, "The Academic Library—Not a Lair for Fiery Dragons," 106.
92 Hauptman, *Ethics and Librarianship*, 134.
93 Foster and McMenemy, "Do Librarians Have a Shared Set of Values?"

At the same time that Gorman is developing a set of values, others are applying empirical approaches for determining LIS values. Koehler and Pemberton examine values statements and ethical codes from across the information professions.[94] In an attempt to deduce a model code that contains a core set of ethical principles for LIS, they identify five values:

1. Whenever possible, place the needs of clients above other concerns.

2. Understand the roles of the information practitioner and strive to meet them with the greatest possible skill and competence.

3. Support the needs and interests of the profession and the professional association(s).

4. Insofar as they do not conflict with professional obligations, be sensitive and responsive to social responsibilities appropriate to the profession.

5. Be aware of and be responsive to the rights of users, employers, fellow practitioners, one's community, and the larger society.

As an extension of this work, Koehler, Hurych, and Dole identify leading values for LIS professionals via a profession-wide survey.[95] Nearly all academic librarians in the United States identify service as their primary ethical principle, followed by preservation and intellectual freedom. In a follow-up study that distributed a similar survey to a wider population covering more geographical regions and types of LIS professionals, service is again the top-rated value, followed most commonly by a combination of information literacy, intellectual freedom, equality, and preservation.[96] Finally, Koehler concludes this line of inquiry by proposing the following six core values for the LIS profession: intellectual freedom, privacy, intellectual property, professional neutrality, preservation, equity of access.[97] Koehler cautions, however, that it is difficult to express a single set of values across the information professions. Similarly, Dole and Hurych observe that despite

---

94 Koehler and Pemberton, "A Search for Core Values."

95 Koehler, Hurych, and Dole, "Values for Librarians in the Information Age."

96 Koehler et al., "Ethical Values of Information and Library Professionals—An Expanded Analysis."

97 Koehler, "Professional Values and Ethics as Defined by 'The LIS Discipline.'"

growing interest at this time in values studies, no standard definitions have emerged.[98] And indeed, the quest to find shared values produced a wide-ranging assortment of potential principles that were proposed by several authors. This again highlights the range of possibilities for what could constitute core values for LIS.

To get a sense of this conversation, I created a tabulation that shows the array of values that were put forward as potential LIS core values. I looked closely at the literature on LIS values published during the period between Ranganathan's Five Laws in 1931 and the publication of the *ALA Core Values of Librarianship* in 2004. The publication of the ALA Core Values is an important turning point in the story of LIS values, and I discuss that process in detail in the next section. At this point in the chapter, I want to demonstrate the range and diversity of core values that were put forward for consideration during this time—beginning with Ranganathan's Five Laws in 1931, running through the highly active period around the turn of the millennium, and concluding with the ALA's entrance into the conversation. I found that 35 different values were proposed in 21 different publications. The following list shows the 35 different values that appear in the published literature from 1931–2003, in descending order of frequency:

- **Service,** *12 appearances* (Ranganathan, 1931; Rothstein, 1968; Shera, 1970; Finks, 1989; Baker, 1992; Buschman et al., 1994; Hisle, 1998; Sager et al., 1999; Koehler and Pemberton, 2000; Koehler, Hurych, and Dole, 2000; Koehler, Hurych, Dole, and Wall, 2000; Gorman, 2000/2015)

- **Access,** *9 appearances* (Ranganathan, 1931; Finks, 1989; Summers, 1989; Rodger, 1998; Sager et al., 1999; Koehler, Hurych, and Dole, 2000; Koehler, Hurych, Dole, and Wall, 2000; Koehler, 2003; Gorman, 2000/2015)

- **Intellectual Freedom,** *6 appearances* (Rothstein, 1968; Baker, 1992; Buschman et al., 1994; Hisle, 1998; Koehler, 2003; Gorman, 2000/2015)

- **Literacy and Learning,** *6 appearances* (Rothstein, 1968; Shera, 1970; Finks, 1989; Rodger, 1998; Sager et al., 1999; Gorman, 2000/2015)

---

98 Dole and Hurych, "Values for Librarians in the Information Age."

- **Professionalism**, 5 *appearances* (Rothstein, 1968; Peterson, 1983; Baker, 1992; St. Clair, 1997; Koehler and Pemberton, 2000)
- **Stewardship**, 5 *appearances* (Ranganathan, 1931; Shera, 1970; Finks, 1989; Buschman et al., 1994; Gorman, 2000/2015)
- **Privacy**, 4 *appearances* (Summers, 1989; Gorman, 2000/2015; Froehlich, 2000; Koehler, 2003
- **Social Responsibility**, 4 *appearances* (Rubin, 1991; Buschman et al., 1994; Koehler and Pemberton, 2000; Rubin and Froehlich, 1996/2010)
- **Individual Autonomy**, 4 *appearances* (Summers, 1989; Rubin, 1991; Baker, 1992; Rubin and Froehlich, 1996/2010)
- **Democracy**, 3 *appearances* (Ranganathan, 1931; Finks, 1989; Gorman, 2000/2015)
- **Preservation**, 3 *appearances* (Koehler, Hurych, and Dole, 2000; Koehler, Hurych, Dole, and Wall, 2000; Koehler, 2003)
- **Justice**, 2 *appearances* (Baker, 1992; Johnson, 1994)
- **People**, 2 *appearances* (Peterson, 1983; Rodger, 1998)
- **The Public Good**, 2 *appearances* (Shera, 1970; Rubin, 1991)
- **Truth**, 2 *appearances* (Finks, 1989; Rubin and Froehlich, 1996/2010)
- **Scholarship**, 1 *appearance* (Shera, 1970)
- **Honesty**, 1 *appearance* (Peterson, 1983)
- **Equality**, 1 *appearance* (Summers, 1989)
- **Survival**, 1 *appearance* (Rubin, 1991)
- **Care**, 1 *appearance* (Baker, 1992)
- **Integrity, Humaneness, Fairness, Excellence**, 1 *appearance each* (St. Clair, 1997)
- **Diversity, Passion**, 1 *appearance each* (Sager et al., 1999)
- **Minimal Well-Being, Protection from Injury, Recognition for One's Work**, 1 *appearance each* (Froehlich, 2000)
- **Tolerance, Beauty**, 1 *appearance each* (Rubin and Froehlich, 1996/2010)
- **Rights**, 1 *appearance* (Koehler and Pemberton, 2000)

- **Intellectual Property, Neutrality**, 1 *appearance each* (Koehler, 2003)
- **Rationalism**, 1 *appearance* (Gorman, 2000/2015).

This literature reveals that 35 different values have been put forward for consideration as core values for libraries, with more than half of those values only appearing once. This list also suggests a lack of agreement within the LIS professional community as to a set of shared values. Relative agreement at the top of the list, however, points to the potential for arriving at an agreed-upon set of "core" values. In arguing for the need to establish core professional values, Baker maintains that identifying profession-wide guidelines is not the work of an individual, but rather a task "best left to a broad-based committee of persons knowledgeable about library administration and about ethical principles."[99] In response to the perceived need to define a shared set of values, the profession's largest and oldest organizing body entered the conversation.

Value Studies in the 21st century: ALA Core Values Task Force and ALA Core Values of Librarianship

As a response to the growing but inconclusive debate around core values, the question of professional values was elevated to a national level with the formation in 1999 of the ALA Core Values Task Force (CVTF1), which was followed in 2001 by the Second Task Force on Core Values (CVTF2). The work of these two committees ultimately produced a document published in 2004 and codified in 2005, the "Core Values of Librarianship." This document represents a key inflection point for the practical and scholarly conversation around enumerating LIS core values. As we have seen above, in publications that pre-date the *ALA Core Values of Librarianship*, practitioners debated the definitions, purposes, and enumerations of LIS professional values. Following its publication, the *ALA Core Values of Librarianship* has become the primary point of reference in discussing and debating LIS professional values. It will be helpful to provide a brief background for the development of the *ALA Core Values of Librarianship*.

The effort to craft a core values statement for the LIS profession was led by Sager, who remarked in 2001, "One of the most contentious

---

99 Baker, "Needed," 96.

professional issues that arose during the past year was the question of whether the American Library Association should adopt a set of core values for the profession, and if so, what those core values would be."[100] Among the already-available, ethics-related documents, Sager finds nuance that justifies a stand-alone Core Values statement, as he remarks on the following documents:

- The *Code of Ethics*, first published in 1939, describes LIS professional obligations and standards.[101]
- The *Library Bill of Rights* first published in 1939, describes obligations to those served.[102]
- The *Libraries: An American Value* statement, first published in 1999, describes LIS commitment to the community.[103]

In contrast and complement to the above documents, a Core Values statement would "summarize the basic beliefs that the members of this profession hold in common." This need was derived from a recommendation that emerged in Spring 1999 at the First Congress on Professional Education. At that meeting, members of ALA identified professional values as an area for further discussion, with a motivation of "defining librarianship for the new millennium."[104] Existing documents were not sufficient for this purpose: "Although the Association has issued a number of documents that imply values for the profession (e.g. the code of ethics, the statement on intellectual freedom, the affirmation of libraries as an American value) there is no clear explication to which members can refer and through which decisions can be assessed; the resulting statement should be developed with partner groups or endorsed by them as the values of librarianship."[105] To lead the drafting of such a statement, Sager served as chair of the first Core Values Task Force. The CVTS1 was appointed "to clarify the core values

---

100 Sager, "The Search for Librarianship's Core Values," 149.

101 American Library Association, "Professional Ethics."

102 American Library Association, "Library Bill of Rights."

103 American Library Association, "Libraries."

104 American Library Association, "ALA | 1st Congress."

105 American Library Association, "Congress on Professional Education – Report of the Core Values Task Force II."

(credo) of the profession."[106] The task force met in person in 1999 to draft a statement, then distributed a sequence of drafts through a variety of communication channels such as email listservs and ALA bureaucratic structures. After receiving hundreds of comments, the task force released its fifth and final draft in 2000. The CVTS1 sought to create a jargon-free, comprehensive, and concise list of values.[107] The initial enumeration included the following values:

- Connection of people to ideas
- Assurance of free and open access to recorded knowledge, information, and creative works
- Commitment to literacy and learning
- Respect for the individuality and the diversity of all people
- Freedom for all people to form, to hold, and to express their own beliefs
- Preservation of the human record
- Excellence in professional service to our communities
- Formation of partnerships to advance these values

Upon release, this initial set of core values was not well received by the wider LIS community. The editor of *Library Journal* objected to the process and the result, saying that the CVTF1 applied a flawed approach to draft a statement containing "vague generalizations" that "weakly" convey how deeply and strongly the LIS community holds these values.[108] The process of the CVTF1 was seen as exclusionary and inconsistent with efforts to further diversify the profession.[109] In an email thread following the release of the draft statement, members of ALA governance and the wider community expressed concern, including the following responses to the statement: it is disappointing, headed in the wrong direction, does not comprehend current issues, is not worthy of endorsement, lacks significance, and adds nothing to the understanding of values.[110] Contributors to this email thread viewed the ALA Core Values statement as a potentially important document that deserved scrutiny and intense development. One ALA Councilor

---

106 American Library Association, "ALA Core Values Task Force – Background and Charge."
107 American Library Association, "ALA Core Values Task Force – Frequently Asked Questions."
108 Berry, "Dumbed-down Core Values."
109 Weissinger, "Competing Models of Librarianship."
110 Rosenzweig et al., "Library Juice 3:14 Supplement – April 12, 2000," 2000.

wrote that the Core Values statement, "as the result of much hard labor, promises to become a PRIMARY POINT OF REFERENCE for a good long time in matters of much moment to the profession and its publics."[111] This impassioned response from the community highlights the anticipated major impact of the ALA Core Values statement.

In response to the continued desire for a clarified Core Values statement, combined with the need for a better process and outcome, ALA convened the Second Core Values Task Force with Patricia Glass Schuman as chair just a few months after the work of the CVTF1 concluded.[112] Whereas the first committee worked for about one year, the second committee worked for 3 years, and employed a more inclusive process with intentional facilitation of profession-wide contributions.[113] The goal of the CVTF2 was to "help librarians and library school students discuss their understanding of, and commitment to, the values that librarianship represents" and that "contribute to our unique perspectives as librarians. [These values] represent essential and enduring beliefs that we uphold over time."[114] In summer 2003, the CVTF2 delivered a set of values, which were adopted in summer 2004 and codified as an official ALA document in January 2005.[115] The *ALA Core Values of Librarianship* articulates the function of values: "The foundation of modern librarianship rests on an essential set of core values which define, inform, and guide our professional practice." The *ALA Core Values of Librarianship* document produced by the CVTF2 is still in effect today. It enumerates the following values (descriptions are quoted directly from the *ALA Core Values of Librarianship*):

Access
All information resources that are provided directly or indirectly by the library, regardless of technology, format, or methods of delivery, should be readily, equally, and equitably accessible to all library users.

---

111 Rosenzweig et al., para. 29.

112 American Library Association, "American Library Association – Congress on Professional Education – Second Task Force on Core Values. Appendix B: Core Values Task Force II, Charge and Membership."

113 Sullivan, "American Library Association Congress on Professional Education – Second Task Force on Core Values – Who We Are – America's Librarians Discuss Their Professional Values – Facilitator's Guide."

114 American Library Association, "American Library Association – Congress on Professional Education – Second Task Force on Core Values – Who We Are – Appendix A, Discussion Guide."

115 Schuman, "Core Values Task Force II Report."

Confidentiality/Privacy
Protecting user privacy and confidentiality is necessary for intellectual freedom and fundamental to the ethics and practice of librarianship.

Democracy
A democracy presupposes an informed citizenry. The First Amendment mandates the right of all persons to free expression, and the corollary right to receive the constitutionally protected expression of others. The publicly supported library provides free and equal access to information for all people of the community the library serves.

Diversity
We value our nation's diversity and strive to reflect that diversity by providing a full spectrum of resources and services to the communities we serve.

Education and Lifelong Learning
ALA promotes the creation, maintenance, and enhancement of a learning society, encouraging its members to work with educators, government officials, and organizations in coalitions to initiate and support comprehensive efforts to ensure that school, public, academic, and special libraries in every community cooperate to provide lifelong learning services to all.

Intellectual Freedom
We uphold the principles of intellectual freedom and resist all efforts to censor library resources.

Preservation
The Association supports the preservation of information published in all media and formats. The association affirms that the preservation of information resources is central to libraries and librarianship.

The Public Good
ALA reaffirms the following fundamental values of libraries in the context of discussing outsourcing and privatization of library services. These values include that libraries are an essential public good and are fundamental institutions in democratic societies.

Professionalism

The American Library Association supports the provision of library services by professionally qualified personnel who have been educated in graduate programs within institutions of higher education. It is of vital importance that there be professional education available to meet the social needs and goals of library services.

Service

We provide the highest level of service to all library users. We strive for excellence in the profession by maintaining and enhancing our own knowledge and skills, by encouraging the professional development of co-workers, and by fostering the aspirations of potential members of the profession.

Social Responsibility

ALA recognizes its broad social responsibilities. The broad social responsibilities of the American Library Association are defined in terms of the contribution that librarianship can make in ameliorating or solving the critical problems of society; support for efforts to help inform and educate the people of the United States on these problems and to encourage them to examine the many views on and the facts regarding each problem; and the willingness of ALA to take a position on current critical issues with the relationship to libraries and library service set forth in the position statement.[116]

There has been one modification to these eleven values. Reflecting the evolving nature of values, the *ALA Core Values of Librarianship* was revised in 2019 with the endorsement of thousands of LIS professionals to include "sustainability" as a newly added core value, with the following description quoted directly from the revised *ALA Core Values of Librarianship*:

Sustainability

ALA is supporting the library community by showing its commitment to assisting in the development of sustainable libraries with the addition of sustainability as a core value of librarianship. This consists of practices that are environmentally sound, economically feasible and socially equitable. Libraries play an important and

---

[116] American Library Association, "Core Values of Librarianship."

unique role in promoting community awareness about resilience, climate change and a sustainable future. They are also leading by example by taking steps to reduce their environmental footprint.

The additional value of sustainability will "inspire, cultivate and encourage" professional action, and will "guide decisions for the future of our society."[117] This language reinforces the concept of a value as an aspirational, time-oriented, and practice-based tool for guiding the ethical conduct and future development of LIS professionals. The Core Values continue to be a point of discussion within the governance of ALA, with renewed effort in 2021 to revisit the Core Values with a re-constituted Core Values committee.[118] This Core Values committee has reaffirmed that the ALA Core Values are intrinsic across most aspects of ALA, reporting further that in a survey of ALA Councilors, 76% (n=81) of respondents marked "yes" to the question, "Are the ALA Core Values currently reflected/ incorporated to your satisfaction in the work done by ALA?"[119] Still, the report identified a few areas of concern that a re-constituted Core Values committee could address: ensuring that Core Values language does not become outdated, ensuring that all values are put into practice (especially diversity and social responsibility), ensuring that all values are centralized in ALA decision-making, ensuring that there are not so many values as to be unworkable, and ensuring that there is alignment between the values and the mission of libraries.

The Core Values in Practice

Core Values as a Practical Guide

Since the release of the *ALA Core Values of Librarianship* in 2004, the values have attracted attention from LIS practitioners and researchers, with a focus on interpreting, critiquing, and operationalizing the values across the various specialties of librarianship. The Core Values articulate professional beliefs for LIS practitioners.[120] The Core Values

---

117 American Library Association, "Resolution for the Adoption of Sustainability as a Core Value of Librarianship."

118 Bowling-Dixon et al., "Forward Together Working Group Report: Snapshot of Work Performed between July 2020 and January 2021."

119 Bowling-Dixon et al., 16.

120 Van der Veer Martens, "New Grounds for Ontic Trust."

can be seen as representing the mission of our profession.[121] In terms of relevancy and purpose, the Core Values have been recognized to "fairly represent the values of LIS professionals in general and provide a sensible framework for how US professionals should conduct themselves."[122] Connaway and Faniel connect the concept of core values back to Ranganathan's original five laws, while also pointing to the continued purpose of professional values as a stabilizing element: "[Ranganathan's laws] establish a framework that keeps us focused on the core values of librarianship—values that have remained remarkably consistent across a time that has seen incredible change in information technology."[123]

In practice, the values are most often invoked when grounding and guiding the work of LIS professionals.[124] This includes professional activities such as outreach and advocacy,[125] social engagement and responsibility,[126] LIS education,[127] information literacy,[128] hiring,[129] disability and access,[130] cataloging and classification,[131] leadership,[132] technology and web development,[133] digital collections and infrastructures,[134] intellectual

---

121 Vinopal, "The Quest for Diversity in Library Staffing."

122 Rubin, "The Values and Ethics of Library and Information Science," 544.

123 Connaway and Faniel, "Reordering Ranganathan," 107.

124 Berg and Jacobs, "Introduction."

125 Berry III, "Inspired by Serving Others"; Hicks, "Advocating for Librarianship."

126 Jaeger, Taylor, and Gorham, *Libraries, Human Rights, and Social Justice*; Oliphant, "Social Justice Research in Library and Information Sciences"; Burgess, "Reconciling Social Responsibility and Neutrality in LIS Professional Ethics: A Virtue Ethics Approach"; Gibson et al., "Libraries on the Frontlines"; Racelis, "Library Services for the Poor."

127 Shockey, "Intellectual Freedom Is Not Social Justice: The Symbolic Capital of Intellectual Freedom in ALA Accreditation and LIS Curricula"; Roberts and Noble, "Empowered to Name, Inspired to Act"; Walther, "Teaching Ethical Dilemmas in LIS Coursework."

128 Jacobs and Berg, "Reconnecting Information Literacy Policy with the Core Values of Librarianship"; Gregory and Higgins, "Reorienting an Information Literacy Program Toward Social Justice"; Saunders, "Connecting Information Literacy and Social Justice: Why and How."

129 Vinopal, "The Quest for Diversity in Library Staffing."

130 Fox and Reece, "Which Ethics?"; Kumbier and Starkey, "Access Is Not Problem Solving."

131 Shoemaker, "No One Can Whistle a Symphony."

132 Farrell, "Leadership and Social Justice."

133 Campbell and Cowan, "The Paradox of Privacy"; Puckett, "Open Source Software and Librarian Values"; Yoon, Dols, and Hulscher, "Applying Inclusive Principles in Web Design to Enhance Accessibility for Disabled Users."

134 Dressler, *Framing Privacy in Digital Collections with Ethical Decision Making*; Owens et al., "Digital Infrastructures That Embody Library Principles: The IMLS National Digital Platform as a Framework for Digital Library Tools and Services."

freedom,[135] labor issues,[136] professional identities,[137] and library administration.[138] Reflecting both the aspirational nature and also the practical application of values, Schroeder and Hollister observe that with "scores of articles devoted to [the values]...it is heartening that librarians, as a professional group, created and abide by the Core Values of Librarianship statement."[139]

Despite the evident usefulness of the Core Values, some have noted their limitations. The Core Values may be overly idealized or too aspirational, to a point that "erases power relations, obfuscates social inequalities, and denies history."[140] The Core Values are also not necessarily accepted as essential. This is evident in studies that attempt to locate a different set of values more relevant for specific areas of practice, such as instruction.[141] In reaching for a more transformative LIS practice, Kumbier and Starkey cast a critical eye on the pragmatism of the *ALA Core Values of Librarianship*, noting that the values reflect existing commitments and functions of librarianship in a way that forecloses other possible avenues for theory and practice.[142]

The main current of conversation regarding professional values and the *ALA Core Values of Librarianship* is characterized by a balance of practical application and contemplative self-reflection. Recalling Drabinski's argument that a value is "continually produced and reproduced in the library discourse," and that values are "ideas to be struggled over in both discourse and practice,"[143] Jacobs and Berg see the Core Values as an important point of reference in developing practices and policies through collaborative dialogue: "the ALA Core Values are reflective of librarians' professional strengths and librarianship's

---

135 Knox, "Supporting Intellectual Freedom"; Oltmann, "Intellectual Freedom and Freedom of Speech"; Oltmann, "Creating Space at the Table."

136 Moeller, "Disability, Identity, and Professionalism."

137 Hicks, "The Construction of Librarians' Professional Identities."

138 Shorb, "Ethical Decision-Making in Library Administration."

139 Schroeder and Hollister, "Librarians' Views on Critical Theories and Critical Practices," 113.

140 Seale, "Compliant Trust," 597.

141 Ziegenfuss, "Using Appreciative Inquiry Methods to Build a Culture of Assessment and Library Instruction Program from the Bottom Up: Uncovering Librarian Values, Assumptions, Beliefs, and Best Practices."

142 Kumbier and Starkey, "Access Is Not Problem Solving."

143 Drabinski, "Valuing Professionalism," 606.

possibilities and thus are a generative place from which to start conversations."[144] Continual examination is necessary because the Core Values—while powerful and inspiring proclamations—are not workable plans of action. A certain amount of translation is required to operationalize the ideas expressed within the *ALA Core Values of Librarianship*. Continual reexamination, reinterpretation, and defense of core values is necessary due to ever-shifting conditions of the wider world.[145] And Budd tells us that "as reflective practitioners we are obliged to examine the assumptions, stated and unstated, that underlie values in general and the values of professionals in particular."[146] Despite these calls for ethical self-examination, Anderson notes that LIS as a discipline still has not followed through with action: "It seems that librarians and other information professionals are falling behind in the field of ethics, in that there is little critical reflection on the customs and traditions (morals) of our profession in light of the changes in the world around us."[147] In following the recommendations of Drabinski, Jacobs and Berg, Preer, Budd, and Anderson, this book will proceed in subsequent chapters to examine LIS values and practices, applying a lens of practical ethics with a view towards the external pressures and conditions that influence the work of LIS professionals.

Core Values and Vocational Awe

The concept of "vocational awe" adds a useful critical dimension to the conversation around core values. The theory of vocational awe presents three main points of critique—that LIS values are canonized, idealized, and weaponized. I briefly discuss these three areas below.

First introduced by Ettarh, vocational awe is "the idea that libraries as institutions are inherently good. It assumes that some or all core aspects of the profession are beyond critique, and it, in turn, underpins many librarians' sense of identity and emotional investment in the profession."[148] Vocational awe theorizes that LIS is seen as a sa-

---

144 Jacobs and Berg, "Reconnecting Information Literacy Policy with the Core Values of Librarianship," 388.

145 Preer, *Library Ethics*, 46.

146 Budd, "Place and Identity."

147 Anderson, "Ethics for Twenty-First Century Librarians," 120.

148 Ettarh, "Vocational Awe?," para. 4.

cred calling, and that its values are canonical and thus incontestable. For example, the core value of access, Ettarh points out, has not been achieved equally in American society, as Black citizens were systematically denied access to libraries for much of the 20th century. When LIS values are positioned as an unquestionable canon, Ettarh argues that such a positioning prevents the profession from examining and addressing its historical and contemporary flaws, including practices that perpetuate race- and gender-based oppressions. Quoting Ettarh: "in fact, each value on which librarianship prides itself is inequitably distributed amongst society."[149]

Vocational awe further shows that LIS values represent a hegemonic ideal of practice that excludes those who may object to or expand beyond the core set of values. Just as certain values are included in the canon, so are others excluded. LIS Core Values reflect a Western, enlightenment perspective.[150] Rather than expressing universal truths from a neutral point of view, the LIS Core Values contain inherent cultural biases that over time have been idealized into a dominant norm of behavior. This normative behavior can exclude LIS practitioners of historically minoritized identities, resulting in negative effects for those who do not conform to the ideal.[151] Similarly, Moeller has applied vocation awe in the context of disability studies, arguing that "the concept of 'vocational awe' within librarianship, like professionalism, is also based upon unacknowledged expectations of normative bodies and minds and thus reinforces this process of displacing those who do not represent the 'ideal' professional."[152]

When values are canonized and idealized, they can then become weaponized against dissenting views that seek to change or challenge dominant modes of librarianship. The literature analysis presented above shows service to be the leading value in LIS. Service may be said to be the dominant mode of LIS work, even to the detriment of LIS workers themselves. Ettarh describes how overwork and under-compensation can result from expectations that the library professional be compensated not in material goods or a healthy workplace, but rather

---

149 Ettarh, "Vocational Awe and Librarianship," para. 9.

150 Froehlich, "Intellectual Freedom, Ethical Deliberation and Codes of Ethics"; de jesus, "Locating the Library in Institutional Oppression."

151 Kendrick and Damasco, "Low Morale in Ethnic and Racial Minority Academic Librarians."

152 Moeller, "Disability, Identity, and Professionalism," 461.

the good feelings of working in a profession that espouses good values and delivers good service.[153] Notably, LIS professionals are compelled into self-sacrificial working conditions in order to uphold the service value, even in cases involving personal health.[154] When service is upheld as the highest priority—taking precedence over mental and physical health, personal relationship-building, or workplace democracy—negative impacts can be seen in staff retention, morale, and productivity.[155] Service first becomes a canonized and irreproachable value, then its expression is idealized through a normative practice of self-sacrifice, and finally those who uphold the value may face diminished personal health while those who challenge the value may face professional exclusion. Through the lens of vocational awe, Gorman's "golden thread" of professional continuity begins to look more like a binding tie of professional conformity.

Taken together, the canonization, idealization, and weaponization of the Core Values complicates the Core Values as potential pathways for professional growth. In this way, Ettarh's theory of vocational awe illuminates the landscape of values-in-conflict. Professional commitments to service, for example, can lead to trade-offs with other values, as when user privacy is affected by tracking software that promises to improve library services. In a case such as this, privacy and intellectual freedom are in conflict with service—but vocational awe blocks the practitioner from considering the harmful implications of this conflict, because a commitment to the service value is seen as inherently good and therefore not in need of critical examination. This and other values-in-conflict are described in depth in the following chapter.

Summary

LIS professional values are aspirational, time-oriented, and practice-based tools for guiding the ethical conduct and professional development of LIS practitioners. Values serve as the underlying principles that inform a practical ethics for the LIS profession. After much debate in the 1990s as to the enumeration of specific values, the American Library Association in 2005 codified a set of professional values

---

153 Ettarh, "Vocational Awe and Librarianship."

154 Kendrick, "This Is How the #service Value Gets Us. Every Time."

155 Ortega, *Academic Libraries and Toxic Leadership*.

that reflect the history and ongoing development of LIS practice. Since that time, the *ALA Core Values of Librarianship* has been a primary point of reference in discussing and applying LIS professional values, often with the focal point of analyzing professional practice vis-à-vis one or more values. The ALA Core Values, however, have also been criticized as overly idealistic, too aspirational, excessively pragmatic, or contributing to effects of vocational awe. Either as a guiding light or as a point of criticism, the Core Values are an important point of reference in understanding ethical practice in LIS. In the next chapter, I will examine several prominent sites of tension that complicate the practical application of LIS professional values.

Bibliography

Abbott, Andrew. "Professionalism and the Future of Librarianship." *Library Trends* 46, no. 3 (Winter 1998): 430–43.

American Library Association. "ALA Core Values Task Force – Background and Charge," 2002. https://web.archive.org/web/20020806122838/http://www.ala.org/congress/corevalues/index.html.

American Library Association. "ALA Core Values Task Force – Frequently Asked Questions," 2002. https://web.archive.org/web/20021027175901/http://www.ala.org/congress/corevalues/faq.html.

American Library Association. "American Library Association – Congress on Professional Education – Second Task Force on Core Values – Who We Are – Appendix A, Discussion Guide," March 15, 2004. https://web.archive.org/web/20040315022036/http://www.ala.org/ala/hrdrbucket/1stcongresspro/1stcongressappendixala.htm.

American Library Association. "American Library Association – Congress on Professional Education – Second Task Force on Core Values. Appendix B: Core Values Task Force II, Charge and Membership," 2004. https://web.archive.org/web/20040523024244/http://www.ala.org/ala/hrdrbucket/1stcongressonpro/1stcongressappendixb.htm.

American Library Association. "Congress on Professional Education – Report of the Core Values Task Force II," September 12, 2002. https://web.archive.org/web/20020912050301/http://www.ala.org/congress/1st_congress/tf2_report.html.

American Library Association. "Congress on Professional Education: Issues in the Profession," 1999. https://web.archive.org/web/20081111183336/http://www.ala.org/ala/educationcareers/education/1stcongressonpro/1stcongressissues.cfm.

American Library Association. "Core Values of Librarianship." Text. Advocacy, Legislation & Issues, 2019. https://web.archive.org/web/20230313120852/https://www.ala.org/advocacy/intfreedom/corevalues.

American Library Association. "Libraries: An American Value." Text. Advocacy, Legislation & Issues, June 30, 2006. http://www.ala.org/advocacy/intfreedom/americanvalue.

American Library Association. "Library Bill of Rights." Text. American Library Association, June 30, 2006. http://www.ala.org/advocacy/intfreedom/librarybill.

American Library Association. "Professional Ethics." Text. American Library Association, May 19, 2017. http://www.ala.org/tools/ethics.

American Library Association. "Resolution for the Adoption of Sustainability as a Core Value of Librarianship." American Library Association, January 2019. https://web.archive.org/web/20190804173435/http://www.ala.org/aboutala/sites/ala.org.aboutala/files/content/ALA%20CD%2037%20RESOLUTION%20FOR%20THE%20ADOPTION%20OF%20SUSTAINABILITY%20AS%20A%20CORE%20VALUE%20OF%20LIBRARIANSHIP_Final1182019.docx.

Anderson, Cokie G. "Ethics for Twenty-First Century Librarians." In *Ethical Decision Making for Digital Libraries*, edited by Cokie G. Anderson, 119–26. Chandos Information Professional Series. Chandos Publishing, 2006. https://doi.org/10.1016/B978-1-84334-149-9.50012-8.

Atherton, Pauline. *Putting Knowledge to Work: An American View of Ranganathan's Five Laws of Library Science*. Delhi: Vikas Publishing House, 1973.

Baker, Sharon L. "Needed: An Ethical Code for Library Administrators." *Journal of Library Administration* 16, no. 4 (1992): 1–17.

Benge, Ronald C. *Libraries and Cultural Change*. London: Clive Bingley, 1970.

Berg, Selinda A., and Heidi LM Jacobs. "Valuing Librarianship: Core Values in Theory and Practice." *Library Trends* 64, no. 3 (April 4, 2016): 459–67.

Berry III, John N. "Inspired by Serving Others." *Library Journal* 141, no. 20 (December 15, 2016): 10.

Berry, John N. "Dumbed-down Core Values." *Library Journal; New York* 125, no. 8 (May 1, 2000): 6.

Blake, Virgil L. P. "Ethics: The Other Dimension of Professionalism." *Public & Access Services Quarterly* 2, no. 1 (September 20, 1996): 13–39. https://doi.org/10.1300/J119v02n01_03.

Bourg, Chris. "Beyond Measure: Valuing Libraries." *Feral Librarian* (blog), May 20, 2013. https://web.archive.org/web/20210427003926/https://chrisbourg.wordpress.com/2013/05/19/beyond-measure-valuing-libraries/.

Bowling-Dixon, Joslyn, Steven Yates, Camila Alire, Stephanie Chase, Sara Dallas, Meg Delaney, Meg Garcia, et al. "Forward Together Working Group Report: Snapshot of Work Performed between July 2020 and January 2021." American Library Association, 2021. http://web.archive.org/web/20220214025132/

https://forwardtogether.ala.org/wp-content/uploads/2021/01/ALA-CD-35-Forward-Together-Working-Group-Final-Report.pdf.

Buchanan, Elizabeth A., and Kathrine A. Henderson. *Case Studies in Library and Information Science Ethics*. Jefferson, N.C: McFarland & Co, 2009.

Budd, John M. "Place and Identity." In *Self-Examination: The Present and Future of Librarianship*, by John M. Budd, 37–72. Westport, CT: Libraries Unlimited, 2008.

Budd, John M. "What's the Right Thing to Do?" In *Self-Examination: The Present and Future of Librarianship*, by John M. Budd, 111–46. Westport, CT: Libraries Unlimited, 2008.

Budd, John M. "Toward a Practical and Normative Ethics for Librarianship." *The Library Quarterly* 76, no. 3 (2006): 251–69. https://doi.org/10.1086/511140.

Burd, Barbara. "The Academic Library—Not a Lair for Fiery Dragons." In *Expectations of Librarians in the 21st Century*, edited by Karl Bridges, 105–9. Westport, CT: Greenwood Press, 2003.

Burgess, John T. F. "Reconciling Social Responsibility and Neutrality in LIS Professional Ethics: A Virtue Ethics Approach." In *Information Cultures in the Digital Age*, edited by Matthew Kelly and Jared Bielby, 307–20. Springer VS, 2016.

Buschman, John, Mark Rosenzweig, and Elaine Harger. "On My Mind: The Clear Imperative for Involvement: Librarians Must Address Social Issues." *American Libraries* 25, no. 6 (1994): 575–76.

Bushing, Mary C. "Acquisition Ethics: The Evolution of Models for Hard Times." *Library Acquisitions: Practice & Theory* 17, no. 1 (January 1, 1993): 47–52. https://doi.org/10.1016/0364-6408(93)90029-6.

Campbell, D. Grant, and Scott R. Cowan. "The Paradox of Privacy: Revisiting a Core Library Value in an Age of Big Data and Linked Data." *Library Trends* 64, no. 3 (April 4, 2016): 492–511. https://doi.org/10.1353/lib.2016.0006.

Christians, Clifford G. "Information Ethics in a Complicated Age." In *Ethics and the Librarian*, edited by F.W. Lancaster, 3–17. Urbana-Champaign, Illinois: University of Illinois Graduate School of Library and Information Science, 1991. https://www.ideals.illinois.edu/handle/2142/596.

Cohen, Morris L. "President's Page: Towards a Philosophy of Law Librarianship." *Law Library Journal* 64 (1971): 1–4.

Connaway, Lynn Silipigni, and Ixchel M. Faniel. "Reordering Ranganathan: Shifting User Behaviors, Shifting Priorities." OCLC Online Computer Library Center, Inc, June 2014. https://eric.ed.gov/?id=ED564831.

Crowe, Lawson, and Susan H. Anthes. "The Academic Librarian and Information Technology: Ethical Issues." *College and Research Libraries* 49, no. 2 (1988): 123–30.

Danner, Richard A. "Redefining a Profession." *Law Library Journal* 90 (1998): 315.

Delaney, Geraldine, and Jessica Bates. "Envisioning the Academic Library: A Reflection on Roles, Relevancy and Relationships." *New Review of*

Academic Librarianship 21, no. 1 (January 2, 2015): 30–51. https://doi.org/10.1080/13614533.2014.911194.

Diamond, Randy, and Martha Dragich. "Professionalism in Librarianship: Shifting the Focus from Malpractice to Good Practice." *Library Trends* 49, no. 3 (2001): 395–414.

Dole, Wanda V., and Jitka M. Hurych. "Values for Librarians in the Information Age." *Journal of Information Ethics; Jefferson* 10, no. 2 (Fall 2001): 38-50,95.

Dougherty, Richard M. "On My Mind: Balancing Technology with Professional Values." *American Libraries* 26, no. 7 (1995): 649–50.

Drabinski, Emily. "Valuing Professionalism: Discourse as Professional Practice." *Library Trends* 64, no. 3 (April 4, 2016): 604–14. https://doi.org/10.1353/lib.2016.0005.

Dressler, Virginia. *Framing Privacy in Digital Collections with Ethical Decision Making*. Chapel Hill, North Carolina: Morgan & Claypool, 2018. https://www.morganclaypool.com/doi/abs/10.2200/S00863ED1V01Y201807ICR064.

Ettarh, Fobazi. "Vocational Awe?" *WTF Is a Radical Librarian, Anyway?* (blog), May 30, 2017. https://web.archive.org/web/20200914181426/https://fobaziettarh.com/2017/05/30/vocational-awe/.

Ettarh, Fobazi. "Vocational Awe and Librarianship: The Lies We Tell Ourselves." *In The Library With The Lead Pipe*, 2018. https://web.archive.org/web/20200908194414/http://www.inthelibrarywiththeleadpipe.org/2018/vocational-awe/.

Farrell, Maggie. "Leadership and Social Justice." *Journal of Library Administration* 56, no. 6 (August 17, 2016): 722–30. https://doi.org/10.1080/01930826.2016.1199147.

Ferguson, Stuart, Clare Thornley, and Forbes Gibb. "Beyond Codes of Ethics: How Library and Information Professionals Navigate Ethical Dilemmas in a Complex and Dynamic Information Environment." *International Journal of Information Management* 36, no. 4 (August 1, 2016): 543–56. https://doi.org/10.1016/j.ijinfomgt.2016.02.012.

Finks, Lee W. "Librarianship Needs a New Code of Professional Ethics." *American Libraries* 22, no. 1 (1991): 84–92.

Finks, Lee W. "What Do We Stand for? Values without Shame." *American Libraries* 20, no. 4 (1989): 352–56.

Fister, Barbara. "Librarians as Agents of Change." Presented at the ACRL-Oregon & Washington Joint Fall Conference 2012, Corbett, Oregon, 2012.

Ford, Barbara J. "ALA President's Message: Visions, Values, and Opportunities." *American Libraries* 29, no. 1 (1998): 54.

Foster, Catherine, and David McMenemy. "Do Librarians Have a Shared Set of Values? A Comparative Study of 36 Codes of Ethics Based on Gorman's Enduring Values." *Journal of Librarianship and Information Science* 44, no. 4 (December 1, 2012): 249–62. https://doi.org/10.1177/0961000612448592.

Fox, Melodie J., and Austin Reece. "Which Ethics? Whose Morality?: An Analysis of Ethical Standards for Information Organization." *Knowledge Organization* 39, no. 5 (2012): 377–83. https://doi.org/10.5771/0943-7444-2012-5-377.

Froehlich, Thomas J. "Intellectual Freedom, Ethical Deliberation and Codes of Ethics." *IFLA Journal* 26, no. 4 (August 2000): 264–72. https://doi.org/10.1177/034003520002600405.

Gibson, Amelia N., Renate L. Chancellor, Nicole A. Cooke, Sarah Park Dahlen, Shari A. Lee, and Yasmeen L. Shorish. "Libraries on the Frontlines: Neutrality and Social Justice." *Equality, Diversity and Inclusion: An International Journal* 36, no. 8 (October 20, 2017): 751–66. https://doi.org/10.1108/EDI-11-2016-0100.

Gorman, Michael. *Our Enduring Values Revisited: Librarianship in an Ever-Changing World*. Chicago: ALA Editions, 2015.

Gorman, Michael. *Our Singular Strengths*. Chicago: American Library Association, 1998.

Gorman, Michael. *The Enduring Library: Technology, Tradition, and the Quest for Balance*. Chicago: ALA Editions, 2003.

Greenwood, Ernest. "Attributes of a Profession." *Social Work* 2, no. 3 (1957): 45–55.

Gregory, Lua, and Shana Higgins. "Reorienting an Information Literacy Program Toward Social Justice: Mapping the Core Values of Librarianship to the ACRL Framework." *Communications in Information Literacy* 11, no. 1 (June 22, 2017): 42–54. https://doi.org/10.7548/cil.v11i1.463.

Hansson, Joacim. "On the Pre-History of Library Ethics: Documents and Legitimacy." In *Information Cultures in the Digital Age*, edited by Matthew Kelly and Jared Bielby, 307–20. Springer VS, 2016.

Hansson, Joacim. "Professional Value and Ethical Self-Regulation in the Development of Modern Librarianship: The Documentality of Library Ethics." *Journal of Documentation* 73, no. 6 (October 4, 2017): 1261–80. https://doi.org/10.1108/JD-02-2017-0022.

Hauptman, Robert. *Ethical Challenges in Librarianship*. Phoenix: Oryx Press, 1988.

Hauptman, Robert. *Ethics and Librarianship*. Jefferson, North Carolina: McFarland & Company, 2002.

Hicks, Deborah. "Advocating for Librarianship: The Discourses of Advocacy and Service in the Professional Identities of Librarians." *Library Trends* 64, no. 3 (April 4, 2016): 615–40. https://doi.org/10.1353/lib.2016.0007.

Hicks, Deborah. "The Construction of Librarians' Professional Identities: A Discourse Analysis." *Canadian Journal of Information and Library Science* 38, no. 4 (December 14, 2014): 251–70. https://doi.org/10.1353/ils.2014.0017.

Hisle, W. Lee. "Values for the Electronic Information Age: Facing the New Millennium." *College & Research Libraries News* 58, no. 11 (1997). https://doi.org/10.5860/crln.58.11.764.

Jacobs, Heidi LM, and Selinda Berg. "Reconnecting Information Literacy Policy with the Core Values of Librarianship." *Library Trends* 60, no. 2 (2011): 383–94. https://doi.org/10.1353/lib.2011.0043.

Jaeger, Paul T., Natalie Greene Taylor, and Ursula Gorham. *Libraries, Human Rights, and Social Justice: Enabling Access and Promoting Inclusion*. Rowman & Littlefield, 2015.

jesus, nina de. "Locating the Library in Institutional Oppression." *In the Library with the Lead Pipe*, 2014. http://www.inthelibrarywiththeleadpipe.org/2014/locating-the-library-in-institutional-oppression/.

Johnson, Wendell G. "The Need for a Value-Based Reference Policy: John Rawls at the Reference Desk." *The Reference Librarian* 22, no. 47 (November 1, 1994): 201–11. https://doi.org/10.1300/J120v22n47_16.

Kendrick, Kaetrena Davis. "This Is How the #service Value Gets Us. Every Time." *KDDK on Twitter* (blog), March 10, 2020. https://web.archive.org/web/20200311013014if_/https://twitter.com/Kaetrena/status/1237474468320038913.

Kendrick, Kaetrena Davis, and Ione T. Damasco. "Low Morale in Ethnic and Racial Minority Academic Librarians: An Experiential Study." *Library Trends* 68, no. 2 (2019): 174–212. https://doi.org/10.1353/lib.2019.0036.

Kern, M. Kathleen. "Continuity and Change, or, Will I Ever Be Prepared for What Comes Next?" *Reference & User Services Quarterly* 53, no. 4 (June 1, 2014): 282–85. https://doi.org/10.5860/rusq.53n4.282.

Knox, Emily J. M. "Supporting Intellectual Freedom: Symbolic Capital and Practical Philosophy in Librarianship." *The Library Quarterly* 84, no. 1 (January 1, 2014): 8–21. https://doi.org/10.1086/674033.

Koehler, Wallace. *Ethics and Values in Librarianship: A History*. Lanham: Rowman & Littlefield Publishers, 2015.

Koehler, Wallace. "Professional Values and Ethics as Defined by 'The LIS Discipline.'" *Journal of Education for Library and Information Science* 44, no. 2 (2003): 99–119. https://doi.org/10.2307/40323926.

Koehler, Wallace. "Trends of Library Associations and Ethics in the US." In *The Ethics of Librarianship: An International Survey*, edited by K.G. Saur, 323–36. Munich: IFLA Publications, 2002.

Koehler, Wallace C., Jitka M. Hurych, and Wanda V. Dole. "Values for Librarians in the Information Age: An Expanded Examination." *Library Management* 21, no. 6 (August 1, 2000): 285–97. https://doi.org/10.1108/01435120010327597.

Koehler, Wallace C., Jitka M. Hurych, Wanda V. Dole, and Joanna Wall. "Ethical Values of Information and Library Professionals—An Expanded Analysis." *International Information & Library Review* 32, no. 3–4 (September 2000): 485–507. https://doi.org/10.1080/10572317.2000.10762533.

Koehler, Wallace C., and J. Michael Pemberton. "A Search for Core Values: Towards a Model Code of Ethics for Information Professionals." *Journal of Information Ethics; Jefferson* 9, no. 1 (Spring 2000): 26-54,96.

Koster, Gregory E. "Ethics in Reference Service: Codes, Case Studies, or Values?" *Reference Services Review*, January 1, 1992. https://doi.org/10.1108/eb049148.

Kumbier, Alana, and Julia Starkey. "Access Is Not Problem Solving: Disability Justice and Libraries." *Library Trends* 64, no. 3 (April 4, 2016): 468–91. https://doi.org/10.1353/lib.2016.0004.

Larson, Magali S. *The Rise of Professionalism: A Sociological Analysis*. University of California Press, 1979.

Levine-Clark, Michael, and Toni Carter Dean, eds. *ALA Glossary of Library and Information Science*. Fourth edition. Chicago: ALA Editions, 2013.

Lindsey, Jonathan A, and Ann E Prentice. *Professional Ethics and Librarians*. Phoenix, Arizona: Oryx Press, 1985.

McMullen, Haynes. "Research in Backgrounds in Librarianship." *Library Trends* 6, no. 2 (1957): 110–19.

Moeller, Christine M. "Disability, Identity, and Professionalism: Precarity in Librarianship." *Library Trends* 67, no. 3 (May 8, 2019): 455–70. https://doi.org/10.1353/lib.2019.0006.

Moon, Eric. "Ethical Bones." *Library Journal* 93 (January 15, 1968): 131.

Oliphant, Tami. "Social Justice Research in Library and Information Sciences: A Case for Discourse Analysis." *Library Trends* 64, no. 2 (2015): 226–45. https://doi.org/10.1353/lib.2015.0046.

Oltmann, Shannon. "Creating Space at the Table: Intellectual Freedom Can Bolster Diverse Voices." *The Library Quarterly* 87, no. 4 (October 1, 2017): 410–18. https://doi.org/10.1086/693494.

Oltmann, Shannon M. "Intellectual Freedom and Freedom of Speech: Three Theoretical Perspectives." *The Library Quarterly* 86, no. 2 (March 17, 2016): 153–71. https://doi.org/10.1086/685402.

Oppenheim, Charles, and Natalie Pollecutt. "Professional Associations and Ethical Issues in LIS." *Journal of Librarianship and Information Science* 32, no. 4 (2000): 187–203. https://doi.org/10.1177/096100060003200404.

Ortega, Alma. *Academic Libraries and Toxic Leadership*. Chandos Publishing, 2017.

Owens, Trevor, Ashley E Sands, Emily Reynolds, James Neal, Stephen Mayeaux, and Maura Marx. "Digital Infrastructures That Embody Library Principles: The IMLS National Digital Platform as a Framework for Digital Library Tools and Services." In *Applying Library Values to Emerging Technology: Decision-Making in the Age of Open Access, Maker Spaces, and the Ever-Changing Library*, edited by Peter D. Fernandez and Kelly Tilton, 73–88. ACRL, 2018.

Peterson, Kenneth G. "Ethics in Academic Librarianship: The Need for Values." *Journal of Academic Librarianship* 9, no. 3 (July 1983): 132–37.

Preer, Jean L. *Library Ethics*. Westport, Conn: Libraries Unlimited, 2008.

Preisig, Amélie Vallotton, Hermann Roesch, and Christoph Stückelberger, eds. *Ethical Dilemmas in the Information Society: Codes of Ethics for Librarians and Archivists*. Geneva: Globethics.net, 2014.

Puckett, Jason. "Open Source Software and Librarian Values." In *Applying Library Values to Emerging Technology: Decision-Making in the Age of Open Access, Maker Spaces, and the Ever-Changing Library*, edited by Peter D. Fernandez and Kelly Tilton, 159–68. Chicago: American Library Association, 2018.

Racelis, Aliza. "Library Services for the Poor: Theoretical Framework for Library Social Responsibility." *Pedagogical Research* 3, no. 2 (2018). https://eric.ed.gov/?id=EJ1180321.

Ranganathan, S. R. *The Five Laws of Library Science*. Madras: Madras Library Association, 1931.

Roberts, Keith A., and Karen A. Donahue. "Presidential Address: Professing Professionalism: Bureaucratization and Deprofessionalization in the Academy." *Sociological Focus* 33, no. 4 (2000): 365–83.

Roberts, Sarah T., and Safiya Umoja Noble. "Empowered to Name, Inspired to Act: Social Responsibility and Diversity as Calls to Action in the LIS Context." *Library Trends* 64, no. 3 (April 4, 2016): 512–32. https://doi.org/10.1353/lib.2016.0008.

Rodger, Joey. "Core Values: Our Common Ground." *American Libraries* 29, no. 9 (1998): 68–71.

Rosenzweig, Mark, Lois Ann Gregory-Wood, GraceAnne A. DeCandido, Al Kagan, Frederick W. Stoss, Christine Lind Hage, Sue Kamm, et al. "Library Juice 3:14 Supplement – April 12, 2000," 2000. https://web.archive.org/web/20160314205501/http://libr.org/juice/issues/vol3/LJ_3.14.sup.html.

Rothstein, Samuel. "In Search of Ourselves." *Library Journal* 93, no. 2 (1968): 156–57.

Rubin, Richard. "Ethical Issues in Library Personnel Management." *Journal of Library Administration* 14, no. 4 (August 16, 1991): 1–16. https://doi.org/10.1300/J111v14n04_01.

Rubin, Richard. "Library and Information Science: An Evolving Profession." In *Foundations of Library and Information Science*, 239–304. Chicago: Neal-Schuman Publishers, 2016.

Rubin, Richard. "The Values and Ethics of Library and Information Science." In *Foundations of Library and Information Science*, 533–79. Chicago: Neal-Schuman Publishers, 2016.

Rubin, Richard A., and Thomas J. Froehlich. "Ethical Aspects of Library and Information Science." In *Encyclopedia of Library and Information Sciences*. New York: Taylor and Francis, 2010.

Sager, Don. "The Search for Librarianship's Core Values." *Public Libraries* 40, no. 3 (June 2001): 149–53.

Sager, Don, Sharon L. Baker, Donna Joy Burke, Nann Baline Hilyard, and Gordon Welles. "A Question of Values." *Public Libraries* 38, no. 4 (1999): 214–18.

Sapp, Gregg, and Ron Gilmour. "A Brief History of the Future of Academic Libraries: Predictions and Speculations from the Literature of the Profession, 1975 to 2000—Part Two, 1990 to 2000." *Portal: Libraries and the Academy* 3, no. 1 (2003): 13–34. https://doi.org/10.1353/pla.2003.0008.

Saunders, Laura. "Connecting Information Literacy and Social Justice: Why and How." *Communications in Information Literacy* 11, no. 1 (2017): 55–75.

Schroeder, Robert, and Christopher V. Hollister. "Librarians' Views on Critical Theories and Critical Practices." *Behavioral & Social Sciences Librarian* 33, no. 2 (April 3, 2014): 91–119. https://doi.org/10.1080/01639269.2014.912104.

Schuman, Patricia Glass. "Core Values Task Force II Report," 2005. https://web.archive.org/web/20151210212223/http://www.ala.org/aboutala/sites/ala.org.aboutala/files/content/governance/policymanual/updatedpolicy-manual/ocrpdfofprm/40-1corevalues.pdf.

Seale, Maura. "Compliant Trust: The Public Good and Democracy in the ALA's 'Core Values of Librarianship.'" *Library Trends* 64, no. 3 (April 4, 2016): 585–603. https://doi.org/10.1353/lib.2016.0003.

Seminelli, Heather. "Librarian as Professional." *The Serials Librarian* 71, no. 1 (July 3, 2016): 63–69. https://doi.org/10.1080/0361526X.2016.1168667.

Shera, Jesse Hauk. *Sociological Foundations of Librarianship*. Bombay: Asia Publishing House, 1970.

Shockey, Kyle. "Intellectual Freedom Is Not Social Justice: The Symbolic Capital of Intellectual Freedom in ALA Accreditation and LIS Curricula." *Progressive Librarian* 44 (2015): 10.

Shoemaker, Elizabeth. "No One Can Whistle a Symphony: Seeking a Catalogers' Code of Ethics." *Knowledge Organization* 42, no. 5 (2015): 353–64. https://doi.org/10.5771/0943-7444-2015-5-353.

Shorb, Stephen. "Ethical Decision-Making in Library Administration." *The Southeastern Librarian* 52, no. 3 (2004): 4–9.

Singer, Peter. *Practical Ethics*. Cambridge: Cambridge University Press, 1993.

Smith, Martha Montague. "Infoethics for Leaders: Models of Moral Agency in the Information Environment." *Library Trends* 40, no. 3 (1992): 553–70.

St. Clair, Guy. *Total Quality Management in Information Services*. London: Bowker-Saur, 1997.

Sullivan, Maureen. "American Library Association Congress on Professional Education – Second Task Force on Core Values – Who We Are – America's Librarians Discuss Their Professional Values – Facilitator's Guide," May 23, 2004. https://web.archive.org/web/20040523015241/http://www.ala.org/ala/hrdrbucket/1stcongressonpro/1stcongresswho.htm.

Summers, F.William. "A Vision of Librarianship." *School Library Journal* 35, no. 14 (October 1989): 25–30.

Symons, Ann K., and Carla J. Stoffle. "When Values Conflict." *American Libraries* 29, no. 5 (May 1998): 56–58.

Tyler, Ralph W. "Educational Problems in Other Professions." In *Education for Librarianship: Papers Presented at the Library Conference, University of Chicago, August 16-21, 1948*, 22–38. Chicago: American Library Association, 1949.

Van der Veer Martens, Betsy. "New Grounds for Ontic Trust: Information Objects and LIS." *Education for Information* 33, no. 1 (January 2017): 37–54. https://doi.org/10.3233/EFI-170988.

Vinopal, Jennifer. "The Quest for Diversity in Library Staffing: From Awareness to Action." *In the Library with the Lead Pipe*, 2016. https://www.inthelibrarywiththeleadpipe.org/2016/quest-for-diversity/.

Walther, James H. "Teaching Ethical Dilemmas in LIS Coursework: An Adaptation on Case Methodology Usage for Pedagogy." *The Bottom Line* 29, no. 3 (September 16, 2016): 180–90. https://doi.org/10.1108/BL-05-2016-0020.

Weissinger, Thomas. "Competing Models of Librarianship: Do Core Values Make a Difference?" *The Journal of Academic Librarianship* 29, no. 1 (January 1, 2003): 32–39. https://doi.org/10.1016/S0099-1333(02)00403-2.

Wilkinson, Lane. "Principlism and the Ethics of Librarianship." *The Reference Librarian* 55, no. 1 (January 2, 2014): 1–25. https://doi.org/10.1080/02763877.2014.853270.

Winter, Michael F. "The Professionalization of Librarianship." In *Occasional Papers*, Vol. 160. University of Illinois Graduate School of Library and Information Science, 1983.

Yerkey, A. Neil. "Values of Library School Students, Faculty, and Librarians: Premises for Understanding." *Journal of Education for Librarianship* 21, no. 2 (1980): 122–34. https://doi.org/10.2307/40368583.

Yoon, Kyunghye, Rachel Dols, and Laura Hulscher. "Applying Inclusive Principles in Web Design to Enhance Accessibility for Disabled Users." In *Applying Library Values to Emerging Technology: Decision-Making in the Age of Open Access, Maker Spaces, and the Ever-Changing Library*, edited by Peter D. Fernandez and Kelly Tilton. Association of College and Research Libraries, 2018.

Young, Scott W. H. "On Ethical Assessment: Locating and Applying the Core Values of Library and Information Science." In *Proceedings of the 2020–2021 Library Assessment Conference*. Association of Research Libraries, 2021. https://www.libraryassessment.org/wp-content/uploads/2021/06/87-Young-On-Ethical-Assessment.pdf.

Ziegenfuss, Donna. "Using Appreciative Inquiry Methods to Build a Culture of Assessment and Library Instruction Program from the Bottom Up: Uncovering Librarian Values, Assumptions, Beliefs, and Best Practices." In *Proceedings of the 2016 Library Assessment Conference*, 2016.

Chapter 3
Sites of Tension for Ethical Decision-Making

Overview

In the practice of everyday information work, a variety of scenarios challenge the LIS practitioner to act in accordance with stated values. These challenges stem from tensions between values and practice, and thus prompt ethical reflection. Many sites of tension exist that compel ethical reflection and ethical decision-making on the part of the practitioner. Sites of tension represent real-world pressures that challenge or complicate a values-based practice, and therefore represent fruitful areas of investigation for identifying relevant values or developing a practical ethical tool, as this book project seeks to accomplish. In the LIS literature, sites of tension are practical conflicts that exert pressures on library values or prevent LIS practitioners from fully operationalizing stated professional values. In this chapter, I investigate ethical dilemmas and decisions in the LIS profession. I begin by providing an overview of two main types of ethical dilemmas—competing external value systems, and competing internal values. I then discuss prominent sites of ethical reflection and action, presented according to these two main types of dilemmas. First, tensions internal to the LIS profession: professional neutrality, library instruction, cataloging and classification, and diversity and equality. Second, tensions external to the LIS profession: market forces, technology, learning analytics and student success, and values assessment and impact studies.

Defining ethical dilemmas

Chapter 2 showed that the predominant approach to a values-based practice in LIS is practical ethics—the act of applying professional values in professional practice.[1] Ethical concerns in LIS are rooted in questions of practice.[2] From this place of practical, ethical concern, professional values become ethical tools to guide practitioners toward ethical conduct.[3] Identifying and applying values improves our professional ability to make ethical decisions that balance competing factors.[4] Now in Chapter 3, we will look closer at these competing factors. We will examine practice-based ethical dilemmas and the sites of tension where values-in-conflict can be found. Let's first frame this discussion by providing a definitional scope for ethical dilemmas.

At the center of an ethical site of tension is some sort of conflict—typically between competing stakeholders who have differing views on values and practices. When different factors compete for priority, ethical analysis can provide a path forward for action by clarifying assumptions and alternatives.[5] Ethical conflict, reflection, and resolution "represents every person's struggle to make the right decisions".[6] Striving towards "the right decision" marks the presence of ethical dilemmas. The LIS literature reveals two main areas of interest in relation to ethical dilemmas—external and internal to the professional—presented in the list below and in more depth in the following sections.

Dilemma Type: Value systems in conflict—external

Description: Disagreements involving competing value systems: personal, professional, institutional, societal.

Example: A librarian's professional values may conflict with the values of a parent-entity institution. A university, for example, may wish to implement student tracking for the purposes of learning analytics or web analytics, thus enacting an institutional value of *student success*, but doing so would be in conflict with the LIS professional value of *privacy*.[7]

---

1 Buchanan and Henderson, *Case Studies in Library and Information Science Ethics*, 95.

2 Wengert, "Some Ethical Aspects of Being an Information Professional."

3 Walther, "Teaching Ethical Dilemmas in LIS Coursework."

4 Rubin and Froehlich, "Ethical Aspects of Library and Information Science," 1750.

5 Smith, "Infoethics for Leaders."

6 Marco, "Ethics for Librarians," 34.

7 Jones and Salo, "Learning Analytics and the Academic Library."

Dilemma Type: Values in conflict—internal

Description: Disagreements involving competing professional values. In these situations, practitioners are faced with multiple paths of action for enacting different professional values. Decisions focus on which value(s) to prioritize for informing action, or whether and how to complete a professional task that is perceived to be in violation of professional values.

Example 1: A library can contract with a prison to conduct large-scale digitization at a low hourly wage. On the one hand, the library can enact the value of *access* by creating digital objects at a low cost. On the other hand, the library can enact the value of *social responsibility* by not engaging in exploitative labor practices.[8]

Example 2: A library vendor maintains a popular database, but the database also includes invasive tracking software. On the one hand, the library can enact the value of *service* by offering this highly-used database. On the other hand, the library can enact the value of *privacy* by not contracting with this vendor and thus preventing user tracking.[9]

Value Systems in Conflict—External

Different value systems can be in conflict: personal, professional, institutional, and societal. When faced with conflicting contexts and competing values, LIS professionals have long encouraged themselves to prioritize professional duties ahead of personal beliefs, and to remain objective in professional service to all users.[10] Objectivity is justified by the service value of LIS, and by the desire to deliver service of similar quality for all library users: "A good librarian must be able, as a professional, to undergo rapid, chameleon-like, changes as one enquirer follows another."[11] But as a complex human actor operating in a multi-stakeholder environment, a librarian balances competing priorities and ultimately makes a decision using their own viewpoint and values. And as we have seen in the prior chapter, the service value is

---

8   Logsdon, "Ethical Digital Libraries & Prison Labor?"
9   Magi, "A Content Analysis of Library Vendor Privacy Policies."
10 Foskett, *The Creed of a Librarian*.
11 Foskett, 11.

just one of many potential values that can be applied when making decisions about how to act.

This complicated environment is demonstrated in a 1954 LIS education report that counts 30 different activities and attitudes that constitute the "characteristics of professional librarianship."[12] The range of expectation and circumstance highlights the complexity of LIS work. The 1954 report also touches briefly on practical ethics—that is, applying values in real-world scenarios—saying that a librarian should possess the "ability to adapt principles to local situations." This point is carried on through the decades, as today's LIS literature includes calls to continuously examine, interpret, and apply professional values within institutional and community contexts that include intersecting political, economic, and cultural factors.[13]

The contemporary LIS landscape is now recognized as ethically complicated, in the sense that competing demands present multiple opportunities for values-based discussion and resolution.[14] As individual actors within larger systems, and even as one profession among many, LIS professionals make ethical decisions in response to multiple external pressures and value perspectives, as expressed by Budd: "If we take [the *ALA Core Values of Librarianship*] to be genuine expressions of the professional ethos, then the reality of external forces—politics, economics, information production, and the public good—must be considered."[15] The ethical complexity of LIS work is further expressed by Smith: "As moral agents (ethical selves) who assume responsibility in their personal, private, professional, and public lives, information professionals balance conflicting loyalties."[16] Smith outlines four main areas of conflict: loyalty to self, loyalty to patrons, loyalty to the profession, and loyalty to the employing institution. McMenemy, Poulter, and Burton similarly outline five ethical influences on librarians:

---

[12] Asheim, *The Core of Education for Librarianship; a Report of a Workshop Held under the Auspices of the Graduate Library School of the University of Chicago, August 10-15, 1953.*

[13] Newton, "The Origins of a Professionalism: Sociological Conclusions and Ethical Implications"; Budd, "Toward a Practical and Normative Ethics for Librarianship"; Budd, "What's the Right Thing to Do?"; Preer, *Library Ethics.*

[14] Rubin, "Ethical Issues in Library Personnel Management"; Marco, "Ethics for Librarians"; Budd, "Toward a Practical and Normative Ethics for Librarianship"; Rubin and Froehlich, "Ethical Aspects of Library and Information Science."

[15] Budd, "Toward a Practical and Normative Ethics for Librarianship," 257.

[16] Smith, "Infoethics for Leaders," 553.

pressure from the patron to provide service, an employer's ethical code, personal ethical beliefs, profession association's ethical code, and society's ethical norms.[17] Jefferson and Contreras note that "professional ethics and principles of an organization may often conflict with societal and personal ethics."[18]

Such external factors exert pressure on ethical professional action, generating a tension between traditional LIS values and contemporary adaptations of practice to suit new demands.[19] Budd explicates further: "Too often the choice we face is between the rock of reduced resources or the hard place of compromised principles. Awareness of the choice can contribute to a conversation among professionals that addresses the fundamental ethical challenge head on."[20] In response to today's media, cultural, and political climate, the LIS profession faces new and additional pressures to act in accordance with professional values.[21]

In analyzing the disparity between the values and actions of librarians, Hauptman offers a number of useful insights.[22] First, Hauptman states, "It is sometimes inconvenient to further [professional values] in the real world."[23] Further: "When two opposing principles vie with each other, it is much easier to capitulate to necessity."[24] Finally, Hauptman observes that LIS professionals "often fail to fully respect or implement" professional values.[25] In this line of thinking, Hauptman recognizes the difficulty that LIS professionals faces in enacting professional values in a broader environment that contains competing value systems that are not aligned with the LIS professional value system. Yousefi builds on these points and identifies this dilemma directly, "We routinely make decisions that oppose our declared

---

17 McMenemy, Poulter, and Burton, *A Handbook of Ethical Practice*.
18 Jefferson and Contreras, "Ethical Perspectives of Library and Information Science Graduate Students in the United States," 66.
19 Buschman, "On Libraries and the Public Sphere," 6.
20 Budd, "What's the Right Thing to Do?," 127.
21 Buschman, "November 8, 2016."
22 Hauptman, *Ethics and Librarianship*.
23 Hauptman, 134.
24 Hauptman, 139–40.
25 Hauptman, 133.

values."[26] Yousefi contends that pressures to act in accordance with external values prevent LIS professionals from enacting internal values. In practice, making an ethical choice among competing value systems involves a considered balance of personal and professional ideals within the perceived constraints and values of external systems.

Values in Conflict—Internal

Different professional values can be in conflict. Where there are multiple values that are considered relevant and applicable for guiding action, professional practice can be in conflict with one or more professional values. This type of ethical dilemma is a choice between two or more paths of action that are similarly acceptable.[27] Rubin offers a description: "'Ethical' considerations are those involved in deciding what is good or right in terms of the treatment of human beings, human actions, and values."[28] In discussing the process of making the right or good choice, Preer directly connects professional practice and professional values: "Ethics is about choices. As a system of principles determining right or wrong conduct; ethics defines the parameters of those choices."[29] Ethical decision-making presumes that an individual actor wants to do what is "right," that they can make thoughtful and reflective decisions, and that their capacities are not diminished or compromised.[30] From that point, the "right decision" may not be clear or obvious, and there may be more than one right decision. The nature of the dilemma is in prioritizing one value over another. The prioritized value then defines a path forward that prioritizes one action over another. It is not always clear which value should be of primary concern, and disagreements may arise between individual practitioners as to the preferred value and preferred course of action.[31] In such cases, professional practice may agree with one value but disagree with another, or there may be a disagreement or lack of alignment among values and

---

26 Yousefi, "On the Disparity Between What We Say and What We Do in Libraries," 92.

27 Severson, *The Principles of Information Ethics*.

28 Rubin, "Ethical Issues in Library Personnel Management," 1.

29 Preer, *Library Ethics*, 1.

30 Buchanan and Henderson, *Case Studies in Library and Information Science Ethics*.

31 Hauptman, *Ethical Challenges in Librarianship*, 7; Fallis, "Information Ethics for Twenty-first Century Library Professionals."

action. As a result of competing values and multiple choices, the path forward is ambiguous.

Ethical ambiguity can be a stimulating aspect of professional practice, in that a diversity of values can illuminate multiple resolutions in response to an ethical problem.[32] Ethical dilemmas in libraries are difficult and complex, and must be confronted on a routine basis.[33] Furthermore, as technology has complicated professional practice, ethical tensions have also become increasingly more complex.[34] Today's LIS professional experiences ethical dilemmas that are made difficult by a lack of clarity about when and how to apply competing professional values towards ethical action. The stakes of ethical action are seen to be professional integrity and the trust of our public community. When stated values are not consistently adhered to, our professional integrity may be called into question.[35] This line of discussion reveals the difficulty of "fully respecting or implementing" values in actual practice.[36] With so many values and value systems contending with the practical constraints of a modern workplace and political climate, enacting the right value at the right time becomes exceedingly difficult.

For LIS practitioners, ethics exist in the context of action—a complex arrangement of stakeholder needs and concerns.[37] Practitioners are encouraged to sensitize themselves to ethically acceptable ways of doing their jobs.[38] With that in mind, let us turn to an examination of specific sites of tension and ethical dilemmas present in contemporary LIS practice. In the following sections, I analyze the scholarly conversation relating to ethical dilemmas. I review the literature through the lens of two overarching pressures on ethical LIS practice: value systems in conflict, and values in conflict. The first section examines *market forces and the LIS profession* as an external pressure that represents value systems in conflict. The literature highlights three specific sites of tension that relate to market forces: 1) value studies and

---

32 Froehlich, "Intellectual Freedom, Ethical Deliberation and Codes of Ethics."
33 Walther, "Teaching Ethical Dilemmas in LIS Coursework."
34 Severson, *The Principles of Information Ethics*.
35 Hauptman, *Ethical Challenges in Librarianship*, 15; Budd, "What's the Right Thing to Do?"
36 Hauptman, *Ethics and Librarianship*.
37 Wengert, "Some Ethical Aspects of Being an Information Professional."
38 Hauptman, "Technological Implementations and Ethical Failures."

impact assessment, 2) information technologies, data, and privacy, and 3) learning analytics and student success. The second section examines the idea of *professional neutrality* as an internal pressure that represents values in conflict. The literature highlights three sites of tension that relate to professional neutrality: 1) social responsibility, 2) critical information literacy, and 3) cataloging and classification.

Value Systems in Conflict: Market Forces and the LIS Profession

The United States operates with a global capitalistic system.[39] People and entities within this system are influenced by the pressures and values of the market economy.[40] The values of a market economy, including efficiency, flexibility, and competition, can stand at odds with stated LIS professional values.[41] This conflict of value systems represents a lens of analysis through which ethical dilemmas may be viewed. As revealed in the LIS literature, a key question the emerges related to this conflict can be stated: Are we valuing our values? As background to this question, we can see a growing influence of market aims and values—including competition, profitability, risk, value for money, entrepreneurship—in public-sector organizations such as libraries and universities.[42] Practicing LIS in a way that enacts LIS values is becoming increasingly difficult in light of continued market pressures in the form of the commodification of information and the erosion of the public sphere.[43] Market forces can pressure libraries to act against their values, and in the face of pressures to prove value, libraries have created success measures that run counter to LIS values, but that align with the market values of parent universities.[44]

---

39 Engerman, "Capitalism."

40 Hayes and Brown, "The Library as a Business: Mapping the Pervasiveness of Financial Relationships in Today's Library"; Sessions, "How College Became a Commodity."

41 McDonald, "Corporate Inroads and Librarianship: The Fight for the Soul of the Profession in the New Millennium"; Quinn, "The McDonaldization of Academic Libraries?"

42 Nicholson, "The Mcdonaldization of Academic Libraries and the Values of Transformational Change."

43 Trosow, "The Commodification of Information and the Public Good: New Challenges for a Progressive Librarianship."

44 Fister, "The Self-Centered Library."

These tensions have today been amplified through a hyper form of capitalism known as neoliberalism. Neoliberalism's central idea is that individual actors can prosper best under conditions of intense market competition.[45] The thinking of neoliberal economics has become embedded in global political and societal structures.[46] Its influence extends to the American university.[47] In this way, neoliberalism is a particularly useful concept for analyzing the ethics of library practice, as it represents the combination of the practices and values of free trade with the practices and values of democracy. This same tense pairing—between the market and the public—is reflected in the history of libraries.[48]

Melvil Dewey founded the ALA in 1876 with the motto, "The best reading for the largest number at the least cost."[49] Even in his own time, Dewey's alignment with market values of return-on-investment and resource efficiency was met with resistance from within the profession, as Mary Salome Cutler Fairchild, Vice Director of ALA, remarked in 1895 that Dewey's motto "smacks of arithmetic and commerce."[50] The LIS profession maintains this century-long, still-unresolved tension: on the one hand, the commercial ideals of efficiency and profit; on the other, competing LIS ideals of social responsibility and community.[51] Yet LIS practice and market values show a long-standing entwinement. Through the history of LIS, there has been a predominant focus on efficient process over abstract purpose, because such a focus aligned with the prevailing logic of business and commercially-oriented outcomes. But altering LIS practice to align with market values is an existential compromise, what Buschman calls a "structural contradiction" between traditional LIS values and current LIS practices as shaped by contemporary market pressures.[52] Tensions deriving therefrom are described as "bone-deep contradictions between our liberal creed and the violent entailments of

---

45 Harvey, *A Brief History of Neoliberalism*.
46 Alvarez, "The End of the End of History."
47 Seal, "How the University Became Neoliberal."
48 Popowich, "Libraries, Labour, Capital."
49 Weigand, *Irrepressible Reformer: A Biography of Melvil Dewey*.
50 Weigand, 207.
51 Gregory and Higgins, "In Resistance to a Capitalist Past: Emerging Practices of Critical Librarianship."
52 Buschman, "On Libraries and the Public Sphere," 6.

industrial capitalism."[53] Despite such deep contradiction, there is ample evidence of libraries operating in service to market values.

In the context of contemporary LIS practice, neoliberal capitalism is expressed in the ideas of education as a commodity, the student as customer, and the importance of measurable evidence in support of delivering economic value.[54] Return-on-investment, for example, is becoming more common as academic libraries integrate a more market-based and entrepreneurial approach to information services, yet such economic measures require a level of precision that does not suit the work of education and libraries.[55] This tension is also revealed through the argument of describing library users as either *patron* or *customer*. For some, framing information services as customer services is correct, and even aligns with library values.[56] For others, perceiving students as customers introduces a consumer-oriented model of value based on the economic exchange of information; such a model presents the library as a material good that conflicts with stated library values of the public good.[57] Moreover, applying the term and concept of *customer* reflects a market-orientation, with the associated goal of achieving customer satisfaction; such a framing is potentially in conflict with the teaching and research mission of a university and library, which involve challenging students through growth and education rather than satisfying customers through product or service delivery.[58]

The literature conveys two main opposing aspects that define this overarching conflict of value systems, namely whether LIS organizations operate as a *public good* or a *market good*, with the attendant values and practices that characterize each. This tension is definitional for ethical practice in LIS. In the subsections below, I describe three specific sites of tension that demonstrate the ethical pressures of market forces in the practice of LIS professionals: 1) value assessment

---

53 Smith, "Vocational Melancholy," 470.

54 Seale, "The Neoliberal Library."

55 Neal, "Stop the Madness: The Insanity of ROI and the Need for New Qualitative Measures of Academic Library Success."

56 Matteson and Boyden, "Old Wine in a New Bottle."

57 Budd, "A Critique of Customer and Commodity."

58 Holley, "Academic Library Users Are Not 'Customers.'"

and impact studies, 2) information technology, data, and privacy, 3) learning analytics and student success.

Site of Tension 1: Value Studies and Impact Assessment

This site of tension is concerned with the rise of and response to value studies and impact assessment in academic libraries. Work in this area was initiated by the president of the Association of College and Research Libraries (ACRL) Division of ALA, who in 2009 established the focus of ACRL in response to the question, "what is our value and who values us?"[59] In response to increased competition for diminishing resources, the president of ACRL remarked, "Demands increase for proving our worth and justifying our existence, resulting in efforts on many of our campuses to demonstrate the value of higher education. In turn, we are being asked how libraries and librarians contribute to that value. How will we respond?"[60] The response to this question is recognized to be the groundbreaking *Value of Academic Libraries: A Comprehensive Research Review and Report.*"[61] In this report, Oakleaf describes and sets forth the practices of studying the value of libraries through the assessment of outcomes and their impacts. This report has since been described as "set[ting] the agenda for assessment in libraries."[62] Oakleaf outlines the main areas of library value: use, return-on-investment, commodity production, impact, and alternative comparison. Following its release, practitioners have diversely applied Oakleaf's concepts of value studies, including in the areas of information literacy,[63] faculty research productivity,[64] student engagement,[65] student retention,[66] graduation rates,[67] and grade point average.[68]

---

59 Goetsch, "What Is Our Value and Who Values Us?," 502.

60 Goetsch, 502.

61 Oakleaf, "The Value of Academic Libraries."

62 Arellano Douglas, "Moving from Critical Assessment to Assessment as Care."

63 Catalano and Phillips, "Information Literacy and Retention."

64 Hollister and Schroeder, "The Impact of Library Support on Education Faculty Research Productivity."

65 Scott, "Academic Library Use Is Positively Related to a Variety of Educational Outcomes."

66 Murray and Ireland, "Communicating Library Impact on Retention."

67 Logan, "Students Who Used the Library in Their First Year of University Are More Likely to Graduate or Still Be Enrolled After Four Years."

68 Tewell, "Use of Library Services Can Be Associated with a Positive Effect on First-Year Students' GPA and Retention."

The past decade of value studies have been continuously motivated by the perceived need for academic libraries to prove value to external stakeholders such as university administration and state boards of regents in order to receive financial resources.[69] Through the COVID-19 pandemic, these pressures have remained or even intensified.[70] Conversations around library value continue to engage and challenge practitioners and researchers in LIS.[71] New assessment practices continue to be developed and applied, because "traditional measures of library success no longer resonate with university leaders, causing academic librarians to seek new methods of determining and demonstrating library value to student success."[72] As the value proposition is typically presented as an exchange for continued financial resources, library value is predominantly presented as a financial matter, with business metrics framing impact assessments.[73] Gregory and Higgins summarize: "Assessment is criticized as a form of neoliberal accountability, as a project that disciplines and controls the workforce and specific communities, and abandons the goal of achieving equitable educational opportunity. It is an attempt to reduce complexity to a quantifiable metric, to link learning to returns on investment and the marketplace, and to fill reports for assessment auditors."[74] In this context, the assessment effort is concerned less with improving or expanding services, and more with demonstrating the worth of existing services to external, market-oriented audiences for the sake of continued financial support.

As these impact areas are drawn from an economic, market-based perspective, Oakleaf acknowledges, "some authors warn that financial values do not mesh easily with the values of higher education."[75] Indeed, much of the counter-discussion around library value studies

---

69 Hufford, "A Review of the Literature on Assessment in Academic and Research Libraries, 2005 to August 2011"; Oakleaf and Kyrillidou, "Revisiting the Academic Library Value Research Agenda"; Murray and Ireland, "Provosts' Perceptions of Academic Library Value & Preferences for Communication."

70 Lembinen, "Academic Libraries' Leaders' Decision-Making during the COVID-19 Crisis."

71 Clarke et al., "Invisible Labor, Invisible Value."

72 Murray, "Academic Libraries and High-Impact Practices for Student Retention," 486.

73 Bourg, "Beyond Measure."

74 Gregory and Higgins, "Reorienting an Information Literacy Program Toward Social Justice," 47.

75 Oakleaf, "The Value of Academic Libraries," 21.

stems from the tension between the values of the financial system that drives assessment and the values of the educational system that produces the work being assessed. Some have voiced concern and criticism of value studies in general and of Oakleaf specifically. Nicholson states of Oakleaf's 2010 report: "The use of capitalist language in higher education is normalized: education is a national resource, learning is a commodity, and degrees are credentials to be exchanged on the job market."[76] For Nicholson, the underlying ideology of market-based metrics that rely on dollars-and-cents calculations is not appropriate for measuring abstract educational outcomes like learning and research. Such arguments further undermine the concept of the library as holding inherent value to a learning and research institution.[77] Because library services are not generally built to produce a stream of revenue, there are conceptual problems for cost-benefit analysis.[78] Seale has also contributed to this critique, contending that neoliberal approaches are antithetical to the missions of both higher education and libraries,[79] and that the core values of libraries are not reflected in dominant impact assessments that focus on efficiency and economic value.[80] Fisher issues a call-to-action for assessment practitioners: "We need to push back on demands to use library data to prove our value."[81]

The assessment tool LibQUAL+ serves as a representative example of this tension. LibQUAL+ is an assessment instrument developed from the commercial sector, and it views libraries as a customer service, emphasizing efficiency, timeliness, and customer satisfaction; it further encourages libraries to competitively rank their scores in relation to those of other libraries.[82] LibQUAL+ is a widely-implemented tool for understanding service quality as measured by user satisfaction.[83] LibQUAL+ has been criticized, however, for narrowly or inaccurately

---

76 Nicholson, "The 'Value Agenda,'" 4.
77 Drabinski and Walter, "Asking Questions That Matter."
78 Urquhart and Turner, "Reflections on the Value and Impact of Library and Information Services."
79 Seale, "Efficiency or Jagged Edges: Resisting Neoliberal Logics of Assessment."
80 Seale, "The Neoliberal Library."
81 Fisher, "Can We Demonstrate Academic Library Value Without Violating Student Privacy?," 36.
82 Thompson, Kyrillidou, and Cook, "Library Users' Service Desires."
83 Atkinson and Walton, "Establishing Quality in University Libraries."

measuring library impact, and for centering market values ahead of academic values.[84] As an ethical dilemma, LibQUAL+ is a useful example. Libraries are compelled to prove their value, and LibQUAL+ is presented as a standard, easy-to-implement tool for doing so. But at the same time, LibQUAL+ may not be the right tool in the context of LIS practice, and implementing the instrument may further entrench a market-based paradigm that undercuts the values and missions of libraries.

In summary, the concept of library value and impact is complex and often abstract or intangible. Due to societal and parent entity pressures, librarians are compelled to quantify and measure library services and usage in ways that may go against organizational or professional values. In these cases, the value system of market forces can come into conflict with the value system of the LIS profession.

Site of Tension 2: Information Technologies, Data, and Privacy

Privacy has become a well-established value among librarians, to the point of being described as a cornerstone of the profession's ethical foundation.[85] Information professionals express high levels of concern for information privacy, with a stated desire to control the access and use of personal information in order to protect library users' ability to read and research without unwanted or unintended surveillance.[86] At the same time, LIS professionals actively seek out and integrate information technologies so as to improve service and enhance access.[87] As a product of human effort, technology is recognized not as neutral, but rather as value-laden by their creators.[88] Information technologies used in LIS settings are often produced and provided by third-party vendors that do not share LIS values related to privacy

---

84 Seale, "Efficiency or Jagged Edges: Resisting Neoliberal Logics of Assessment"; Urquhart and Turner, "Reflections on the Value and Impact of Library and Information Services"; Lilburn, "Ideology and Audit Culture."

85 Witt, "The Evolution of Privacy within the American Library Association, 1906–2002."

86 Zimmer, "Librarians' Attitudes Regarding Information and Internet Privacy."

87 Nicols Hess, LaPorte-Fiori, and Engwall, "Preserving Patron Privacy in the 21st Century Academic Library."

88 Owens et al., "Digital Infrastructures That Embody Library Principles: The IMLS National Digital Platform as a Framework for Digital Library Tools and Services"; Reidsma, *Masked by Trust*.

and are therefore more likely to expose user data.[89] LIS practitioners have recognized certain ethical tensions resulting from third-party information technologies, particularly regarding the potentially invasive collection of data related to user behavior.[90]

At the center of this tension are competing professional commitments to privacy, access, and service, each of which is included in the *ALA Core Values of Librarianship*. Third-party vendors, typically operating as for-profit companies, are compelled by market forces to collect and monetize user data, yet many of these technologies—while promising better access—also compromise privacy. In these instances, the core value of access is overweighted and misapplied vis-à-vis privacy.[91] A few examples can illustrate this tension. First, librarians were shown to be strong defenders of privacy following USA PATRIOT ACT-related requests for user information from United States governmental agencies such as the National Security Agency.[92] In this case, librarians demonstrated a values clarity on this issue because the USA PATRIOT ACT did not also appear as beneficial to service or access.

When a technology also enacts values such as service or access, the ethical uncertainty with respect to privacy becomes more apparent. Assessment technologies and practices such as data warehousing, for example, offer a more complicated case. In these instances, the financial pressures of data-driven decision making in support of service improvements and impact assessments drive libraries to leverage technologies for user data collection and analysis. Libraries are encouraged to resolve this tension by acting responsibly to protect user privacy while at the same time attending to organizational needs for service evaluation.[93] In another example, the third-party search tools used by libraries to enhance access may not operate in accordance with values such as privacy or social responsibility. Reidsma provides an in-depth examination of the search algorithms that drive the

---

89   Galvan, "Architecture of Authority"; O'Brien et al., "Protecting Privacy on the Web: A Study of HTTPS and Google Analytics Implementation in Academic Library Websites"; Lamdan, "Librarianship at the Crossroads of ICE Surveillance."

90   Valentine and Barron, "An Examination of Academic Library Privacy Policy Compliance with Professional Guidelines."

91   Buschman, "The New Technocracy."

92   Carpenter, "Librarians Versus the NSA."

93   Yoose, "Balancing Privacy and Strategic Planning Needs."

operation of a third-party Integrated Library System (ILS): "Algorithms are sold to us as disinterested, objective, neutral information gathering tools that find us answers. But a closer look at algorithms shows us that corporate profit motives, the nature of computer science and mathematics, reductive models of the world, and a fetish for speed and efficiency are also factors that help shape how they are designed and how they work."[94] While offering high quality web service and access to thousands of library records, search algorithms also produce results that include cultural biases and harmful stereotypes, all while passively tracking and collecting activity data on users.

LIS professionals have proposed a number of responses to this ethical tension between the values of service/access and privacy. Professional trainings, collective actions, and public awareness can be one path forward for critically engaging with information technologies, as demonstrated by professional organizations and initiatives such as the Library Freedom Project,[95] Data for Black Lives,[96] and the Digital Library Federation Privacy and Ethics in Technology Working Group.[97] Organizational policies in support of privacy are another option, including public statements on patron privacy and identifying behind-the-scenes issues with the collection, storage, and disposal of library patrons' private information.[98] Others have called for the profession to refine and strengthen notions of privacy and other core values in light of contemporary technologies such as linked data and big data,[99] and machine learning and artificial intelligence.[100]

Professional discourse focuses chiefly on critical engagement as a way to approach ethical tensions. But when privacy is in tension with service or access, the path forward is murkier as compared to the more straightforward case of the USA PATRIOT ACT, in which the predominant response was a clear-cut denial of record requests. Ultimately,

---

94 Reidsma, *Masked by Trust*, 26.
95 "Library Freedom Project."
96 "Data 4 Black Lives."
97 Digital Library Federation, "Technologies of Surveillance."
98 Nicols Hess, LaPorte-Fiori, and Engwall, "Preserving Patron Privacy in the 21st Century Academic Library."
99 Campbell and Cowan, "The Paradox of Privacy."
100 Lorang et al., "Digital Libraries, Intelligent Data Analytics, and Augmented Description: A Demonstration Project"; Padilla, "A Mutualistic View of AI in the Library or a Continuation of Craft."

the way to ensure tools and services reflect LIS values is for LIS professionals to deeply engage in the design, implementation, and administration of information technologies.[101] Even more strongly, Bignoli et al. propose a framework of refusal in the face of ubiquitous data collection that violates privacy.[102]

Across the history of the LIS profession, privacy has been an enduring value. But contemporary information technologies threaten privacy even as they offer advantages for service and access. Where new technologies promise to enhance access and improve service—but at the potential cost of user privacy—a site of tension emerges. While LIS organizations do not typically operate for profit, they often implement technologies built by for-profit third parties that track user behavior, thereby forcing LIS organizations into a larger business model that supports some LIS values while simultaneously being antithetical to others. Despite the increasing difficulty in achieving privacy, however, LIS professionals continue to think critically and ethically about privacy, and work to protect the privacy of library users.

Site of Tension 3: Learning Analytics and Student Success

Tensions around technology extend to a specific practice of assessing student success in higher education—learning analytics. Learning analytics is the practice of aggregating and analyzing data related to student activity so as to better understand student success and improve services.[103] In order to maintain alignment with university strategic goals and initiatives, academic libraries have pursued and implemented learning analytics software and practices.[104] The motivation to implement learning analytics stems from perceived market-style competition for limited resources and the related pressure to demonstrate library contributions to student success so as to justify resource

---

101 Matz, "Libraries and the USA PATRIOT Act"; Owens et al., "Digital Infrastructures That Embody Library Principles: The IMLS National Digital Platform as a Framework for Digital Library Tools and Services"; Reidsma, *Masked by Trust*.

102 Bignoli et al., "Resisting Crisis Surveillance Capitalism in Academic Libraries."

103 Jones and Salo, "Learning Analytics and the Academic Library"; Jones, "Just Because You Can Doesn't Mean You Should"; Travis and Ramirez, "Big Data and Academic Libraries: The Quest for Informed Decision-Making."

104 Association of College and Research Libraries, "Standards for Libraries in Higher Education"; Murray, "Academic Libraries and High-Impact Practices for Student Retention"; Jones, "Learning Analytics, the Academic Library, and Positive Intellectual Freedom."

allocations within the larger context of the university.[105] Professional discourse indicates a mainstream acceptance that university efforts to collect student data—including libraries' participation in such efforts—are important to student success, thus framing learning analytics as necessary for ensuring the health of both the library and the wider institution.[106] Many examples of learning analytics studies are present in the LIS literature, including those attempting to relate student library usage to retention,[107] first-year student success,[108] graduate rates,[109] grade point average,[110] and improving library services.[111]

Despite its prevalence and appearance of inevitability, others have argued that the ethical dimensions of learning analytics have not been given sufficient attention.[112] Learning analytics have been shown to complicate ethical practice across several dimensions. Foremost among these dimensions are LIS professional commitments to privacy and intellectual freedom. Learning analytics can compromise intellectual freedom when its results are applied as interventions that limit students' access to learning materials; the practice also impinges privacy when student information related to the use of research materials is recorded, analyzed, and shared with a variety of first-party and third-party entities.[113] Learning analytics potentially affects learning and democracy, either positively by supporting students and achieving learning outcomes, or negatively by alienating students and undermining educational goals.[114] Learning analytics have been criticized as detracting from pedagogical aims by simplifying the student into a

---

105 Oakleaf, "The Problems and Promise of Learning Analytics for Increasing and Demonstrating Library Value and Impact."

106 Nicholson, Pagowsky, and Seale, "Just-in-Time or Just-in-Case?"

107 Haddow, "Academic Library Use and Student Retention"; Murray, Ireland, and Hackathorn, "The Value of Academic Libraries."

108 Soria, Fransen, and Nackerud, "Stacks, Serials, Search Engines, and Students' Success."

109 Soria, Fransen, and Nackerud, "The Impact of Academic Library Resources on Undergraduates' Degree Completion."

110 Wong and Webb, "Uncovering Meaningful Correlation between Student Academic Performance and Library Material Usage."

111 Beile, Choudhury, and Wang, "Hidden Treasure on the Road to Xanadu."

112 Viberg et al., "The Current Landscape of Learning Analytics in Higher Education"; Rabinowitz, "Learning Analytics, Surveillance, Student Success, and the Library."

113 Jones and Salo, "Learning Analytics and the Academic Library."

114 Oliphant and Brundin, "Conflicting Values."

quantifiable numerical entity, thereby commodifying learning for the sake of competitive analysis among institutions and departments.[115] Learning analytics reinforces a market-oriented view of student success, which in turn limits the assessment approaches that libraries can implement.[116] Moreover, the datasets, tools, and processes related to learning analytics are often modeled or borrowed from the private sector, and thus are not suitable for measuring the complexities of educational outcomes, nor do they reflect the values of educational institutions.[117] A leading voice in learning analytics, Oakleaf acknowledges a number of limitations in the approach, noting especially that learning analytics is correlational, and thus cannot "definitively demonstrate that student library interactions cause students to learn more or attain success markers."[118] It has been shown that library involvement in learning analytics has increased over time, even as the outcomes of learning analytics have produced findings of limited efficacy, thereby calling into question whether learning analytics justify the loss of privacy and risk borne by students and institutions.[119]

Collecting and analyzing personal data presents an uneasy balance of ethics and privacy, with the potential disaster of data leakage and misapplication of analysis.[120] From this place of uncertainty, an emerging ethical question for learning analytics is how to pursue the potential benefits of academic data mining while accounting for the potential harms.[121] For some in the profession, learning analytics should be embraced[122] For others, the current model of learning analytics does not align with ethical standards of LIS practice.[123] When privacy-violating learning analytics promises to advance key goals like library service

---

115 Nicholson, Pagowsky, and Seale, "Just-in-Time or Just-in-Case?"

116 Beilin, "Student Success and the Neoliberal Academic Library."

117 Oliphant and Brundin, "Conflicting Values."

118 Oakleaf, "The Problems and Promise of Learning Analytics for Increasing and Demonstrating Library Value and Impact," 21.

119 Viberg et al., "The Current Landscape of Learning Analytics in Higher Education"; Robertshaw and Asher, "Unethical Numbers?"

120 Travis and Ramirez, "Big Data and Academic Libraries: The Quest for Informed Decision-Making."

121 Jones and Salo, "Learning Analytics and the Academic Library."

122 Oakleaf and Kyrillidou, "Revisiting the Academic Library Value Research Agenda."

123 Fisher, "Can We Demonstrate Academic Library Value Without Violating Student Privacy?"; Hathcock, "Learning Agency, Not Analytics"; Jones, "Just Because You Can Doesn't Mean You Should."

and student success, tensions arise. The right approach is not obvious or objective, and our professional discourse, practices, and attitudes are evolving as our field continues to work more in this area.[124] Though there are no clear steps or profession-wide ethical boundaries, practitioners desire a definite path forward that offers "bright-line rules" for either the ethical practice of learning analytics or a response strategy for choosing not to implement learning analytics.[125]

A number of such responses have been proposed for engaging with or countering learning analytics. The first is to reject learning analytics and other passive surveillance techniques, and instead work more closely and directly with research subjects such as students in order to determine and measure success.[126] Students have been shown to be generally unaware of the data and information their institutions have access to about themselves, and students think such data should be more restricted than current practice accommodates.[127] Approaches that recognize student agency are more in accordance with LIS values of learning, democracy, privacy, and intellectual freedom. If libraries choose to move forward with learning analytics, Jones and Salo suggest that LIS professionals advocate for embedding LIS values into the systems, policies, and programs of learning analytics so as to aid in their ethical implementation.[128] Additional professional development is needed to help LIS workers become fluent and effective in the practices of learning analytics so that sound procedures are put into place.[129]

In summary, learning analytics represent a clear ethical tension. On the one hand, market forces of contemporary higher education demand accountability and always-improving services, and student tracking software has emerged as a seemingly effective method for achieving these results. On the other hand, libraries wish to preserve

---

124 Simms and Paschke-Wood, "Academic Librarians and Student Success."

125 Jones, "Just Because You Can Doesn't Mean You Should."

126 Beilin, "Student Success and the Neoliberal Academic Library"; Hathcock, "Learning Agency, Not Analytics."

127 Jones et al., "In Their Own Words: Student Perspectives on Privacy and Library Participation in Learning Analytics Initiatives."

128 Jones and Salo, "Learning Analytics and the Academic Library."

129 Robertshaw and Asher, "Unethical Numbers?"; Travis and Ramirez, "Big Data and Academic Libraries: The Quest for Informed Decision-Making."

privacy and other values. Robertshaw and Asher express the tension of learning analytics: "since we are presently in an era where the businessification of higher education is quickening, academic libraries will likely find it difficult to completely resist the quantification of their impacts."[130] Despite much debate and continued pressure to implement learning analytics from parent entities, no consensus has yet emerged for ethical guidelines or responses among the LIS professional community. As we have seen in other sites of tension and in the prior chapter, multiple right answers may be available. If we understand ethics as a matter of choice, then the values that we choose to apply determine the outcome. And we have many values from which to choose. Learning analytics provides an instructive example. On the one hand, a practitioner can choose to apply a service value in joining a learning analytics assessment program. On the other hand, a different practitioner could choose to apply a privacy value in not joining a learning analytics program. Both practitioners can be said to be following a values-based practice. The tension is located where values conflict.

Values in Conflict: Professional Neutrality

Within the LIS profession, the concept of professional neutrality is a fertile ground of discussion related to ethical professional practice. Libraries have a long-held position of neutrality in the design and delivery of LIS services and systems; such a position is understood to be a basic assumption underlying modern librarianship, dating to Dewey's founding of the ALA in 1876.[131] Though not counted among the ALA's core values, neutrality serves as a precondition to officially-recognized core values of intellectual freedom and democracy.[132] The positioning of neutrality as possible and desirable is driven by a multi-faceted motivation. Neutrality is seen as a way to maintain objectivity and eliminate bias in the relationship between library professional and library patron.[133] The foundation of this point rests on the argument that the personal beliefs of a librarian must not influence

---

130 Robertshaw and Asher, "Unethical Numbers?," 95.

131 Mai, "Ethics, Values and Morality in Contemporary Library Classifications."

132 Burgess, "Reconciling Social Responsibility and Neutrality in LIS Professional Ethics: A Virtue Ethics Approach."

133 Berninghausen, "Antithesis in Librarianship: Social Responsibility vs. The Library Bill of Rights"; Wilson, *Second-Hand Knowledge*.

professional duties, so as to ensure a continuity of service for patrons of different cultural identities.[134] This position has been held as a traditional marker of the profession, even being called "timeless" because it looks to the core purpose of LIS.[135] Some literature suggests that neutrality is an achievable standard because it supports library claims to be a public good,[136] ensures equal concern and respect for patrons,[137] and promotes political choice and freedom.[138]

But professionals today are re-engaging with and re-evaluating the concept and application of neutrality. To view a library as neutral is to "view it as 'beyond' the reach of politics.[139] But a library is not beyond politics, nor is it out of reach from critical self-examination.[140] The ALA President's Program at the 2017 Midwinter Meeting centered on neutrality, prompting self-examination through a series of questions:

- Were libraries ever neutral?
- Has the time come to question neutrality?
- Are libraries through their practices, collections, services and technologies able to be neutral?
- Can libraries be neutral as part of societies and systems that are not neutral?
- Rather than neutral, should we advocate for a distinct set of values?
- How can we do so and maintain trust in our communities?[141]

These questions are representative of the contemporary, critical re-examination of LIS neutrality.[142] The question of values is particularly

---

134 Foskett, *The Creed of a Librarian*.

135 Brewerton, "The Creed of a Librarian."

136 Matz, "Libraries and the USA PATRIOT Act."

137 Wenzler, "Neutrality and Its Discontents."

138 Burgess, "Reconciling Social Responsibility and Neutrality in LIS Professional Ethics: A Virtue Ethics Approach."

139 Santamaria, "Concealing White Supremacy through Fantasies of the Library," 435.

140 Ettarh, "Vocational Awe and Librarianship."

141 American Library Association, "The ALA President's Program at the Midwinter Meeting Debates Neutrality in Libraries."

142 Chiu, Ettarh, and Ferretti, "Not the Shark, but the Water: How Neutrality and Vocational Awe Intertwine to Uphold White Supremacy."

relevant for practical ethics and professional practice. From a values viewpoint, neutrality is defined as not taking a stand or a side in a debate.[143] The neutrality discussion in the LIS literature is itself polarized, with discourse focused on first scrutinizing the coherence of neutrality as a concept and second whether neutrality has a positive or negative effect when applied in practice.[144] Some hold that neutrality is achievable, positive, and reinforces LIS values; others hold that neutrality is nonviable, negative, and undermines LIS values.

The contemporary view of neutrality begins with a re-examination of its history and social context. A contemporary view sees neutrality as a contrived posture meant to maintain financial support in an unstable market environment in which the appearance of political objectivity renders libraries unobjectionable to established and powerful stakeholders such as federal funders—but "by perpetuating the myth that their profession should be politically neutral, librarians have created a value vacuum… being filled by the prevailing political and economic ethos."[145] The main thrust found in recent LIS literature on this topic involves challenging the myth of neutrality. If we understand LIS to be a profession of values and action, the notion of neutrality is rendered "an impossible construct."[146]

The apparent impossibility of neutrality is thoroughly expounded by others. Neutrality is seen to be an incoherent and untenable position, because LIS is a profession with a specific social history that includes specific political and social contexts.[147] Specifically, LIS comes from a Western, enlightenment tradition.[148] LIS stems from and reinforces the values and sensibilities of a socio-economic middle-class.[149] With this history in mind, it is argued that neutrality functions not as an objective stance, but rather as a position that reinforces and encourages

---

143 Bourg, "Debating Y/Our Humanity, or Are Libraries Neutral?"

144 Macdonald and Birdi, "The Concept of Neutrality."

145 Blanke, "Librarianship and Political Values," 40.

146 Samek, *Librarianship and Human Rights*, 1.

147 Jensen, "The Myth of the Neutral Professional"; Honma, "Trippin' Over the Color Line"; Rosenzweig, "Politics and Anti-Politics in Librarianship"; Ettarh, "Making a New Table"; Nowviskie, "From the Grass Roots."

148 Froehlich, "Intellectual Freedom, Ethical Deliberation and Codes of Ethics"; de jesus, "Locating the Library in Institutional Oppression."

149 Popowich, *Confronting the Democratic Discourse of Librarianship*.

already-dominant worldviews and values, and in such a way that obscures the dominance of those values.[150] Since it passively reinforces the status quo, a posture of neutrality in fact takes as clear a stand as directly addressing social issues.[151]

By implicitly upholding historically dominant societal values, neutrality hinders LIS practitioners from enacting professional values with intention and effectiveness.[152] In order to achieve a more ethical practice, Wengert implores LIS professionals to take a stronger stand against neutrality and in favor of enacting professional values for the betterment of the wider communities: "Our sole goal ought not be to be morally blameless; we would also like to contribute to making better the lives of those around us and who share our communities."[153]

The conversation today indicates that LIS cannot be a profession of values and also a profession of neutrality. Enacting professional values explicitly requires taking a stand.[154] Neutrality therefore gives rise to a number of ethical dilemmas, stemming from the following question: how can LIS professionals resolve the tension between, on the one hand, adhering to a sense of neutrality, and, on the other hand, enacting a values-based practice? In the subsections below, I describe three sites of tension that highlight the pressures and contradictions of professional neutrality: 1) social responsibility, 2) critical information literacy, and 3) cataloging and classification.

Site of Tension 4: Social Responsibility

LIS professionals demonstrate an interest in enacting the stated professional value of social responsibility, notably through social justice—the practice of addressing historical imbalances of rights, resources, and representation among different groups in our society, often

---

150 Sparanese, "Activist Librarianship: Heritage or Heresy?"; Macdonald and Birdi, "The Concept of Neutrality."

151 Ferretti, "Neutrality Is Hostility."

152 Gibson et al., "Libraries on the Frontlines"; Nicholson, Pagowsky, and Seale, "Just-in-Time or Just-in-Case?"

153 Wengert, "Some Ethical Aspects of Being an Information Professional," 500.

154 Good, "The Hottest Place in Hell: The Crisis of Neutrality in Contemporary Librarianship."

focused on race, gender, and class.[155] As related by Schroeder and Hollister, "many librarians are concerned with social justice issues as they relate to the library…It is heartening that librarians, as a professional group, created and abide by the Core Values of Librarianship (ALA 2004) statement, which includes a commitment to social responsibility."[156] More broadly, "the information professions have long been associated with inclusiveness, civic-mindedness, and concern for the poor and underserved."[157] Academic libraries' main pathway to social justice is through the work of diversity, equity, and inclusion, which focuses on increasing cultural representation and the capacity for understanding and supporting different cultural identities, leading to an equality of outcomes.[158]

As a counterweight to social responsibility, neutrality stands in tension to the aims of social justice, diversity, inclusion, and equity: "The extent that the LIS profession can claim to be politically neutral decreases as efforts to right political injustices increase."[159] It is further argued that maintaining positions of neutrality and addressing social injustice are incompatible.[160] Porter points out that wider social and political conditions are continually and inescapably acting upon the work of LIS, and that postures of neutrality enable a marginalization that in turn limits equity, intellectual freedom, and democracy for vulnerable populations; moreover, to uphold LIS professional values, LIS professionals "must be advocates against marginalization and inequity, and for justice and equity."[161]

To uphold library values is to engage directly with social inequality. Enacting the justice-oriented LIS value of social responsibility means

---

155 Sparanese, "Activist Librarianship: Heritage or Heresy?"; Morales, Knowles, and Bourge, "Diversity, Social Justice, and the Future of Libraries"; Jaeger, Taylor, and Gorham, *Libraries, Human Rights, and Social Justice*; Mehra, "Introduction"; Roberts and Noble, "Empowered to Name, Inspired to Act."

156 Schroeder and Hollister, "Librarians' Views on Critical Theories and Critical Practices," 113.

157 Rioux, "Metatheory in Library and Information Science," 9.

158 Mathuews, "Moving Beyond Diversity to Social Justice"; Hudson, "On 'Diversity' as Anti-Racism in Library and Information Studies."

159 Burgess, "Reconciling Social Responsibility and Neutrality in LIS Professional Ethics: A Virtue Ethics Approach," 169.

160 Jensen, "The Myth of the Neutral Professional"; Samek, *Librarianship and Human Rights*; Nowviskie, "From the Grass Roots."

161 Porter, "Radical Collaboration: Allied Media Conference in Detroit," para. 6.

being attuned to power dynamics and working to improve the material and social conditions of traditionally marginalized people.[162] Conversely, in advancing the position of neutrality, LIS professionals fail to confront harmful racial injustices and colonial oppressions.[163] In these instances, neutrality acts to remove LIS workers from the issues that are important to their wider communities.[164] As expressed by Gibson: "Libraries have clung to a colorblind philosophy of neutrality that has allowed for disengagement from communities of color."[165] Still, the argument persists that social issues exist outside of the realm of LIS issues, and that neutrality should be upheld and defended.[166]

This site of tension is therefore defined by the embrace or rejection of neutrality as it applies to the values of social responsibility and social justice. Two key examples illustrate this tension in practice: 1) diversity, equity, and inclusion, and 2) library spaces. Beginning with diversity, one avenue towards accomplishing diversity is through diversifying the cultural profile of the LIS profession itself—in the field and in the classroom—through recruitment, retention, and promotion of diverse LIS students and professionals that can serve diverse populations. Leaving social responsibility out of the LIS curriculum, for example, does not equip students for their real-world working environments.[167] In analyzing diversity-related content of LIS program websites, Ndumu and Betts-Green find that much can be improved, and that "rather than approaching diversity as the right thing to do...it must be positioned as a value so integral to our profession that it is grafted within LIS programs and workplaces."[168] Some in the field call for deeply embracing social responsibility by confronting past historical injustices such as white supremacy: "Interventions in public libraries, academic libraries, law libraries, and medical libraries are also needed, sending

---

162 de jesus, "Locating the Library in Institutional Oppression"; Stoytcheva, "Steven Salaita, the Critical Importance of Context, and Our Professional Ethics."

163 de jesus, "Locating the Library in Institutional Oppression"; Gibson et al., "Libraries on the Frontlines."

164 Jensen, "The Myth of the Neutral Professional"; Good, "The Hottest Place in Hell: The Crisis of Neutrality in Contemporary Librarianship."

165 Gibson et al., "Libraries on the Frontlines," 11.

166 Berninghausen, "Antithesis in Librarianship: Social Responsibility vs. The Library Bill of Rights"; Wenzler, "Neutrality and Its Discontents."

167 Roberts and Noble, "Empowered to Name, Inspired to Act."

168 Ndumu and Betts-Green, "First Impressions," 92.

a strong message that equity and inclusion are library values."[169] Kendrick and Damasco note that, as a way to enact its values of diversity, equity, and social responsibility, the ALA has acknowledged and recalibrated the disproportionate whiteness of the LIS field by engaging in diversity work.[170]

Yet despite such measures, results have not materialized: "Given that three decades of discussion of the urgent need for diversity in our field in order to make good on our professional ethics and commitment to equity has nonetheless yielded little direct action or change."[171] Although a number of programs exist to support diverse hiring in academic librarianship, race and gender representation has remained the same for decades.[172] Looking at the structural roots of LIS, the library profession and library workplaces continue to express a deeply-ingrained antagonism toward employees of color.[173] Neutrality is relevant again here as a factor that impedes progress towards diversity and equity. It is difficult to confront and counteract white culture in LIS because many in the field perceive white culture to be invisible and neutral.[174] From a position of neutrality, there is no evident need for any initiatives that would change hiring in libraries. In this context, neutrality manifests as unacknowledged whiteness in such a way as to prevent urgency or action that would impact diversity or advance social justice.[175] Neutrality is seen as an underlying default—a subaltern yet more powerful value that supersedes the more espoused value of diversity.[176]

The second case for review—library spaces—follows a similar trajectory of tension, with neutrality serving as a counterbalance to stated values. Numerous cases demonstrate that the physical space of a library building is politicallycharged territory: when a library space is occupied by one group that expresses hostility to another group, an

---

169 Espinal, Sutherland, and Roh, "A Holistic Approach for Inclusive Librarianship," 156.

170 Kendrick and Damasco, "Low Morale in Ethnic and Racial Minority Academic Librarians."

171 Collins, "Language, Power, and Oppression in the LIS Diversity Void," 49.

172 Kung, Fraser, and Winn, "Diversity Initiatives to Recruit and Retain Academic Librarians."

173 Guss, Stout, and Cunningham, "#NotAllLibraries."

174 Brook, Ellenwood, and Lazzaro, "In Pursuit of Antiracist Social Justice."

175 Honma, "Trippin' Over the Color Line."

176 Espinal, Sutherland, and Roh, "A Holistic Approach for Inclusive Librarianship."

operational difficulty arises and an ethical tension emerges. On the one hand, the ALA maintains a position of neutrality with respect to room reservations, saying that no person should be denied space usage due to origin, age, background, or views.[177] This approach of objectivity is presented as supporting equity and fulfilling social responsibility by allowing library space to be used by all.[178] But such a posture is a discursive twist that distances library services from the needs of library users. Here, "neutrality is framed as disengagement from community crises, and is defined in opposition to active engagement with community."[179]

Many marginalized groups have in historical fact been oppressed and continue to be oppressed in and by libraries, and "to claim libraries are neutral, in aspiration or practice, is to be blind to the realities of violence and oppression that marginalized groups face every day."[180] Instead of achieving social responsibility, library space neutrality functions as a political stand that favors dominant groups, as when library space is used by a far-right hate group to organize against non-white users or when a Transexclusionary Radical Feminist (TERF) group organizes against transgender users. In these instances, when one group actively advocates for the disenfranchisement of another group, and both are treated as equivalent when occupying library space, neutrality is shown to be a fiction that is socially harmful, not socially responsible.[181] The issue of space is instructive for values-in-conflict: for some, opening library space to hate groups is an ethical stance that upholds the value of intellectual freedom and diversity; to others, the same action is a violation of the value of social responsibility and of that very same value of diversity.[182]

The examples of LIS diversity and library spaces both demonstrate the complexities and contradictions of enacting the library value of social responsibility in practice. Ethical reflection and dedicated

---

177 American Library Association, "Meeting Rooms: An Interpretation of the Library Bill of Rights."

178 Bowles, "A Librarian's Timeless Mission: Supporting Social Justice Through Freedom of Speech – Quillette."

179 Gibson et al., "Libraries on the Frontlines," 6.

180 Jones, "Institutional Neutrality Isn't Reality," para. 6.

181 Teal, "Library Meeting Rooms for All, for Real."

182 Thomas, "Intellectual Freedom and Inclusivity."

thoughtfulness can help balance these competing priorities.[183] Professional neutrality and social responsibility will remain an ongoing site of complexity and tension as librarians continue to debate the role of LIS in society.

Site of Tension 5: Critical Information Literacy

Critical information literacy is a socially-engaged, politically-aware mode of library instructional pedagogy. Critical information literacy differs from traditionally-accepted definitions of information literacy (such as locating, evaluating, and applying information) in that it centers the social, political, economic, and corporate systems that have power and influence over information.[184] This approach to teaching about information is a profession-wide response to perceived limitations of traditional information literacy in addressing the social and political dimensions of information and education in libraries, specifically "taking issue with the notion of libraries as ideologically neutral spaces, arguing for an understanding of information literacy that accounts for sociopolitical dynamics, and seeking ways to involve library users in the politics of information access and use."[185] Critical information literacy understands that neutrality and social justice are at odds, and so this approach seeks to investigate libraries' active participation in systems of oppression, to develop ways for LIS professionals and students to critically engage with these systems, and ultimately to bring about social change.[186]

In explicitly engaging with political issues and taking a stand against historical injustices, the practice of critical information literacy is in tension with a neutrality position. Critical practitioners note this tension and address it directly. Ferretti argues that practicing neutrality implicitly upholds dominant cultural narratives such as white patriarchy, saying,

> If discussions of race, gender, sexuality, economic status, etc. are not discussed when information literacy and critical thinking are

---

183 Fister, "Libraries and the Practice of Freedom in the Age of Algorithms."

184 Gregory and Higgins, *Information Literacy and Social Justice*.

185 Tewell, "The Practice and Promise of Critical Information Literacy," 12.

186 Pagowsky and Wallace, "Black Lives Matter!"

main objectives, you're making a conscious decision to leave [women of color] out, thereby not actually being neutral, but effectively privileging one group over others.[187]

For Ferretti, neutral librarianship intentionally ignores marginalized communities and experiences, and is thus incompatible with social responsibility and equity values that could be fulfilled via critical information literacy. Likewise for Tewell, who underscores this ethical dilemma with the following prompt:

> The question is whether librarians will fight inequalities alongside the rest of the world, or whether we wish to pretend that we can maintain neutrality in the midst of social issues that affect us, our patrons, and our planet.[188]

LIS professional values are seen as a guiding light that can illuminate this question, with the ALA Core Values serving as a foundation upon which LIS professionals can examine and achieve the broader social goals of information literacy.[189] In this way, a crucial question for ethical LIS practice is which values a practitioner chooses to apply in their setting. An LIS practitioner can choose to embrace and apply neutrality, or to embrace and apply social responsibility, diversity, and equity.

A few examples in practice showcase the potential of critical information literacy for those LIS practitioners who choose to reject neutrality. Pagowsky and Wallace describe an initiative to create race-aware, politically-conscious learning and outreach content that takes an explicit stand in support of the Black Lives Matter social justice movement.[190] Pagowsky and Wallace call on LIS professionals to examine their own practice more critically by looking inward and considering what policies, practices, and systems replicate systems of oppression and are hostile to marginalized groups. Neutrality is in direct conflict to this approach of critical librarianship, for in "trying to remain 'neutral,' by showing all perspectives have value—even those that violently

---

187 Ferretti, "Neutrality Is Hostility," para. 68.

188 Tewell, "The Practice and Promise of Critical Information Literacy," 27.

189 Jacobs and Berg, "Reconnecting Information Literacy Policy with the Core Values of Librarianship."

190 Pagowsky and Wallace, "Black Lives Matter!"

disregard black existence–is harmful to our community and does not work to dismantle racism."[191]

LIS practitioners have seen further connections between LIS values and the Framework for Information Literacy for Higher Education.[192] By eschewing rigid, reductive educational standards in favor of local, contextual approaches, the Framework allows critical information literacy to be applied by those who choose to do so.[193] But social justice does not appear explicitly in the Framework, which marks a related site of tension regarding values-in-practice. When asked directly to take a stronger stand on social justice, the Task Force authors who drafted the Framework replied, "The Task Force members are sympathetic to the views expressed about social justice…the Task Force felt that social justice was not its own frame."[194] This omission was criticized; Battista et al., for example, notes that despite a relationship between social justice and information literacy previously articulated by many LIS scholars, the Framework lacks a cogent statement that connects information literacy to social justice.[195]

While not appearing explicitly, the ALA Core Value of social responsibility can be mapped to phrases in three different frames—Authority Is Constructed and Contextual, Information Has Value, Research as Inquiry. Through this mapping exercise, the Framework can be activated for enacting LIS values of social responsibility.[196] And by allowing practitioners to develop learning outcomes specific to their local contexts, the Framework gives space for social justice interpretations.[197] Social justice aspects can also be seen in the Framework, as the Framework discusses social issues related to information and describes how information literacy can address those issues.[198] For example, the "Information Has Value" frame indicates that value may be wielded by

---

191 Pagowsky and Wallace, 198.

192 American Library Association, "Framework for Information Literacy for Higher Education."

193 Drabinski, "A Kairos of the Critical."

194 Task Force, ACRL Framework, "Framework for Information Literacy for Higher Education, Frequently Asked Questions," para. 43.

195 Battista et al., "Seeking Social Justice in the ACRL Framework."

196 Gregory and Higgins, "Reorienting an Information Literacy Program Toward Social Justice."

197 Branch, "Illuminating Social Justice in the Framework."

198 Saunders, "Connecting Information Literacy and Social Justice: Why and How," 64.

powerful interests in ways that marginalize certain voices. Still, the Framework could go further in explicating the connection between social justice and information literacy, such as including additional frame that focuses specifically on "information social justice."[199]

In summary, the critical information literacy site of tension demonstrates a key insight: ethical practice in LIS is a matter of choosing which values to apply in a given situation. Rather than marking a clear path forward, practical ethics in LIS are framed by a question—which paths should be followed? In this case, the choice is between two options: follow a theory of neutrality to practice traditional information literacy, or follow a theory of social justice to practice critical information literacy. From this viewpoint, library instruction can be an expression of professional values—whichever ones we choose.

Site of Tension 6: Cataloging and Classification

Classification is a significant component of the LIS profession. The work of building and maintaining an access catalog is highly impactful for a library's user community. Catalogers are trained to organize information by encoding, describing, analyzing for subject content (naming), classifying, controlling, and sharing.[200] In the course of this work, catalogers have what Olson has notably described as "the power to name"—the ability to describe and represent an information object, which in turn affects access and use of the object.[201] The function of our classification systems is to serve as a conceptual and practical structure in which relationships among objects are identified, recorded, and made accessible to users.[202] Throughout the complexities of these classification procedures, "the decisions that catalogers have to make are not always so clear."[203]

The ethical decisions of cataloging and classification are many. Catalogers first consider various groups when making decisions: other catalogers, other LIS professionals, their institution, the public, and wider

---

199 Saunders, "Connecting Information Literacy and Social Justice: Why and How."

200 Bair, "Toward a Code of Ethics for Cataloging."

201 Olson, *The Power to Name*.

202 Furner, "Dewey Deracialized."

203 Bair, "Toward a Code of Ethics for Cataloging," 17.

community of users who access the library's materials through the catalog.[204] Decisions related to assigning subject headings, in particular, can help or harm a user and thus represent a key ethical point of reflection.[205] From this point of reflection, a practice of ethical cataloging has emerged as a means of reexamining and reclassifying library materials with a critical view towards the assumptions and perspectives of the world and society.[206]

Neutrality is again at the center for this site of tension. For some, neutrality operates as a guiding principle through these decision points. In the work of deciding subject headings, "objectivity is generally valued."[207] As LIS professionals, catalogers respond to the "the basic assumption underlying modern librarianship—that libraries and librarians should embrace the position of neutrality."[208] Neutrality is especially entrenched in information organization due to the desired appearance of a positivist, rational, scientific, and technical objectivity for a key professional practice in information science.[209] Such a knowable and known universe of knowledge from which a book could be drawn was a practical construct seen as beneficial from the viewpoint of customer service efficiency, an approach dating back to Dewey.[210]

In counterpoint, classification schemes are a product of individual human effort, thus inherently subjective and political. The appearance of a logical system, however, elides and obscures any subjectivity: "In its fixity, every classification scheme is an objective representation of a subjective point of view."[211] In striving towards neutrality and objectivity, catalogers of eras past have failed "to accurately and respectfully organize library materials about social groups and identities that lack

---

[204] Ferris, "The Ethics and Integrity of Cataloging."

[205] Bair, "Toward a Code of Ethics for Cataloging."

[206] Mai, "Ethics, Values and Morality in Contemporary Library Classifications."

[207] CannCasciato, "Ethical Considerations in Classification Practice," 413.

[208] Mai, "Ethics, Values and Morality in Contemporary Library Classifications," 246.

[209] Adler and Harper, "Race and Ethnicity in Classification Systems."

[210] Olson, *The Power to Name*; Mai, "Ethics, Values and Morality in Contemporary Library Classifications"; Maret and Eagle, "Situating the Customer: The Genealogy of Customer Language in Libraries"; Gregory and Higgins, "In Resistance to a Capitalist Past: Emerging Practices of Critical Librarianship."

[211] Furner, "Dewey Deracialized," 154.

social and political power."²¹² But LIS classification systems in fact reflect the points of view of their creators, and thus feature built-in biases and contradictions.²¹³ For catalogers who wish to engage the ethical dilemmas and contradictions of classification, "there is no view from nowhere. Any act of naming or classifying is an act of saying something about the world, and such an act is always done from a particular perspective."²¹⁴ The classification and the organization of information are directly connected to issues surrounding social justice, diversity, and inclusion, with researchers observing racism, imperialism, sexism, ableism, and heterosexism in the stacks.²¹⁵ Libraries' attempts at neutrality obscure a long history of racism in cataloging practices.²¹⁶ Neutrality is therefore unattainable and undesirable in the context of information organization, and "librarians who understand libraries as spaces that advance equality and justice often view neutrality as an obstacle to those goals."²¹⁷ To engage critically with reclassification as harm reduction or as an act of values-based anti-oppression is to stand against neutrality. Indeed, classifications are a powerful technology, and deserve political and social sensitivities.²¹⁸ When ethical decisions are confronted, catalogers also look to the stated core values of the LIS profession—such as social responsibility, diversity, and equity—which can come into tension with positions of neutrality.

In further examining the ethical decisions of catalogers we can look to leading classification schemas and organizations: Library of Congress Subject Headings (LCSH), Dewey Decimal System (Dewey), Resource Description and Access (RDA), and the Subject Authority Cooperative Program (SACO). Each of these areas offer different demonstrations of the ethical complexities of cataloging. Biases and subjectivities have been found to be present in a number of LCSH headings, including

---

212 Drabinski, "Queering the Catalog," 95.

213 Mai, "Ethics, Values and Morality in Contemporary Library Classifications."

214 Mai, 246.

215 Adler, "Classification Along the Color Line"; Adler and Harper, "Race and Ethnicity in Classification Systems."

216 Hobart, "Ethical Cataloging and Racism in Special Collections."

217 Adler and Harper, "Race and Ethnicity in Classification Systems," 57.

218 Bowker and Star, *Sorting Things Out*.

those related to religion,[219] nationality,[220] gender and sex,[221] and social justice movements.[222] One of the earliest to draw attention to the cultural injustices embedded in subject headings is Berman, who as a cataloger working in Zambia in 1960s came to understand that certain LCSH subject headings—created from the American perspective and presented as a universal vocabulary—in fact perpetuated harmful, racist language in the Zambian context.[223]

Likewise, the Dewey Decimal System contains its own biases. Information objects relating to religion, for example, are overwhelmingly Christian.[224] More broadly, Olson describes how the appearance of Dewey as an objective information system is in fact "a harmful characteristic in the sense that it marginalizes and excludes Others—concepts outside of a white, male, Eurocentric, Christocentric, heterosexual, able-bodied, bourgeois mainstream."[225] Upon further examination, the aim of classification schemes such as LCSH and Dewey to provide a value-neutral snapshot of an objective reality is revealed to be unattainable.[226] Other systems of information organization are revealed to be similarly faulty, as with RDA and gender bias,[227], and with SACO and race[228] and immigration.[229] In one instance, an academic library updated their local catalog to replace the subject heading for "illegal aliens" with "undocumented immigrants" following a rejection to do the same across the nationally-shared LCSH catalog.[230] Such an act of local resistance to wide-spread norms illustrates the real-world ethical decision-making of catalogers.

---

219 Idrees and Mahmood, "Devising a Classification Scheme for Islam."

220 Ferris, "The Ethics and Integrity of Cataloging."

221 Johnson, "Transgender Subject Access."

222 Adler and Harper, "Race and Ethnicity in Classification Systems."

223 Berman, *Prejudices and Antipathies*.

224 Berman.

225 Olson, *The Power to Name*, 142.

226 Furner, "Dewey Deracialized."

227 Billey, Drabinski, and Roberto, "What's Gender Got to Do with It?"

228 Espinal, Sutherland, and Roh, "A Holistic Approach for Inclusive Librarianship."

229 Adler and Harper, "Race and Ethnicity in Classification Systems."

230 Proctor, "Falvey Memorial Library."

In summary, the classification systems used within the LIS profession have historically been constructed by members of dominant groups, and can perpetuate certain biases and stereotypes that harm or exclude users of traditionally marginalized identities. Maintaining a posture of neutrality does not allow for these exclusions to be addressed. Classification schemas have been built as objective tools for accessing a stable universe of knowledge, but they should now be reexamined as sites of political and ethical work.[231] There is no way to fully correct a catalog, as cultural ideas and vocabularies are constantly in flux, but a more socially-aware approach to classification opens new possibilities for more inclusive, accurate, and socially-responsible collections.[232]

Most Pressing Sites of Tensions for Library Assessment

Among the examples discussed in this chapter, a few sites of tension are particularly relevant to consider for library assessment. I offer four here to highlight: market forces, technology, neutrality, and social responsibility.

Market forces exert significant pressure on the work of library assessment. Often the practices, goals, and outcomes of library assessment are conditioned by the expectations of external entities that may not share or understand library values. This creates a profound tension at the center of assessment work. How is success defined? Who defines success? As assessment practitioners, we may not be able to convey the most compelling strengths of our libraries if our assessments rely on market-oriented success measures such as efficiency and return-in-investment. Business measures aren't well suited for the library because the library isn't designed to operate as a business. Libraries are educational institutions that support imagination, creativity, and collaboration. These more intangible aspects of our value are challenging or even impossible to capture with neatly digestible measures. And yet universities and libraries—existing within larger market-based systems—still are called to account for effort and output in such terms. Assessment practitioners operate in this complex, multi-stakeholder environment, balancing the views of university and

---

231 Mai, "Ethics, Values and Morality in Contemporary Library Classifications."

232 Johnson, "Transgender Subject Access"; Drabinski, "Queering the Catalog."

library administrators alongside professional values and a personal sense of best practice. How can we design assessments that speak to the unique purpose, strengths, and values of libraries in a way that also resonates with and meets the needs of external or parent entities?

Technology presents similar tensions within the practice of library assessment. The software tools that we use are often made by people or organizations whose own values may not map to ours. Web analytics software, for example, is typically built by for-profit companies whose service and values are optimized for e-commerce and other business applications. In libraries, web analytics can help improve web services, but the software also impinges on the data privacy of users—how do we resolve this tension between service and privacy? The most easily-implemented or widely-adopted tools are often the tools that would violate our values or harm our users. And so it takes extra effort to build or implement non-mainstream tools that are more suitable for library applications, which points to another tension: the privacy value and the sustainability value. Can our technical and personnel infrastructure support the search for more outlier technologies that would align with our values? Google Analytics, for instance, is the most common tool for web analytics in libraries. Support documentation is plentiful, and the library web services and assessment communities have a deep knowledge base regarding this software. Yet Google Analytics complicates our commitment to privacy.[233] It becomes notable when a library takes a different approach to install a more privacy-oriented analytics software.[234] Similar to other sites of tension, this dilemma is one of dueling choices: do we install readily-available tools that can improve services, but may negatively impact user privacy? Or do we dedicate additional capacity to investigate and implement alternative tools that are less well documented and supported? Based on which values are prioritized and applied to this question, the response will be different—and there's no right answer.

Neutrality is another overarching tension for library assessment. In this book, I put forward the argument that we can practice ethical assessment by applying the right values at the right time. To accomplish

---

233 O'Brien et al., "Protecting Privacy on the Web: A Study of HTTPS and Google Analytics Implementation in Academic Library Websites."

234 Chandler and Wallace, "Using Piwik Instead of Google Analytics at the Cornell University Library."

this, we must first know and name our values. And this requires us as practitioners to acknowledge the unique viewpoints that influence the choices that we make. Neutrality is an important choice for us to make as practitioners and as a field. This choice represents a central tension for library assessment. Can we hold neutrality as a value, when that one value functions to negate other values? As individual practitioners or as a profession, do we choose to reject neutrality? Which other values do we choose to embrace?

This leads to a tension related to social responsibility. Embracing social responsibility means taking an honest look at our history and our practices, and asking whether our work supports social justice outcomes for our assessment participants and our wider communities. Assessment practice is often institution-centered, which can tend to prioritize the status quo and foreclose more difficult but important questions about social inequality and social justice. When practicing from an institution-centric perspective, assessment is more likely to fall into extractive paradigms by viewing research participants as subjects to be studied in a one-way transfer of information. To illuminate other paths, we can ask—what does a participant-centered assessment practice look like? How can a participant-centered practice prioritize the voices of historically marginalized students? How can we conduct collaborative assessments that produce social benefit for our communities? These questions underscore some existing tensions within our field, but they also point to more a politically-aware, socially-responsible assessment practice.[235]

Summary

LIS professionals are challenged to act ethically by two primary factors: market forces and the concept of professional neutrality. In this chapter, I examined six sites of tension that demonstrate the effect of market forces and professional neutrality on ethical LIS professional practice. Regarding market forces, LIS values are often superseded by the values of a parent institution and of the larger society of the United States and the global economic system of capitalism. Market forces complicate ethical action in three key areas: measuring success

---

[235] Magnus, Belanger, and Faber, "Towards a Critical Assessment Practice"; Magnus, Faber, and Belanger, "A Consideration of Power Structures (and the Tensions They Create) in Library Assessment Activities."

according to externally-defined economic principles as opposed to internally-defined professional principles, implementing privacy-invading technology services, and collecting behavioral data related to student activity. Regarding neutrality, the LIS professional stance of neutrality prevents the LIS professional from taking a values-based stance in three key areas: social responsibility, information literacy, and cataloging and classification. In sum, this chapter provided a discussion of the main sites of ethical tension encountered by LIS professionals—but what are the responses that our field has developed for addressing these tensions? In the next chapter, we will take a closer look at ethical practices of the library assessment community.

Bibliography

Adler, Melissa. "Classification Along the Color Line: Excavating Racism in the Stack." *Journal of Critical Library and Information Studies* 1, no. 1 (2017). https://doi.org/10.24242/jclis.v1i1.17.

Adler, Melissa, and Lindsey M. Harper. "Race and Ethnicity in Classification Systems: Teaching Knowledge Organization from a Social Justice Perspective." *Library Trends* 67, no. 1 (October 25, 2018): 52–73. https://doi.org/10.1353/lib.2018.0025.

Alvarez, Maximillian. "The End of the End of History." Text. Boston Review, March 22, 2019. https://bostonreview.net/print-issues-politics/maximillian-alvarez-end-end-history.

American Library Association. "Framework for Information Literacy for Higher Education." Text. Association of College & Research Libraries (ACRL), February 9, 2015. https://web.archive.org/web/20200214223440/http://www.ala.org/acrl/standards/ilframework.

American Library Association.. "Meeting Rooms: An Interpretation of the Library Bill of Rights," January 29, 2019. https://web.archive.org/web/20200215182556/http://www.ala.org/advocacy/intfreedom/librarybill/interpretations/meetingrooms.

American Library Association. "The ALA President's Program at the Midwinter Meeting Debates Neutrality in Libraries." Text. News and Press Center, November 8, 2017. https://web.archive.org/web/20190512004718/ttp://www.ala.org/news/member-news/2017/11/ala-president-s-program-midwinter-meeting-debates-neutrality-libraries.

Arellano Douglas, Veronica. "Moving from Critical Assessment to Assessment as Care." *Communications in Information Literacy* 14, no. 1 (June 2020): 46–65.

Asheim, Lester. *The Core of Education for Librarianship; a Report of a Workshop Held under the Auspices of the Graduate Library School of the University of Chicago, August 10-15, 1953*. Chicago: American Library Association, 1954.

Association of College and Research Libraries. "Standards for Libraries in Higher Education," 2011.

Atkinson, Jeremy, and Graham Walton. "Establishing Quality in University Libraries: Role of External Frameworks." *New Review of Academic Librarianship* 23, no. 1 (January 2, 2017): 1–5. https://doi.org/10.1080/13614533.2016.1271238.

Bair, Sheila. "Toward a Code of Ethics for Cataloging." *Technical Services Quarterly* 23, no. 1 (September 13, 2005): 13–26. https://doi.org/10.1300/J124v23n01_02.

Battista, Andrew, Dave Ellenwood, Lua Gregory, Shana Higgins, Jeff Lilburn, Yasmin Harker, and Christopher Sweet. "Seeking Social Justice in the ACRL Framework." *Communications in Information Literacy* 9, no. 2 (December 1, 2015). https://doi.org/10.15760/comminfolit.2015.9.2.188.

Beile, Penny, Kanak Choudhury, and Morgan C. Wang. "Hidden Treasure on the Road to Xanadu: What Connecting Library Service Usage Data to Unique Student IDs Can Reveal." *Journal of Library Administration* 57, no. 2 (February 17, 2017): 151–73. https://doi.org/10.1080/01930826.2016.1235899.

Beilin, Ian. "Student Success and the Neoliberal Academic Library." *Canadian Journal of Academic Librarianship* 1 (January 28, 2016): 10–23. https://doi.org/10.33137/cjal-rcbu.v1.24303.

Berman, Sanford. *Prejudices and Antipathies: A Tract on the LC Subject Heads Concerning People*. McFarland & Company, 1993.

Berninghausen, David. "Antithesis in Librarianship: Social Responsibility vs. The Library Bill of Rights." *Library Journal* 97, no. 20 (November 15, 1972): 3675–81.

Bignoli, Callan, Sam Buechler, Deborah Caldwell, and Kelly McElroy. "Resisting Crisis Surveillance Capitalism in Academic Libraries." *Canadian Journal of Academic Librarianship* 7 (December 15, 2021): 1–25. https://doi.org/10.33137/cjalrcbu.v7.36450.

Billey, Amber, Emily Drabinski, and K. R. Roberto. "What's Gender Got to Do with It? A Critique of RDA 9.7." *Cataloging & Classification Quarterly* 52, no. 4 (May 19, 2014): 412–21. https://doi.org/10.1080/01639374.2014.882465.

Blanke, Henry T. "Librarianship and Political Values: Neutrality or Commitment?" *Library Journal* 114, no. 12 (1989): 39–43.

Bourg, Chris. "Beyond Measure: Valuing Libraries." *Feral Librarian* (blog), May 20, 2013. https://web.archive.org/web/20210427003926/https://chrisbourg.wordpress.com/2013/05/19/beyond-measure-valuing-libraries/.

Bourg, Chris. "Debating Y/Our Humanity, or Are Libraries Neutral?" *Feral Librarian* (blog), February 12, 2018. https://web.archive.org/web/20190623090117/https://chrisbourg.wordpress.com/2018/02/11/debating-y-our-humanity-or-are-libraries-neutral/.

Bowker, Geoffery C., and Susan Leigh Star. *Sorting Things Out*. Cambridge, Massachusetts: The MIT Press, 1999.

Bowles, Vickery. "A Librarian's Timeless Mission: Supporting Social Justice Through Freedom of Speech – Quillette." Quillette, March 17, 2020. https://web.archive.org/web/20200318140749/https://quillette.com/2020/03/17/a-librarians-timeless-mission-supporting-social-justice-through-freedom-of-speech/.

Branch, Nicole. "Illuminating Social Justice in the Framework: Transformative Methodology, Concept Mapping and Learning Outcomes Development for Critical Information Literacy." *Communications in Information Literacy* 13, no. 1 (2019): 4–22. https://doi.org/10.15760/comminfolit.2019.13.1.2.

Brewerton, A. "The Creed of a Librarian: A Review Article." *Journal of Librarianship and Information Science* 35, no. 1 (March 2003): 47–55. https://doi.org/10.1177/096100003763880315.

Brook, Freeda, Dave Ellenwood, and Althea Eannace Lazzaro. "In Pursuit of Antiracist Social Justice: Denaturalizing Whiteness in the Academic Library." *Library Trends* 64, no. 2 (2015): 246–84.

Buchanan, Elizabeth A., and Kathrine A. Henderson. *Case Studies in Library and Information Science Ethics*. Jefferson, N.C: McFarland & Co, 2009.

Budd, John M. "A Critique of Customer and Commodity." *College & Research Libraries* 58, no. 4 (1997): 309–20. https://doi.org/10.5860/crl.58.4.309.

Budd, John M. "What's the Right Thing to Do?" In *Self-Examination: The Present and Future of Librarianship*, by John M. Budd, 111–46. Westport, CT: Libraries Unlimited, 2008.

Budd, John M. "Toward a Practical and Normative Ethics for Librarianship." *The Library Quarterly* 76, no. 3 (2006): 251–69. https://doi.org/10.1086/511140.

Burgess, John T. F. "Reconciling Social Responsibility and Neutrality in LIS Professional Ethics: A Virtue Ethics Approach." In *Information Cultures in the Digital Age*, edited by Matthew Kelly and Jared Bielby, 307–20. Springer VS, 2016.

Buschman, John. "November 8, 2016: Core Values, Bad Faith, and Democracy." *The Library Quarterly* 87, no. 3 (June 8, 2017): 277–86. https://doi.org/10.1086/692305.

Buschman, John. "On Libraries and the Public Sphere." *Library Philosophy and Practice* 11 (2005). https://digitalcommons.unl.edu/libphilprac/11.

Buschman, John. "The New Technocracy: Positioning Librarianship's Core Values in Relationship to Technology Is a Much Taller Order Than We Think." In *Applying Library Values to Emerging Technology: Decision-Making in the Age of Open Access, Maker Spaces, and the Ever-Changing Library*, edited by Peter D. Fernandez and Kelly Tilton, 1–25. ACRL, 2018. https://works.bepress.com/john_buschman/82/.

Campbell, D. Grant, and Scott R. Cowan. "The Paradox of Privacy: Revisiting a Core Library Value in an Age of Big Data and Linked Data." *Library Trends* 64, no. 3 (April 4, 2016): 492–511. https://doi.org/10.1353/lib.2016.0006.

CannCasciato, Daniel. "Ethical Considerations in Classification Practice: A Case Study Using Creationism and Intelligent Design." *Cataloging & Classification Quarterly* 49, no. 5 (June 1, 2011): 408–27. https://doi.org/10.1080/01639374.2011.589221.

Carpenter, Zoë. "Librarians Versus the NSA," May 6, 2015. http://web.archive.org/web/20160222003128/http://www.thenation.com/article/librarians-versus-nsa/.

Catalano, Amy Jo, and Sharon Rose Phillips. "Information Literacy and Retention: A Case Study of the Value of the Library." *Evidence Based Library and Information Practice* 11, no. 4 (December 15, 2016). https://doi.org/10.18438/B82K7W.

Chandler, Adam, and Melissa Wallace. "Using Piwik Instead of Google Analytics at the Cornell University Library." *The Serials Librarian* 71, no. 3–4 (November 16, 2016): 173–79. https://doi.org/10.1080/0361526X.2016.1245645.

Chiu, Anastasia, Fobazi M. Ettarh, and Jennifer A. Ferretti. "Not the Shark, but the Water: How Neutrality and Vocational Awe Intertwine to Uphold White Supremacy." In *Knowledge Justice: Disrupting Library and Information Studies through Critical Race Theory*, edited by Sofia Y. Leung and Jorge R. López-McKnight, 49–72. The MIT Press, 2021. https://doi.org/10.7551/mitpress/11969.001.0001.

Clarke, Rachel Ivy, Katerina Lynn Stanton, Alexandra Grimm, and Bo Zhang. "Invisible Labor, Invisible Value: Unpacking Traditional Assessment of Academic Library Value" 83, no. 6 (2022): 926–45. https://doi.org/10.5860/crl.83.6.926.

Collins, Anastasia M. "Language, Power, and Oppression in the LIS Diversity Void." *Library Trends* 67, no. 1 (October 25, 2018): 39–51. https://doi.org/10.1353/lib.2018.0024.

Data 4 Black Lives. "Data 4 Black Lives." Data 4 Black Lives, 2020. http://d4bl.org.

Digital Library Federation. "Technologies of Surveillance." Technologies of Surveillance, 2020. https://wiki.diglib.org/Technologies_of_Surveillance.

Drabinski, Emily. "A Kairos of the Critical: Teaching Critically in a Time of Compliance." *Communications in Information Literacy* 11, no. 1 (June 22, 2017): 76–94. https://doi.org/10.7548/cil.v11i1.452.

Drabinski, Emily. "Queering the Catalog: Queer Theory and the Politics of Correction." *The Library Quarterly* 83, no. 2 (April 1, 2013): 94–111. https://doi.org/10.1086/669547.

Drabinski, Emily, and Scott Walter. "Asking Questions That Matter." *College & Research Libraries* 77, no. 3 (2016). https://crl.acrl.org/index.php/crl/article/view/16508/17954.

Engerman, Stanley L. "Capitalism." In *The Oxford Encyclopedia of American Cultural and Intellectual History*, edited by Joan Shelley Rubin and Scott E. Casper, 166–68. Oxford: Oxford University Press, 2013.

Espinal, Isabel, Tonia Sutherland, and Charlotte Roh. "A Holistic Approach for Inclusive Librarianship: Decentering Whiteness in Our Profession."

Library Trends 67, no. 1 (October 25, 2018): 147–62. https://doi.org/10.1353/lib.2018.0030.

Ettarh, Fobazi. "Making a New Table: Intersectional Librarianship." In The Library With The Lead Pipe, 2014. http://www.inthelibrarywiththeleadpipe.org/2014/making-a-new-table-intersectional-librarianship-3/.

Ettarh, Fobazi. "Vocational Awe and Librarianship: The Lies We Tell Ourselves." In The Library With The Lead Pipe, 2018. http://www.inthelibrarywiththeleadpipe.org/2018/vocational-awe/.

Fallis, Don. "Information Ethics for Twenty-first Century Library Professionals." Library Hi Tech 25, no. 1 (March 13, 2007): 23–36. https://doi.org/10.1108/07378830710735830.

Ferretti, Jennifer A. "Neutrality Is Hostility: The Impact of (False) Neutrality in Academic Librarianship." Medium (blog), February 13, 2018. https://web.archive.org/web/20191111183943/https://medium.com/librarieswehere/neutrality-is-hostility-the-impact-of-false-neutrality-in-academic-librarianship-c0755879fb09.

Ferris, Anna M. "The Ethics and Integrity of Cataloging." Journal of Library Administration 47, no. 3–4 (July 1, 2008): 173–90. https://doi.org/10.1080/01930820802186514.

Fisher, Zoe. "Can We Demonstrate Academic Library Value Without Violating Student Privacy?" Presented at the Colorado Academic Library Association: Intellectual and Academic Freedom and the Academic Library, University of Denver, July 21, 2017. https://docs.google.com/presentation/d/1maJmk4a-LO13oCe-tk0bEzeOF299oKEMhtE5tvGG0oM.

Fister, Barbara. "Libraries and the Practice of Freedom in the Age of Algorithms." Presented at the Electronic Resources and Libraries, Austin, TX, March 2020. https://barbarafister.net/libraries/libraries-and-the-practice-of-freedom-in-the-age-of-algorithms/.

Fister, Barbara. "The Self-Centered Library: A Paradox." Inside Higher Ed, August 28, 2012. https://www.insidehighered.com/blogs/library-babel-fish/self-centered-library-paradox.

Foskett, Douglas John. The Creed of a Librarian: No Politics, No Religion, No Morals. London: The Library Association, 1962.

Froehlich, Thomas J. "Intellectual Freedom, Ethical Deliberation and Codes of Ethics." IFLA Journal 26, no. 4 (August 2000): 264–72. https://doi.org/10.1177/034003520002600405.

Furner, Jonathan. "Dewey Deracialized: A Critical Race-Theoretic Perspective." Knowledge Organization 34, no. 3 (2007). https://works.bepress.com/furner/14/.

Galvan, A. Scarlet. "Architecture of Authority." Scarlet Fixes Things (blog), December 5, 2016. https://web.archive.org/web/20190123185145/https://asgalvan.com/2016/12/05/architecture-of-authority/.

Gibson, Amelia N., Renate L. Chancellor, Nicole A. Cooke, Sarah Park Dahlen, Shari A. Lee, and Yasmeen L. Shorish. "Libraries on the Frontlines: Neutrality and Social Justice." *Equality, Diversity and Inclusion: An International Journal* 36, no. 8 (October 20, 2017): 751–66. https://doi.org/10.1108/EDI-11-2016-0100.

Goetsch, Lori A. "What Is Our Value and Who Values Us?: The 2009–10 ACRL President's Focus." *College & Research Libraries News* 70, no. 9 (2009): 502–3. https://doi.org/10.5860/crln.70.9.8249.

Good, Joseph. "The Hottest Place in Hell: The Crisis of Neutrality in Contemporary Librarianship." *Progressive Librarian* 28 (Winter /2007 2006): 25–29.

Gregory, Lua, and Shana Higgins. "In Resistance to a Capitalist Past: Emerging Practices of Critical Librarianship." In *The Politics of Theory and the Practice of Critical Librarianship*, edited by Karen P. Nicholson and Maura Seale, 21–38. Sacramento, California: Library Juice Press, 2017.

Gregory, Kua, and Shana Higgins, eds. *Information Literacy and Social Justice: Radical Professional Praxis*. Sacramento, CA: Library Juice Press, 2013.

Gregory, Kua, and Shana Higgins. "Reorienting an Information Literacy Program Toward Social Justice: Mapping the Core Values of Librarianship to the ACRL Framework." *Communications in Information Literacy* 11, no. 1 (June 22, 2017): 42–54. https://doi.org/10.7548/cil.v11i1.463.

Guss, Samantha, Jennifer Stout, and Sojourna Cunningham. "#NotAllLibraries: Toxicity in Academic Libraries and Retention of Librarians." In *Forging the Future: The Proceedings of the ACRL 2023 Conference*, 125–36. Pittsburgh, PA: ACRL, 2023. https://web.archive.org/web/20230321214059/https://www.ala.org/acrl/sites/ala.org.acrl/files/content/conferences/confsand-preconfs/2023/NotAllLibraries.pdf.

Haddow, Gaby. "Academic Library Use and Student Retention: A Quantitative Analysis." *Library & Information Science Research* 35, no. 2 (April 1, 2013): 127–36. https://doi.org/10.1016/j.lisr.2012.12.002.

Harvey, David. *A Brief History of Neoliberalism*. Oxford: Oxford University Press, 2007.

Hathcock, April. "Learning Agency, Not Analytics." *At The Intersection* (blog), January 24, 2018. http://web.archive.org/web/20180203034400/https://aprilhathcock.wordpress.com/2018/01/24/learning-agency-not-analytics/.

Hauptman, Robert. *Ethical Challenges in Librarianship*. Phoenix: Oryx Press, 1988.

Hauptman, Robert. *Ethics and Librarianship*. Jefferson, North Carolina: McFarland & Company, 2002.

Hauptman, Robert. "Technological Implementations and Ethical Failures." *Library Trends* 49, no. 3 (2001): 433–40.

Hayes, Sherman, and Don Brown. "The Library as a Business: Mapping the Pervasiveness of Financial Relationships in Today's Library." *Library Trends* 42, no. 3 (Winter 1994): 404–19.

Hobart, Elizabeth. "Ethical Cataloging and Racism in Special Collections." In *Archives and Special Collections as Sites of Contestation*, edited by Mary Kandiuk, 203–21. Duluth, Minnesota: Library Juice Press, 2020.

Holley, Robert P. "Academic Library Users Are Not 'Customers': A Response to Steven Bell." *Journal of Library Administration* 60, no. 1 (January 2, 2020): 88–96. https://doi.org/10.1080/01930826.2019.1685272.

Hollister, Christopher V., and Robert Schroeder. "The Impact of Library Support on Education Faculty Research Productivity: An Exploratory Study." *Behavioral & Social Sciences Librarian* 34, no. 3 (July 3, 2015): 97–115. https://doi.org/10.1080/01639269.2015.1062584.

Honma, Todd. "Trippin' Over the Color Line: The Invisibility of Race in Library and Information Studies." *InterActions: UCLA Journal of Education and Information Studies* 1, no. 2 (June 21, 2005). https://escholarship.org/uc/item/4nj0w1mp.

Hudson, David James. "On 'Diversity' as Anti-Racism in Library and Information Studies: A Critique." *Journal of Critical Library and Information Studies* 1, no. 1 (2017). http://libraryjuicepress.com/journals/index.php/jclis/article/view/6.

Hufford, Jon R. "A Review of the Literature on Assessment in Academic and Research Libraries, 2005 to August 2011." *Portal: Libraries and the Academy* 13, no. 1 (February 12, 2013): 5–35. https://doi.org/10.1353/pla.2013.0005.

Idrees, Haroon, and Khalid Mahmood. "Devising a Classification Scheme for Islam: Opinions of LIS and Islamic Studies Scholars." *Library Philosophy and Practice*, November 5, 2009. https://digitalcommons.unl.edu/libphilprac/308.

Jacobs, Heidi LM, and Selinda Berg. "Reconnecting Information Literacy Policy with the Core Values of Librarianship." *Library Trends* 60, no. 2 (2011): 383–94. https://doi.org/10.1353/lib.2011.0043.

Jaeger, Paul T., Natalie Greene Taylor, and Ursula Gorham. *Libraries, Human Rights, and Social Justice: Enabling Access and Promoting Inclusion*. Rowman & Littlefield, 2015.

Jefferson, Renée N., and Sylvia Contreras. "Ethical Perspectives of Library and Information Science Graduate Students in the United States." *New Library World*, January 1, 2005. https://doi.org/10.1108/03074800510575357.

Jensen, Robert. "The Myth of the Neutral Professional." *Progressive Librarian* 24 (Winter 2004): 28–34.

jesus, nina de. "Locating the Library in Institutional Oppression." *In the Library with the Lead Pipe*, 2014. http://www.inthelibrarywiththeleadpipe.org/2014/locating-the-library-in-institutional-oppression/.

Johnson, Matt. "Transgender Subject Access: History and Current Practice." *Cataloging & Classification Quarterly* 48, no. 8 (September 27, 2010): 661–83. https://doi.org/10.1080/01639370903534398.

Jones, Julie. "Institutional Neutrality Isn't Reality." *American Libraries Magazine*, May 1, 2018. https://web.archive.org/web/20190511040435/https://americanlibrariesmagazine.org/2018/05/01/institutional-neutrality-isnt-reality/.

Jones, Kyle M. L. "'Just Because You Can Doesn't Mean You Should': Practitioner Perceptions of Learning Analytics Ethics." *Portal: Libraries and the Academy* 19, no. 3 (July 10, 2019): 407–28. https://doi.org/10.1353/pla.2019.0025.

Jones, Kyle M.L.. "Learning Analytics, the Academic Library, and Positive Intellectual Freedom." *Journal of Intellectual Freedom and Privacy* 2, no. 2 (October 12, 2017): 7–10. https://doi.org/10.5860/jifp.v2i2.6305.

Jones, Kyle M. L., Michael R. Perry, Abigail Goben, Andrew Asher, Kristin A. Briney, M. Brooke Robertshaw, and Dorothea Salo. "In Their Own Words: Student Perspectives on Privacy and Library Participation in Learning Analytics Initiatives." In *Recasting the Narrative: The Proceedings of the ACRL 2019 Conference*, 262–74. Cleveland, OH: ACRL, 2019.

Jones, Kyle M. L., and Dorothea Salo. "Learning Analytics and the Academic Library: Professional Ethics Commitments at a Crossroads." *College & Research Libraries* 79, no. 3 (2018): 304–23. https://doi.org/10.5860/crl.79.3.304.

Kendrick, Kaetrena Davis, and Ione T. Damasco. "Low Morale in Ethnic and Racial Minority Academic Librarians: An Experiential Study." *Library Trends* 68, no. 2 (2019): 174–212. https://doi.org/10.1353/lib.2019.0036.

Kung, Janice Y., K.-Lee Fraser, and Dee Winn. "Diversity Initiatives to Recruit and Retain Academic Librarians: A Systematic Review." *College & Research Libraries* 81, no. 1 (2020): 96–108. https://doi.org/10.5860/crl.81.1.96.

Lamdan, Sarah. "Librarianship at the Crossroads of ICE Surveillance." *In the Library with the Lead Pipe*, November 2019. http://www.inthelibrarywiththeleadpipe.org/2019/ice-surveillance/.

Lembinen, Liisi. "Academic Libraries' Leaders' Decision-Making during the COVID-19 Crisis." *The Journal of Academic Librarianship* 49, no. 3 (May 1, 2023): 102709. https://doi.org/10.1016/j.acalib.2023.102709.

"Library Freedom Project," May 9, 2017. https://libraryfreedomproject.org/.

Lilburn, Jeff. "Ideology and Audit Culture: Standardized Service Quality Surveys in Academic Libraries." *Portal: Libraries and the Academy* 17, no. 1 (January 6, 2017): 91–110. https://doi.org/10.1353/pla.2017.0006.

Logan, Judith. "Students Who Used the Library in Their First Year of University Are More Likely to Graduate or Still Be Enrolled After Four Years." *Evidence Based Library and Information Practice* 13, no. 4 (December 12, 2018): 108–10. https://doi.org/10.18438/eblip29477.

Logsdon, Alexis. "Ethical Digital Libraries & Prison Labor?" Presented at the Digital Library Federation Forum, Tampa, Florida, October 2019. https://osf.io/yqpkr/.

Lorang, Elizabeth, Leen-Kiat Soh, Yi Liu, and Chulwoo Pack. "Digital Libraries, Intelligent Data Analytics, and Augmented Description: A Demonstration Project." Library of Congress: University Libraries & Department of Computer Science and Engineering, University of Nebraska–Lincoln, 2020.

Macdonald, Stephen, and Briony Birdi. "The Concept of Neutrality: A New Approach." *Journal of Documentation* 76, no. 1 (January 1, 2019): 333–53. https://doi.org/10.1108/JD-05-2019-0102.

Magi, Trina J. "A Content Analysis of Library Vendor Privacy Policies: Do They Meet Our Standards?" *College & Research Libraries* 71, no. 3 (2010): 254–72. https://doi.org/10.5860/0710254.

Magnus, Ebony, Jackie Belanger, and Maggie Faber. "Towards a Critical Assessment Practice." *In the Library With the Lead Pipe*, 2018. http://www.inthelibrarywiththeleadpipe.org/2018/towards-critical-assessment-practice/.

Magnus, Ebony, Maggie Faber, and Jackie Belanger. "A Consideration of Power Structures (and the Tensions They Create) in Library Assessment Activities." In *Proceedings of the 2018 Library Assessment Conference: Building Effective, Sustainable, Practical Assessment: December 5–7, 2018, Houston, TX*, 600–606. Association of Research Libraries, 2019. https://doi.org/10.29242/lac.2018.55.

Mai, Jens-Erik. "Ethics, Values and Morality in Contemporary Library Classifications." *Knowledge Organization* 40, no. 4 (2013): 242–53. https://doi.org/10.5771/0943-7444-2013-4-242.

Marco, Guy A. "Ethics for Librarians: A Narrow View." *Journal of Librarianship and Information Science* 28, no. 1 (1996): 33–38. https://doi.org/10.1177/096100069602800105.

Maret, Susan, and Ben Eagle. "Situating the Customer: The Genealogy of Customer Language in Libraries." *Progressive Librarian* 41 (2013): 18–38.

Mathuews, Katy. "Moving Beyond Diversity to Social Justice." *Progressive Librarian*, no. 44 (2016).

Matteson, Miriam, and Cynthia Boyden. "Old Wine in a New Bottle: Customer Orientation in Librarianship." *Reference Services Review* 42, no. 3 (January 1, 2014): 433–45. https://doi.org/10.1108/RSR-02-2014-0003.

Matz, Chris. "Libraries and the USA PATRIOT Act: Values in Conflict." *Journal of Library Administration* 47, no. 3–4 (July 2008): 69–87. https://doi.org/10.1080/01930820802186399.

McDonald, Peter. "Corporate Inroads and Librarianship: The Fight for the Soul of the Profession in the New Millennium." *Progressive Librarian* 12/13 (Spring/Summer 1997): 32–44.

McMenemy, David, Alan Poulter, and Paul Burton. *A Handbook of Ethical Practice: A Practical Guide to Dealing with Ethical Issues in Information and Library Work*. Oxford: Chandos Publishing, 2007.

Mehra, Bharat. "Introduction." *Library Trends* 64, no. 2 (2015): 179–97. https://doi.org/10.1353/lib.2015.0042.

Morales, Myrna, Em Claire Knowles, and Chris Bourge. "Diversity, Social Justice, and the Future of Libraries." *Portal: Libraries and the Academy* 14, no. 3 (July 2014): 439–51.

Murray, Adam. "Academic Libraries and High-Impact Practices for Student Retention: Library Deans' Perspectives." *Portal: Libraries and the Academy* 15, no. 3 (July 6, 2015): 471–87. https://doi.org/10.1353/pla.2015.0027.

Murray, Adam, and Ashley Ireland. "Provosts' Perceptions of Academic Library Value & Preferences for Communication: A National Study." *College & Research Libraries* 79, no. 3 (2018): 336–65.

Murray, Adam, Ashley Ireland, and Jana Hackathorn. "The Value of Academic Libraries: Library Services as a Predictor of Student Retention." *College & Research Libraries* 77, no. 5 (November 12, 2015): 631–42. https://doi.org/10.5860/crl.77.5.631.

Murray, Adam L., and Ashley P. Ireland. "Communicating Library Impact on Retention: A Framework for Developing Reciprocal Value Propositions." *Journal of Library Administration* 57, no. 3 (April 3, 2017): 311–26. https://doi.org/10.1080/01930826.2016.1243425.

Ndumu, Ana, and Crystal Betts-Green. "First Impressions: A Review of Diversity-Related Content on North American LIS Program Websites." *The International Journal of Information, Diversity, & Inclusion (IJIDI)* 2, no. 3 (July 24, 2018). https://doi.org/10.33137/ijidi.v2i3.32193.

Neal, James G. "Stop the Madness: The Insanity of ROI and the Need for New Qualitative Measures of Academic Library Success." In *Declaration of Interdependence: The Proceedings of the ACRL 2011 Conference*, 424–29. Philadelphia, Pennsylvania: Association of Research Libraries, 2011.

Newton, Lisa. "The Origins of a Professionalism: Sociological Conclusions and Ethical Implications." In *Ethics, Information, and Technology: Readings*, edited by Richard N. Stichler and Robert Hauptman, 261–72. Jefferson, North Carolina: McFarland & Company, 1998.

Nicholson, Karen P. "The Mcdonaldization of Academic Libraries and the Values of Transformational Change." *College & Research Libraries* 76, no. 3 (March 2015): 328–38. https://doi.org/10.5860/crl.76.3.328.

Nicholson, Karen P.. "The 'Value Agenda': Negotiating a Path Between Compliance and Critical Practice." Presented at the Canadian Libraries Assessment Workshop, University of Victoria, 2017. https://ir.lib.uwo.ca/fimspres/49.

Nicholson, Karen P., Nicole Pagowsky, and Maura Seale. "Just-in-Time or Just-in-Case? Time, Learning Analytics, and the Academic Library." *Library Trends* 68, no. 1 (October 24, 2019): 54–75. https://doi.org/10.1353/lib.2019.0030.

Nicols Hess, Amanda, Rachelle LaPorte-Fiori, and Keith Engwall. "Preserving Patron Privacy in the 21st Century Academic Library." *The Journal of Academic Librarianship* 41, no. 1 (December 2014): 105–14. https://doi.org/10.1016/j.acalib.2014.10.010.

Nowviskie, Bethany. "From the Grass Roots." *Bethany Nowviskie* (blog), March 24, 2019. https://web.archive.org/web/20190822165354/http://nowviskie.org/2019/from-the-grass-roots/.

Oakleaf, Megan. "The Problems and Promise of Learning Analytics for Increasing and Demonstrating Library Value and Impact." *Information and Learning Sciences* 119, no. 1/2 (January 5, 2018): 16–24. https://doi.org/10.1108/ILS-08-2017-0080.

Oakleaf, Megan. "The Value of Academic Libraries: A Comprehensive Research Review and Report." Chicago, IL: Association of College and Research Libraries, American Library Association, 2010.

Oakleaf, Megan, and Martha Kyrillidou. "Revisiting the Academic Library Value Research Agenda: An Opportunity to Shape the Future." *The Journal of Academic Librarianship* 42, no. 6 (November 2016): 757–64. https://doi.org/10.1016/j.acalib.2016.10.005.

O'Brien, Patrick, Scott W. H. Young, Kenning Arlitsch, and Karl Benedict. "Protecting Privacy on the Web: A Study of HTTPS and Google Analytics Implementation in Academic Library Websites." *Online Information Review* 42, no. 6 (October 8, 2018): 734–51. https://doi.org/10.1108/OIR-02-2018-0056.

Oliphant, Tami, and Michael R. Brundin. "Conflicting Values: An Exploration of the Tensions between Learning Analytics and Academic Librarianship." *Library Trends* 68, no. 1 (October 24, 2019): 5–23. https://doi.org/10.1353/lib.2019.0028.

Olson, Hope A. *The Power to Name: Locating the Limits of Subject Representation in Libraries*. Springer, 2002.

Owens, Trevor, Ashley E Sands, Emily Reynolds, James Neal, Stephen Mayeaux, and Maura Marx. "Digital Infrastructures That Embody Library Principles: The IMLS National Digital Platform as a Framework for Digital Library Tools and Services." In *Applying Library Values to Emerging Technology: Decision-Making in the Age of Open Access, Maker Spaces, and the Ever-Changing Library*, edited by Peter D. Fernandez and Kelly Tilton, 73–88. ACRL, 2018.

Padilla, Thomas. "A Mutualistic View of AI in the Library or a Continuation of Craft." *Thomas Padilla* (blog), March 6, 2023. https://web.archive.org/web/20230307064712/https://tgpadillajr.medium.com/a-mutualistic-view-of-ai-in-the-library-or-a-continuation-of-craft-289a3e9f6d49.

Pagowsky, Nicole, and Niamh Wallace. "Black Lives Matter!: Shedding Library Neutrality Rhetoric for Social Justice." *College & Research Libraries News* 76, no. 4 (2015): 196–200. https://doi.org/10.5860/crln.76.4.9293.

Popowich, Sam. *Confronting the Democratic Discourse of Librarianship: A Marxist Approach*. Sacramento, CA: Library Juice Press, 2019.

Popowich, Sam. "Libraries, Labour, Capital." *Journal of Radical Librarianship* 4 (March 28, 2018): 6–19.

Porter, Christopher. "Radical Collaboration: Allied Media Conference in Detroit." *Ann Arbor District Library* (blog), May 19, 2017. http://web.archive.org/web/20220614182611/https://aadl.org/node/360351.

Preer, Jean L. *Library Ethics*. Westport, Conn: Libraries Unlimited, 2008.

Proctor, Shawn. "Falvey Staff Members Work Together to 'Change the Subject' on the Term 'Illegal Aliens.'" *Falvey Memorial Library Blog* (blog), January 13, 2020. https://web.archive.org/save/https://blog.library.villanova.edu/2020/01/13/falvey-staff-members-work-together-to-change-the-subject-on-the-term-illegal-aliens/.

Quinn, Brian. "The McDonaldization of Academic Libraries?" *College & Research Libraries* 61, no. 3 (2000): 248–61. https://doi.org/10.5860/crl.61.3.248.

Rabinowitz, Celia. "Learning Analytics, Surveillance, Student Success, and the Library." *Open Librarianship* (blog), April 22, 2019. https://web.archive.org/web/20190924150037/http://celiarabinowitz.kscopen.org/uncategorized/learning-analytics-surveillance-student-success-and-the-library/.

Reidsma, Matthew. *Masked by Trust: Bias in Library Discovery*. Sacramento, CA: Library Juice Press, 2019.

Rioux, Kevin. "Metatheory in Library and Information Science: A Nascent Social Justice Approach." *Journal of Education for Library and Information Science* 51, no. 1 (Winter 2010): 9–17.

Roberts, Sarah T., and Safiya Umoja Noble. "Empowered to Name, Inspired to Act: Social Responsibility and Diversity as Calls to Action in the LIS Context." *Library Trends* 64, no. 3 (April 4, 2016): 512–32. https://doi.org/10.1353/lib.2016.0008.

Robertshaw, M. Brooke, and Andrew Asher. "Unethical Numbers? A Meta-Analysis of Library Learning Analytics Studies." *Library Trends* 68, no. 1 (October 24, 2019): 76–101. https://doi.org/10.1353/lib.2019.0031.

Rosenzweig, Mark. "Politics and Anti-Politics in Librarianship." In *Questioning Neutrality*, edited by Alison Lewis, 4–7. Library Juice Press, 2008.

Rubin, Richard. "Ethical Issues in Library Personnel Management." *Journal of Library Administration* 14, no. 4 (August 16, 1991): 1–16. https://doi.org/10.1300/J111v14n04_01.

Rubin, Richard A., and Thomas J. Froehlich. "Ethical Aspects of Library and Information Science." In *Encyclopedia of Library and Information Sciences*. New York: Taylor and Francis, 2010.

Samek, Toni. *Librarianship and Human Rights: A Twenty-First Century Guide*. Oxford, England: Chandos Publishing, 2007.

Santamaria, Michele R. "Concealing White Supremacy through Fantasies of the Library: Economies of Affect at Work." *Library Trends* 68, no. 3 (April 2, 2020): 431–49.

Saunders, Laura. "Connecting Information Literacy and Social Justice: Why and How." *Communications in Information Literacy* 11, no. 1 (2017): 55–75.

Schroeder, Robert, and Christopher V. Hollister. "Librarians' Views on Critical Theories and Critical Practices." *Behavioral & Social Sciences Librarian* 33, no. 2 (April 3, 2014): 91–119. https://doi.org/10.1080/01639269.2014.912104.

Scott, Rachel E. "Academic Library Use Is Positively Related to a Variety of Educational Outcomes." *Evidence Based Library and Information Practice* 14, no. 3 (September 12, 2019): 144–46. https://doi.org/10.18438/eblip29583.

Seal, Andrew. "How the University Became Neoliberal." *The Chronicle of Higher Education*, June 8, 2018. http://www.chronicle.com/article/How-the-University-Became/243622.

Seale, Maura. "Efficiency or Jagged Edges: Resisting Neoliberal Logics of Assessment." *Progressive Librarian* 46 (2016): 140–45.

Seale, Maura. "The Neoliberal Library." In *Information Literacy and Social Justice: Radical Professional Praxis*, edited by Shana Higgins and Lua Gregory, 39–61. Sacramento, CA: Library Juice Press, 2013. http://eprints.rclis.org/20497/.

Sessions, David. "How College Became a Commodity." The Chronicle of Higher Education, January 14, 2020. https://web.archive.org/web/20200114224643/https://www.chronicle.com/interactives/how-college-became-a-commodity.

Severson, Richard W. *The Principles of Information Ethics*. Armonk, N.Y: Routledge, 1997.

Simms, Sarah, and Jeremiah Paschke-Wood. "Academic Librarians and Student Success: Examining Changing Librarian Roles and Attitudes." *Journal of Library Administration* 62, no. 8 (November 17, 2022): 1017–44. https://doi.org/10.1080/01930826.2022.2127585.

Smith, Dolsy. "Vocational Melancholy." *Library Trends* 68, no. 3 (April 2, 2020): 450–81.

Smith, Martha Montague. "Infoethics for Leaders: Models of Moral Agency in the Information Environment." *Library Trends* 40, no. 3 (1992): 553–70.

Soria, Krista M., Jan Fransen, and Shane Nackerud. "Stacks, Serials, Search Engines, and Students' Success: First-Year Undergraduate Students' Library Use, Academic Achievement, and Retention." *The Journal of Academic Librarianship* 40, no. 1 (January 2014): 84–91. https://doi.org/10.1016/j.acalib.2013.12.002.

Soria, Krista M., Jan Fransen, and Shane Nackerud . "The Impact of Academic Library Resources on Undergraduates' Degree Completion." *College & Research Libraries* 78, no. 6 (2017): 812–23. https://doi.org/10.5860/crl.78.6.812.

Sparanese, Ann. "Activist Librarianship: Heritage or Heresy?" In *Questioning Library Neutrality: Essays from Progressive Librarian*, edited by Alison Lewis, 67–87. Duluth, Minnesota: Library Juice Press, 2008.

Stoytcheva, Sveta. "Steven Salaita, the Critical Importance of Context, and Our Professional Ethics." *Canadian Journal of Academic Librarianship* 1 (January 28, 2016): 92–103. https://doi.org/10.33137/cjal-rcbu.v1.24309.

Task Force, ACRL Framework. "Framework for Information Literacy for Higher Education, Frequently Asked Questions." Association of College and Research Libraries, 2015. https://alair.ala.org/handle/11213/8657.

Teal, Wesley. "Library Meeting Rooms for All, for Real." Beardbrarian, July 14, 2018. http://web.archive.org/web/20180715125947/https://beardbrarian.com/blog/hate.html.

Tewell, Eamon C. "The Practice and Promise of Critical Information Literacy: Academic Librarians' Involvement in Critical Library Instruction." *College & Research Libraries* 79, no. 1 (2018): 10–34. https://doi.org/10.5860/crl.79.1.10.

Tewell, Eamon C. "Use of Library Services Can Be Associated with a Positive Effect on First-Year Students' GPA and Retention." *Evidence Based Library and Information Practice* 10, no. 1 (March 6, 2015): 79–81. https://doi.org/10.18438/B8RP6R.

Thomas, Deborah A. "Intellectual Freedom and Inclusivity: Opposites or Partners?" *Journal of Intellectual Freedom & Privacy* 4, no. 3 (2019): 7–10. https://doi.org/10.5860/jifp.v4i3.7129.

Thompson, Bruce, Martha Kyrillidou, and Colleen Cook. "Library Users' Service Desires: A LibQUAL+ Study." *The Library Quarterly* 78, no. 1 (January 1, 2008): 1–18. https://doi.org/10.1086/523907.

Travis, Tiffany A., and Christian Ramirez. "Big Data and Academic Libraries: The Quest for Informed Decision-Making." *Portal: Libraries and the Academy* 20, no. 1 (2020): 33–47.

Trosow, Samuel E. "The Commodification of Information and the Public Good: New Challenges for a Progressive Librarianship." *Progressive Librarian*, no. 43 (Winter 2014): 17–29.

Urquhart, Christine, and Jenny Turner. "Reflections on the Value and Impact of Library and Information Services: Part 2: Impact Assessment." *Performance Measurement and Metrics* 17, no. 1 (January 1, 2016): 5–28. https://doi.org/10.1108/PMM-01-2016-0001.

Valentine, Greta, and Kate Barron. "An Examination of Academic Library Privacy Policy Compliance with Professional Guidelines." *Evidence Based Library and Information Practice* 17, no. 3 (September 19, 2022): 77–96. https://doi.org/10.18438/eblip30122.

Viberg, Olga, Mathias Hatakka, Olof Bälter, and Anna Mavroudi. "The Current Landscape of Learning Analytics in Higher Education." *Computers in Human Behavior* 89 (December 1, 2018): 98–110. https://doi.org/10.1016/j.chb.2018.07.027.

Walther, James H. "Teaching Ethical Dilemmas in LIS Coursework: An Adaptation on Case Methodology Usage for Pedagogy." *The Bottom Line* 29, no. 3 (September 16, 2016): 180–90. https://doi.org/10.1108/BL-05-2016-0020.

Weigand, Wayne A. *Irrepressible Reformer: A Biography of Melvil Dewey*. Chicago, IL: American Library Association, 1996.

Wengert, Robertg. "Some Ethical Aspects of Being an Information Professional." *Library Trends* 49, no. 3 (Winter 2001): 486–509.

Wenzler, John. "Neutrality and Its Discontents: An Essay on the Ethics of Librarianship." *Portal: Libraries and the Academy* 19, no. 1 (January 29, 2019): 55–78. https://doi.org/10.1353/pla.2019.0004.

Wilson, Patrick. *Second-Hand Knowledge: An Inquiry into Cognitive Authority*. Westport, Conn: Praeger, 1983.

Witt, Steve. "The Evolution of Privacy within the American Library Association, 1906–2002." *Library Trends* 65, no. 4 (September 8, 2017): 639–57. https://doi.org/10.1353/lib.2017.0022.

Wong, Shun Han Rebekah, and T. D. Webb. "Uncovering Meaningful Correlation between Student Academic Performance and Library Material Usage." *College & Research Libraries* 72, no. 4 (2011): 361–70. https://doi.org/10.5860/crl-129.

Yoose, Becky. "Balancing Privacy and Strategic Planning Needs: A Case Study in De-Identification of Patron Data." *Journal of Intellectual Freedom & Privacy* 2, no. 1 (July 7, 2017): 15–22. https://doi.org/10.5860/jifp.v2i1.6250.

Yousefi, Baharak. "On the Disparity Between What We Say and What We Do in Libraries." In *Feminists Among Us: Resistance and Advocacy in Library Leadership*, edited by Shirley Lew and Baharak Yousefi, 91–105. Sacramento, CA: Library Juice Press, 2017.

Zimmer, Michael. "Librarians' Attitudes Regarding Information and Internet Privacy." *The Library Quarterly* 84, no. 2 (April 1, 2014): 123–51. https://doi.org/10.1086/675329.

Chapter 4
Characteristics of Ethical Assessment Practice

Overview

In Chapter 2, we looked at the extensive work that our field has undertaken in grappling with the values of our profession, and in Chapter 3 we identified ethical tensions that library assessment faces. Now, Chapter 4 turns toward ethical responses to those tensions. In this chapter, I discuss five areas of ethical library assessment where values are articulated and applied. Following this discussion, I present an inductive analysis of the five areas that reveals a set of characteristics shared across the practice areas. These characteristics bring into view a picture of ethical library assessment.

Ethical Practices in Library Assessment

We've seen across the last two chapters that ethical practice in LIS involves the application of values, and where values conflict, we can find sites of tension in our work. Those sites of tension involve market forces and neutrality, and they affect diverse areas of practice, including instruction, the archives, cataloging, and assessment. Now, this chapter is framed around two key questions: how do practitioners respond when faced with these ethical tensions? What assessment practices have been developed in response to the sites of tensions discussed in Chapter 3? What does a values-based, ethical practice look like? To answer these questions, and to help illuminate ethical practices and resolutions in library assessment, I examine five areas of assessment practice: critical assessment, co-design, strategic planning, norms and regulations, and care ethics. We will take a closer look at these areas of assessment because they each seek to enact values in support of an ethical practice. These five practice areas will be instructive for further examining library assessment through the lens of practical ethics and applied values.

Critical Assessment

Critical assessment in libraries is a newly-emerging area that focuses on bringing forward critical viewpoints related to traditional library assessment. From this place of critical inquiry, critical assessment seeks to build new communities of practice for library assessment. Critical assessment can be understood through the following three aspects: 1) practitioner self-reflection on issues of individual and institutional power and privilege, 2) applying qualitative and community-based methods in balance with quantitative approaches, with a focus on social impacts, and 3) foregrounding subjects of assessment as co-equal participants in the research process—all in support of advancing an alternative vision and practice for LIS assessment.[1]

Critical assessment stems from the wider foundation of critical librarianship, which provides the groundwork for examining the structures and systems that shape LIS work.[2] For example, critically reconsidering established library assessment practices such as EZ proxy logins, ID card swipes, article downloads, circulation records, and tracking the amount of time students spend in physical and online spaces.[3] From a critical assessment perspective, these practices—many of which have been developed from Oakleaf's influential report on library assessment[4]—can be seen as surveillance efforts that do not fully or accurately capture a student's experience in the library. Such self-reflective, self-critical viewpoints are applied toward a useful questioning of prevailing practices, as with Hodge, who encourages LIS practitioners

---

1 Magnus, Belanger, and Faber, "Towards a Critical Assessment Practice."
2 Drabinski, "What Is Critical about Critical Librarianship?"
3 Fisher, Magnus, and Branch, "Critical Assessment Practices: A Discussion of When and How to Use Student Learning Data Without Doing Harm."
4 Oakleaf, "The Value of Academic Libraries."

to work from a place of cultural humility and self-reflection: "To provide the best possible service, we must start with ourselves first."[5]

Through a process of self-reflection, critical insights are possible. Sentance, for instance, illuminates the long history of extractive methodologies common in libraries and archives that have resulted in harms to Indigenous peoples while benefiting Western researchers and practitioners.[6] A key point of self-reflection is that assessment practice cannot be divorced from its history and context, and that assessment is always a political and social act, whether the socio-political agenda is made explicit or not.[7] DeLuca Fernández offers four main aspects that further define critical assessment: 1) expose and address power, privilege, and structures; 2) consider thoughtfully histories and contexts; 3) make explicit assumptions and intentions; 4) eschew color-blind and ideological neutral claims.[8] DeLuca Fernández's work builds on important work from Wall, Hursh, and Rodgers III, who offer a comprehensive critical analysis of assessment and call on practitioners to deeply reflect on the ethical and operational aspects of assessment, particularly focusing on who benefits from prevailing norms, standards, and hierarchies:

> By raising consciousness of the ethical and value-based decisions implicit in any assessment context, the practice of assessment truly becomes a complex social practice rather than a collection of technical data gathering approaches that might unwittingly serve power interests unintended by well-meaning individuals.[9]

In situating assessment as predominantly a tool of managerial and market-based accountability, Wall, Hursh, and Rodgers III describe a revised assessment practice that is socially-aware, politically-attuned, and functions "first and foremost as an ethical and valuing practice."[10] Where traditional assessment approaches have focused on technical methods and a neutral objectivity of result, the critical assessment

---

5   Hodge, "Integrating Cultural Humility into Public Services Librarianship," 268.

6   "Engaging with the Uncomfortable."

7   DeLuca Fernández, "Critical Assessment."

8   DeLuca Fernández.

9   Wall, Hursh, and Rodgers III, "Assessment for Whom," 13.

10 Wall, Hursh, and Rodgers III, 11.

practitioner considers the effects of wider systems of power, privilege, and market forces in a way that surfaces the social position and political viewpoint of the practitioner.[11] Critical assessment is an important but challenging turn for LIS professionals, because librarians are not necessarily oriented toward a reflective practice, in part because LIS professional values of objectivity and neutrality can inhibit critical self-reflection.[12] But LIS is a profession that espoused values, as established in prior chapters. When practitioners explicitly acknowledge and transparently apply values, assessment can be further developed in support of social justice.[13]

Critical assessment is rooted in ongoing conversations around the challenges and successes of those communities who are researched, expressed through qualitative, ethnographic, and longitudinal methods.[14] Critical assessment shifts the focus from the institution to the participant through community-oriented, empathic approaches that reinforces *power with*, rather than *power over* as a way to inscribe new, more equitable power relations.[15] In practice, assessment research should be developed with and from the community in question, with results flowing beneficially back to the community.[16] Critical assessment is characterized through the continual act of reflection-in-action, and with the alignment of method with goals and values, especially with an investment in qualitative approaches to counterbalance quantitative methods.[17] Participatory approaches are another mark of critical assessment, the motivations for which are captured by Montenegro and Jankowski: "One of the easiest means by which to check

---

11 Wall, Hursh, and Rodgers III, "Assessment for Whom"; DeLuca Fernández, "Critical Assessment."

12 Graf and Harris, "Reflective Assessment."

13 Doucette, "Acknowledging the Political, Economic, and Values-Based Motivators of Assessment Work: An Analysis of Publications on Academic Library Assessment."

14 Fisher, Magnus, and Branch, "Critical Assessment Practices: A Discussion of When and How to Use Student Learning Data Without Doing Harm."

15 Douglas et al., "A Practice of Connection: Applying Relational Cultural Theory to Librarianship"; McCartin and Dineen, *Toward a Critical-Inclusive Assessment Practice for Library Instruction*.

16 Gaudry, "Insurgent Research."

17 Macaluso, "Incorporating Self-Assessment and Peer Assessment into Library Instructional Practice"; Badia, "Combining Critical Reflection and Action Research to Improve Pedagogy"; Reale, *Becoming a Reflective Librarian and Teacher: Strategies for Mindful Academic Practice*; Deitering, Rempel, and Jensen, "Reflective Information Literacy."

assumptions is to actively involve participants in the process of assessment."[18]

For community-based, participatory assessment practices, helpful examples can be found in the field of archives and digital collections. Archives professionals have been critically re-evaluating the history and practice of archives, and offering alternative conceptualizations of an archives as open and empowering to more stakeholders, as articulated by Gilliland: "Participatory archives acknowledge that multiple parties have rights, responsibilities, needs and perspectives with regard to the record."[19] LIS professionals in the archive have focused a critical lens on the long history of exclusion, misrepresentation, oppression, and injustice in the archives, as well as the more recent pressures of neoliberal market forces.[20] Critical assessment is expressed in the archives through participatory archives,[21] and through community-based approaches.[22] This ethical practice involves bringing in members of the wider community to the process of creating, maintaining, and assessing archival descriptions and digital collections.[23]

In the context of assessment, there is an effort to identify and include a wider range of stakeholders and apply more community-attuned measures to the process of assessing digital collections. In moving beyond counting clicks and likes, Punzalan, Marsh, and Cools demonstrate an approach for assessing ethnographic digital collections that focus on narrative storytelling and change-oriented impact areas as a more community-attuned practice.[24] Beyond numeric metrics of use that reinforce colonial practices of objectification, this approach involves qualitative research with those impacted by the use of the collections, thereby offering more nuanced portraits of

---

18 Montenegro and Jankowski, "A New Decade for Assessment: Embedding Equity into Assessment Praxis," 10.

19 Gilliland and McKemmish, "The Role of Participatory Archives in Furthering Human Rights, Reconciliation and Recovery," 80.

20 Caswell et al., "'To Be Able to Imagine Otherwise'"; Drake, "Diversity's Discontents."

21 Iacovino, "Shaping and Reshaping Cultural Identity and Memory"; Rolan, "Agency in the Archive."

22 Jules, Summers, and Mitchell, Jr., "Ethical Considerations for Archiving Social Media Content Generated by Contemporary Social Movements: Challenges, Opportunities, and Recommendations."

23 Zavala et al., "'A Process Where We're All at the Table.'"

24 Punzalan, Marsh, and Cools, "Beyond Clicks, Likes, and Downloads."

engagement that focus on material benefits and social change.[25] The rationale for a participatory, community-determined assessment practice is expressed by Shilton and Srinivasan: "By approaching appraisal in collaboration with community members, archivists are given the chance to assess the value of community records as the community understands them."[26]

Further examples of community-oriented archival assessments include the collections reuse project, which seeks to assess the impacts not of use (defined by, for example, the download count of an object), but of reuse (defined by the application of an object).[27] For this assessment project, "ethical considerations and community values should be at the forefront of all discussions."[28] Critical assessment in the archives is comprehensively summarized by Caswell et al. in describing a vision for putting forward an alternative practice of archival activity and assessment:

> The ultimate goal to which we hope this research contributes in some small part is to 'imagine otherwise,' that is to conceive of and build a world in which communities that have historically been and are currently being marginalized due to white supremacy, patriarchy, capitalism, gender binaries, colonialism and ableism are fully empowered to represent their past, construct their present and envision their futures as forms of liberation.[29]

Looking very briefly to an adjacent field to illustrate this concept, we can see that museum professionals have also applied the principle of *otherwise* as a practice of "think[ing] and do[ing] museums and heritage differently from the ways in which they have more recently or more usually been done."[30] Archives professionals, archives scholars, and related practitioners offer promising models for ethical

---

25 Marsh et al., "Stories of Impact."
26 Shilton and Srinivasan, "Participatory Appraisal and Arrangement for Multicultural Archival Collections," 93.
27 Muglia et al., "How We Talk about Assessment."
28 O'Gara et al., "Barriers and Solutions to Assessing Digital Library Reuse," 138.
29 Caswell et al., "'To Be Able to Imagine Otherwise,'" 6.
30 Macdonald, "Otherwise: Rethinking Museums and Heritage," 3.

assessment, especially related to participatory and community-based assessments that think beyond currently established practice.

In sum, critical assessment offers a promising framework for ethical assessment in LIS. Critical assessment is a reflective practice that is systems-attuned, people-oriented, socially-engaged, politically-aware, and change-driven. The concept of "imagining otherwise" is central to the reflective and transformative goals of critical assessment, for "critical librarianship knows that the world could be different."[31]

Co-Design

The traditions of design offer compelling approaches for ethical library assessment. Design offers a set of practical methods rooted in values-based theories and is thus a promising area to examine through the lens of practical ethics. Designers recognize that "core values matter in shaping people's attitudes and behavior" and "values-driven practices seek change in complex systems."[32] At the center of the design process is people, as expressed by industrial designer Dieter Rams: "If you do not understand people, you cannot understand good design."[33]

Co-design—and its related practices of participatory design and service design—is a subfield of design that is especially committed to involving and understanding the people involved in and impacted by the design process and the design result. Co-design and participatory design work to identify and involve representatives of key stakeholder groups so as to "challenge power relationships and transform patterns of exclusion and social injustice."[34] Participatory design is guided by a set of principles: equalizing power relations, democratic practices, situation-based actions, mutual learning, and the application of tools and techniques that can realize these principles.[35] In the process of participatory co-design, practitioners explicitly take a stand for justice and often work on projects that involve and elevate

---

31 Drabinski, "What Is Critical about Critical Librarianship?," 53.

32 Davis, "Design Futures Trend: Core Values Matter," 2–8.

33 Hustwit, *Rams*, 1:01.

34 Robertson and Wagner, "Ethics: Engagement, Representation and Politics-in-Action," 68.

35 Kensing and Greenbaum, "Heritage: Having a Say."

members of groups who have been historically marginalized, disempowered, or oppressed.[36]

In LIS, design is manifested in multiple ways: as service design, co-design, participatory design, user experience design, and design thinking. These approaches are united through common elements, including self-reflection, co-creating the outcome with participants and stakeholders, co-determination in the process, empathy for the people who use and deliver a service, and an explicit articulation of both professional and personal values. Service design tools have been applied, for example, in the area of data ethics to operationalize values such as the public good.[37] A design methodology can be applied to create an open access statement, with an integration of a self-reflective component that questioned traditional neutrality.[38] Co-design can be effective in developing library policy and services, by bringing together multiple stakeholder groups for a shared purpose, guided by shared values.[39] Clarke has argued that LIS is primed to accommodate design as a central theoretical and practical tenet of the profession, as LIS already involves key aspects of design, including reflection, problem solving, knowledge through making, criteria-based assessments, and practice-as-scholarship.[40]

Participation and collaboration in the process of designing and assessing library services allows LIS professionals to build on core values such as service, equity, social justice, and lifelong learning.[41] Design ways have been adopted by practitioners who invite tensions that arise from the explicitly political nature of co-design, as expressed by Bats, who studied participatory techniques in information literacy: "Political action seems to be in conflict with some traditional values of libraries like neutrality."[42] As a response to neutrality, co-design offers

---

36 Ehn, "Scandinavian Design: On Participation and Skill."

37 Drew, "Design for Data Ethics."

38 Rigling, Waugh, and Carlisle, "In Pursuit of Equity."

39 Rigling, Waugh, and Carlisle, para. 27.

40 Clarke, "Toward a Design Epistemology for Librarianship"; Clarke, "How We Done It Good."

41 Clarke, "Toward a Design Epistemology for Librarianship"; Clarke, "From 'Library Science' to 'Library Design': Recasting the Narrative of Academic Librarianship."

42 Bats, "Information Literacy, Participatory Projects and the Development of Political Roles for Librarians," 33.

a theory and a practice that allows librarians to take a stand for values and to enact an ethical practice.

Design offers an apt model of practical ethics for library assessment. Design practitioners in LIS such as Reidsma, a UX Librarian, invoke the central self-reflective question of practical ethics: "The questions we face now lean more toward 'is this the right thing to do?' than 'am I doing this right?'"[43] Reidsma describes scenario-based ethical dilemmas in library service design, and posits an attunement to values as an ethical way forward. Indeed, co-design challenges the status quo by posing and attempting to solve troublesome design problems that encourage reflection and discourse while at the same time rejecting neutrality and objectivity.[44] The connection between ethics, values, and practice is drawn clearly by LIS design practitioners, with a recognition that all of our designs necessarily reflect our values.[45] Hanson specifically calls for a greater values-oriented viewpoint in library software design.[46] And service design has been shown as a method for achieving the service value of LIS.[47]

Design then becomes a pathway to ethical assessment, with the principles and practices of co-design applied to better understand user needs and goals, as well as to achieve an ethical practice that brings to life core values. A few examples can illustrate this point. At the University of Michigan, a process of co-design was followed for space assessment in order to "help our department hold ourselves accountable to our intentions of transparency, participation, and creating a data gathering program that is useful, timely, and relevant to colleagues across the entire organization."[48] Davis used participatory paper prototyping to design and assess web interfaces in an academic library, demonstrating that inviting students into the design and assessment process can provide in-roads for student expertise, leading to user empowerment and a better-researched final product.

---

43 Reidsma, "Keynote 1: Ethical UX," 9.

44 Robinson, "Critical Design in Librarianship."

45 Orphanides, "Architecture Is Politics: The Power and the Perils of Systems Design."

46 Hanson, "Libraries Are Software."

47 Marquez and Downey, "Service Design."

48 Puckett-Rodgers, Leyton, and King, "Participatory Data-Gathering and Community Building," 243.

[49] Gamboni applied a reflective, participatory process to assess the skills of librarians in developing an e-book service, concluding that participation in assessment was effective for growth-through-reflection, personal and professional development, and change-making in an academic setting.[50]

Further examples demonstrate the application of design in support of diversity and social responsibility. Tewell applied a participatory photovoice method in a co-designed assessment of reference services involving librarians and students from historically marginalized groups.[51] The motivation for participation in this project comes from the recognition that "people's experiences and information practices are unique and shaped by their diverse life experiences."[52] In following the tradition of participatory design, this project sought results that could positively impact the lives of the participants, not only by creating better library services that better meet the needs of marginalized students, but also by empowering those students through a process of co-determination and mutual learning in the assessment process. Importantly, the results were "determined by the community studied instead of solely the researcher."[53]

In a similar study, Neurohr and Bailey applied photo-elicitation—a participatory research method—to assess how Native American students "perceived the role of the academic library in their lives, and which elements of the library students depicted and described as holding meaning for them."[54] In this instance, participatory assessment proved valuable for engaging diverse users in support of designing and assessing library services. The process of participatory co-determination seeks to build relationships of mutual benefit and trust with participants.[55] And Belanger et al. applied participatory design to

---

49 Davis, "Participatory Paper Prototyping."

50 Gamboni, "Developing Academic Librarians' Skills in e-Book Services through Participatory Action Research."

51 Tewell, "Reframing Reference for Marginalized Students."

52 Tewell, 173.

53 Tewell, 164.

54 Neurohr and Bailey, "Using Photo-Elicitation with Native American Students to Explore Perceptions of the Physical Library," 56.

55 Delaney and Bates, "Envisioning the Academic Library"; Gamboni, "Developing Academic Librarians' Skills in e-Book Services through Participatory Action Research."

understand the needs of students enrolled in online programs, finding that the approach generated feelings of connectedness among participants, but also that the deeper goal of equal participation was limited by well-established organizational structures and dynamics that reinforce existing hierarchies.[56]

As an approach rooted in values, co-design is especially suited for pursuing an ethical assessment practice. Co-design shares certain characteristics of critical assessment, especially relating to questioning neutrality and the status quo, involving the subjects of assessment as equal participants, and working towards social change for the benefit of people who have historically been under-resourced or marginalized.

Strategic Planning

Strategic planning also offers a model for achieving an ethical library assessment practice, in that the strategic planning process incorporates a values-orientation. Strategic planning in higher education dates back to the 1960s, and assessment is a key part of strategic planning.[57] Strategic plans set the collective direction for a library, and provide a structure for generating insight into how libraries are prioritizing goals and the extent to which they are assessing those goals.[58] The basic formulation of strategic planning assessment follows a multi-part cycle: identify objectives, measures, and targets; gather data; analyze data; identify improvements and action plans; implement improvements to close the loop and restart the cycle.[59] Underlying this cycle is the identity of the organization, including the vision, mission, and values. A library's organizational vision "will include a clearly articulated guiding philosophy that includes core values and beliefs and a statement of purpose."[60] Strategic planning therefore provides a structure for articulating and assessing values.[61] Importantly, strategic planners recognize that planning and assessment unfold from particular

---

56 Belanger et al., "We're All Online Students Now: Using Participatory Design to Meet the Needs of Students at the University of Washington Libraries."
57 Dole, "Strategic Planning and Assessment."
58 Saunders, "Room for Improvement."
59 Crowe, "Strategic Library Assessment."
60 Harland, Stewart, and Bruce, "Aligning Library and University Strategic Directions," 278.
61 Dole, "Strategic Planning and Assessment."

viewpoints—indeed, in allocating resources and articulating values, strategic planning is a political activity.[62]

Some key examples can show strategic planning in action and demonstrate its relevance for ethical assessment, particularly as connected to the practice of defining, embedding, and assessing values. The practice of assessing values can be found in Baich, who defines a "values-based vision" for the scholarly communications activities of Indiana University–Purdue University Indianapolis.[63] This vision draws upon evidence gathered through participatory activities and focus groups, culminating in an "Open Values Statement" that articulates values such as openness, transparency, and equity. Baich then develops a set of evaluation criteria to measure the degree to which library tools and services are aligned with the values of the vision statement. Baich presents a useful model for values-based planning and assessment using the strategic planning formulation of setting goals and measuring progress. In another similar example, Galvan describes a process of developing a values-driven license for library e-resources.[64] Galvan articulates a set of library strategic values—including inquiry, inclusiveness, sustainability, and community—and then poses the question, "How does licensing impact those values?" By mapping licensing terms to stated values, the project seeks to answer this ethical question by assessing the alignment of library licenses with library values.

Another example can be seen in HuMetricsHSS, the Humane Metrics Initiative.[65] This project "proposes that metrics only be used to measure one's progress towards embodying five core values that initial research suggests are central to all humanities and social science disciplines: Collegiality, Quality, Equity, Openness, and Community."[66] The HuMetricsHSS initiative builds on the premise that common quantitative metrics like citation counts capture only a limited scope of activity, and that an assessment model based on values can better capture output and impact. Articulating and enacting core values becomes "an

---

62 Saunders, "Room for Improvement."
63 Baich, "Guided by Values."
64 Galvan, "The Values Driven Library Resource License."
65 Agate et al., "The Transformative Power of Values-Enacted Scholarship"; Agate, "Walking the Talk"; "HuMetricsHSS."
66 Konkiel et al., "Exploring Values-Based (Alt)Metrics to Enhance Library Services," 1.

alternative means of enabling people to tell textured stories about their professional development through the lens of the values they uphold, adhere to, and respect as members of an institution."[67]

Moving further in the direction of values assessment, we can draw from the body of work of Town, who offers perhaps the strongest example of values-based assessment in strategic planning.[68] Over the course of several years, Town developed a values-based assessment approach that leveraged the Balanced Scorecard, a prominent strategic planning framework. Town acknowledges that libraries are under pressure to "prove their worth" through value and impact studies; he then posited that answers to value contributions can be found by expanding the concept of value to include values: "Because values are manifested, there will be something that we can measure arising from the way values are enacted in our libraries and the way value is generated as a result."[69] Beyond "mere espousal," libraries should contextualize values, resolve conflicts among values, and ultimately "provide evidence of contribution to values achievement."[70] The evidence for achieving values can be measured because values are manifested in what people do and the choices they make. This values-based approach to value measurement may be summarized by the following: "value reflects values."[71] Next, Town and Kyrillidou developed a practical tool—the "Value Scorecard"—to give a practical expression to the concept of a values-based approach to value measurement.[72]

The Value Scorecard is structured according to the basic operations of strategic planning: set goals, measure progress, report results. In the Values Scorecard framework, the library's goals are the library's values. And by linking the library's future vision—the goals—back to the library's foundation—the values—the Values Scorecard formulates values as the key indicator of the library's alignment with and worth to the parent institution. The Values Scorecard is thus a framework for centering library values as library value. As Town writes, "Because a

---

67 Agate, "Humane Metrics and the Value of Values," para. 2.

68 Town, "Value, Impact, and the Transcendent Library."

69 Town, 114.

70 Town, 120.

71 Town, 122.

72 Town and Kyrillidou, "Developing a Values Scorecard."

value represents a slogan for the rationalization of action, values will be key to correct actions, which then lead to value creation."[73] Town then implemented and tested the Value Scorecard in an academic library, positing that "the ultimate test of the Value Scorecard is the contribution to the achievement of value as defined by institutional values, rather than the achievement of strategy alone; hence whilst the centre of the Balanced Scorecard is vision and strategy, the centre of the Value Scorecard is values."[74] In practice, the Values Scorecard was found to be a "practical success, collecting a rich range of data and evidence of the worth of the library."[75] In a subsequent analysis of the Value Scorecard, Town argues that the application of this tool combined with a commitment to organizational development can generate positive results for the library.[76] The Values Scorecard builds on other strategic planning scorecard models to direct values-based activities related to measurements, assessment, and advocacy.

The Values Scorecard offers an inspiring example for engaging with the ethical tensions of market forces and neutrality that we discussed in the prior chapter. The Value Scorecard encourages a broader vision of library value and impact that goes beyond immediate, market-conditioned outcomes in a way that captures the knowledge-based after-effects of library usage. The realization of aspirational values becomes the goal; demonstrating the realization of values becomes the demonstration of value. Town's model has since been described as a compelling advancement of assessment practice, as the Values Scorecard provides a broader, higher-level view of library resources, services, and facilities.[77] Town's approach of situating values as the centerpiece of library value stands as a productive point of reference for practical ethics and values-based assessment. Bourg has similarly called for LIS values to be the driver of LIS practice, and to "re-inject the core values of libraries and of our parent institutions into our work and our decision-making."[78] The examples from Town and others show that libraries can leverage the structure of strategic planning to articulate and

---

73 Town, "Value, Impact, and the Transcendent Library," 120.

74 Town, "Implementing the Value Scorecard," 239.

75 Town, 248.

76 Town, "The Value Scorecard."

77 Corrall, "Seven Stories of Performativity and Advocacy."

78 Bourg, "Beyond Measure," para. 11.

manifest values in support of ethical library assessment. In this approach, LIS values themselves can be the key to demonstrating value and for resolving the tension between library values and library value.

Norms and Regulations

The practice of ethical assessment can also be informed through an examination of legislative regulations and subsequent effects on normative behaviors. The relationship between norm and regulation derives from the passage of a law that reflects societal values and goals, followed by a community commitment to establishing and reinforcing best practices in support of the law.[79] Two case studies can help illustrate the effects of regulation on normative community behavior: first, the effects of the General Data Protection Regulation (GDPR) on data collection and web privacy; second, the effects of the Americans with Disabilities Act (ADA) on physical and digital accessibility.

The GDPR aims to ensure a harmonized, unified and sustainable approach to European Union (EU) citizens' data protection by implementing privacy protection practices in the European Union, effectively giving more control to citizens over their personal data.[80] The law went into effect in May 2018, and it sets out a number of standards that apply directly to the processing of personal data within the EU's territory or market, with fines for non-compliance; subsequent to the passage of this law, many companies and organizations prioritized meeting the standards of the GDPR.[81] GDPR is a response to the need for large-scale changes in order to improve normative behaviors related to privacy practices in the digital environment.[82] By creating more transparency and greater opportunity for people to determine how their data is collected and shared, the GDPR helps engage citizens as active participants in society and democracy.[83]

---

79 Nissenbaum, *Privacy in Context*, 242.

80 Almeida Teixeira, Mira da Silva, and Pereira, "The Critical Success Factors of GDPR Implementation."

81 Albrecht, "How the GDPR Will Change the World."

82 Kalbag, "This One Weird Trick Tells Us Everything About You."

83 Hoel and Chen, "Privacy and Data Protection in Learning Analytics Should Be Motivated by an Educational Maxim—Towards a Proposal."

Yet the practical implementation of GDPR standards has been inconsistent, indicating that norms are still developing for this regulation. A study of post-GDPR cookie notices, for example, revealed that cookie notices have been implemented with varying designs that lead to correspondingly varying results in terms of user interactions, pointing to "the importance for regulation to not just require consent, but also provide clear requirements or guidance for how this consent has to be obtained in order to ensure that users can make free and informed choices."[84] The work of Utz et al. highlight a gap that persists between espousing values and implementing values. Consent is an example of this gap. Consent is required by GDPR law, but implementation of cookie consent notifications is inconsistent across the jurisdiction, and to date a standardized cookie notice has not been developed. The outcome is an inconsistent patchwork of consent notifications that hinders the practical implementation of the consent value. The evolving relationship between regulation and norm is summarized by Hoel and Chen: "Even if the concern for data privacy is shared among the general public around the world there is a long way to go from concern, at least in the abstract, to finding a common normative basis for establishing data protection policies."[85] The GDPR provides motivation and a high-level framework for implementation, but the wider community of web developers and policy-makers must support the development of more detailed norms of behavior to support consistent outcomes for citizens.

The gap between abstract value and normative practice becomes evident when looking closer at data protection practices in US academic libraries. Despite the global impacts of GDPR, there remains a long-standing divide between the cultures of privacy in the EU and in the US.[86] Practitioners in the US do not benefit from the motivation and framework of GDPR to prompt the development of shared norms around data protection and privacy. Due to a lack of clear direction at the national level, privacy practices across the US—like US privacy laws themselves—are patchwork, inconsistent, and non-normative.[87]

---

84 Utz et al., "(Un)Informed Consent," 973.

85 Hoel and Chen, "Privacy and Data Protection in Learning Analytics Should Be Motivated by an Educational Maxim—Towards a Proposal," 5.

86 Penney, "Chilling Effects and Transatlantic Privacy."

87 Cox, "Legal Landscape of Consumer/ User Data Privacy and Current Policy Discussions."

Bamberger and Mulligan describe a landscape of US privacy practices that "are dynamic, are at times contradictory, can diverge both up and down from the law on the books, and vary contextually."[88]

Without a consequential regulatory mandate regarding privacy and data protection, libraries in the US rely on suggestions for behavior that leverage existing values as the primary motivation for action. IFLA, for example, encourages libraries to comply with GDPR while also invoking core values: "Libraries' continued commitment to the values of privacy can easily be seen in the many, many initiatives they dedicate to helping protect their users' data privacy inside and outside of the library."[89] But GDPR likely doesn't impact US libraries directly if their activities do not occur within the jurisdiction of the EU.[90] For libraries in the US, GDPR can lead to more values-driven data collection practices—but primarily on an opt-in basis.[91]

At the University of Denver, for instance, Cox led an initiative to update privacy practices related to the institutional repository (IR).[92] Though it was recognized that GDPR does not directly affect the IR, Cox opted to work towards partial GDPR compliance so as to apply standards, reduce risk, and build trust. A leading value in this project was transparency, with Cox reviewing and revising the library's privacy policy to ensure clear communication with users regarding activity across the library's website, online catalog, physical spaces, and databases. This work was self-initiated, with the intention to "show our patrons we care."[93] Cox also poses self-reflective questions to help guide implementation: What data do we collect? Why do we collect it? Is it justified? By assessing and improving privacy within the context of GDPR—but in a voluntary, site-specific approach—this project demonstrates that in the US, without a GDPR-style national regulation, implementation of privacy protection standards will continue to be ad hoc and opt-in, with users experiencing a patchwork of different approaches at

---

88 Bamberger and Mulligan, "Privacy in Europe," 1641.

89 International Federation of Library Associations, "What Data Privacy Means for Libraries in 2020," para. 10.

90 Hannay et al., "Legally Speaking—U.S. Libraries and the GDPR."

91 Heller, "Keeping Up With… General Data Protection Regulation (GDPR)."

92 Cox, "Understanding GDPR."

93 Cox, 8.

different libraries. Library norms around online privacy will continue to be shaped less by national standards that carry legal consequences, and more by guidance statements from professional organizations that leverage professional values to further motivate the practice. On-the-ground practical implementation will continue to vary widely.[94]

The Americans with Disabilities Act offers a contrasting case study. Since its passage in 1990 with a jurisdiction that affects most companies and organizations in the US, discourse and practice around the ADA has blossomed into a rich conversation and a set of normative behaviors related to access and disability. The ADA requires organizations with public facilities to make reasonable accommodations for those with disabilities.[95] The law prompted awareness and action of accessibility issues across the public and private sectors.[96] Within LIS, the ADA has been influential in initiating a conversation "about the importance of access to librarianship and educating us all regarding the needs of the disabled population."[97] Before the ADA, "very little thought was given to functional diversity."[98]

Today, the ADA directly supports the development of normative behaviors in the form of best practices for library users in a variety of settings, including instructional contexts,[99] web services,[100] and staff training in support of differently-abled users.[101] The ADA has also prompted critical reflection and action focused on LIS professionals themselves, as demonstrated by an emerging literature examining the experience of disabled librarians with a view towards addressing inequities and injustices.[102]

---

94 Corrado, "Libraries and Protecting Patron Privacy."
95 Peters and Bradbard, "Web Accessibility."
96 Kimura, "Defining, Evaluating, and Achieving Accessible Library Resources."
97 Brown and Sheidlower, "Claiming Our Space," 473.
98 Pionke, "Beyond ADA Compliance," 9.
99 Whitver, "Accessible Library Instruction in Practice."
100 Yoon, Hulscher, and Dols, "Accessibility and Diversity in Library and Information Science"; Ng, "A Practical Guide to Improving Web Accessibility."
101 Wade, "Serving the Visually Impaired User."
102 Schomberg, "Disability at Work"; Brown and Sheidlower, "Claiming Our Space"; Moeller, "Disability, Identity, and Professionalism"; Pionke, "Library Employee Views of Disability and Accessibility"; Schomberg and Highby, *Beyond Accommodation: Creating an Inclusive Workplace for Disabled Library Workers*.

For both library users and library workers, the regulatory aspects of the ADA have given rise to normative practices that are values-based and justice-oriented, seeking equity of access and service for both library users and library staff.[103] Accessibility is now seen as a system of values and goals that information professionals can "bring to everything we do, from collections to services to hiring...accessibility can help promote values of diversity and social responsibility, and can serve us in the work of making our workplaces and profession more equitable and just."[104]

The ADA has motivated a practice of "imagining otherwise" described above by Caswell et al.[105] This practice, rooted in LIS values, helps promote an "access that both responds to the pragmatic needs of the American Library Association's 'Core Values of Librarianship' (to guide professional practice and education) and helps librarians and library workers imagine how we might transform the systems, beliefs, and practices that make libraries and the profession inaccessible and inequitable."[106] Now thirty years beyond its passage, the ADA has helped direct libraries to enhance access across the spectrum of information services: physical space, services, databases, instruction, policies, trainings, management, education, attitudes and interactions with differently abled patrons, empathy-building, and staff representation.[107] The ADA is a regulation that has influenced normative behavior and today functions as an essential point of reference in developing best practices and norms for accessibility and disability justice.

For the assessment of accessibility in LIS, the ADA establishes standards for practitioners, with compliance being a focus since the law was enacted.[108] But while many libraries meet the basic letter of the law in terms of physical space access (e.g., elevators and doorways), they can go still further in understanding disability, empowering

---

103 Hill, "Disability and Accessibility in the Library and Information Science Literature"; Pereyaslavska, "Accessibility Librarian Competencies"; Kumbier and Starkey, "Access Is Not Problem Solving."

104 Rosen, "Accessibility for Justice," para. 37.

105 Caswell et al., "'To Be Able to Imagine Otherwise.'"

106 Kumbier and Starkey, "Access Is Not Problem Solving," 468.

107 Pionke, "Library Employee Views of Disability and Accessibility."

108 Foos and Pack, *How Libraries Must Comply with the Americans with Disabilities Act (ADA)*.

disabled users and staff, and building a fair library accessible to all.[109] In this way, the ADA further functions as an important bedrock for building a normative assessment practice that goes beyond compliance. LIS professionals recognize, for example, that ADA standards are often restrictive or exclusionary, treating disabled persons as objects to be controlled and managed.[110]

In response, accessibility practitioners have advanced an assessment practice that doesn't view disabled users as existing outside the assessment process, but rather as essential participants in the assessment process. In a literature review covering the years 2000–2010, Hill finds that LIS professionals express a commitment to enhancing accessibility, but that accessibility efforts could benefit further from increased direct participation of people with disabilities in designing and assessing the accessibility of information services.[111] Kumbier and Starkey reinforce the call to "recruit, educate, hire, and support library workers with disabilities" so as to make the LIS profession accessible and equitable.[112] Kimura further amplifies the call to involve disabled people in the assessment of information services.[113] With the normative standards set by these practitioners, disabled users become vital participants in the assessment lifecycle through a process of co-determination that supports positive social change for the disabled community through the implementation of information services made accessible with and for community members themselves.

Both the GDPR and the ADA demonstrate the limits and possibilities of regulation in setting norms and best practice, representing two sides of the same coin. On the one hand, the GDPR is unenforceable in the US and functions on an opt-in basis. On the other hand, the ADA is legally enforceable and sets a standard for practice. In both cases, the regulations serve as important points of reference that influence norms within practitioner communities. The ADA showcases the promise and power of regulation-driven norm development—over three decades of implementation, accessibility assessment within LIS has matured into

---

109 Pionke, "Beyond ADA Compliance."

110 Schomberg, "Disability at Work."

111 Hill, "Disability and Accessibility in the Library and Information Science Literature."

112 Kumbier and Starkey, "Access Is Not Problem Solving," 482.

113 Kimura, "Defining, Evaluating, and Achieving Accessible Library Resources."

a justice-oriented practice that deeply involves members of the disabled community in the practice of assessing information services. As a newer regulation, the GDPR hasn't yet reached this stage of maturity, but as more practitioners respond to the standards, the practitioner community around privacy may grow over time to develop its own set of normative behaviors.

These insights can be applied to the practice of ethical assessment: without a comprehensive regulation that sets clear, enforceable, consequential rules for library assessment, the practical implementation of an ethical assessment framework would likely resemble privacy more than accessibility—varying in application, motivated not by law but by a commitment to values, and ultimately opt-in and unenforceable. This book proposes a new *Values Classification for Library Assessment* and offers an accompanying toolkit for implementing values in practice—these new contributions will not have the regulatory and norm-setting power of the ADA; yet, as a point of reference for guiding practice, assessment-specific values could over time lead to the development of normative behaviors in support of ethical assessment.

Care Ethics

The ethics of care is the fifth and final area of practice examined here for its applicability to library assessment. The theory and practice of care ethics derives from the wider field of feminist ethics. Feminist ethics recognizes that individuals are woven together in a social fabric, and therefore have relational responsibilities to one another in an interconnected community.[114] "Feminist Ethics" first appeared in the 1980s as a term to define a movement within philosophy that acknowledged women and gender as indispensable to adequately understanding many issues in practical ethics.[115] Feminist ethics challenges the status quo of philosophy, especially focusing on the disproportionate representation of male-identifying thinkers and traditionally masculine ideas such as objectivity and individualism. In working to define the multiple dimensions of feminist ethics, prominent areas of attention have included care, empathy, and the cultivation of relationships

---

114 Noddings, *Caring*.

115 Jaggar, "Feminist Ethics."

as an important ethical action.[116] In LIS contexts, feminist ethics has been applied in several ways, including in the archives,[117] through management and leadership,[118] and in reference services.[119]

Feminist ethics offers a potent response to our key tensions of neutrality and market forces. Olson, for example, couches the act of classification in the language of feminist thought.[120] Rather than seeing the world of information organization as hierarchical, Olson encourages a view of connected knowing: first, a rejection of a universal, objective model of truth based on pyramidal hierarchy; then, a focus on relationships as connected through a web-like structure that highlights situatedness, or the consideration of context and experience. Olson further underscores the importance of involving different communities in LIS practice, and a recognition of power as a factor in knowing. Furthermore, Hathcock and Vinopal find through interviews with feminist-identifying library administrators: "For our interviewees, there is no room for neutrality in feminist leadership."[121] Clements likewise views neutrality as incompatible for the delivery of authentic and justice-oriented reference services, as neutrality works to uphold the status quo of social inequality.[122] In rejecting the existing paradigm of objectivity and neutrality, feminist ethics offers alternative visions for work and the world. In the context of library instruction, we find a vision and practice of feminist pedagogy, which can be characterized as collaborative, democratic, and transformative; consciousness raising about sexism and oppression; applying an ethic of care; valuing personal testimony and lived experience as valid ways of knowing.[123]

As a subfield of feminist ethics, the ethics of care focuses on seeing people not as individuals only, but as relational entities in society;

---

116 Slote, *The Ethics of Care and Empathy*; Jaggar, "Feminist Ethics."

117 Cifor and Wood, "Critical Feminism in the Archives"; Arnold, "Practicing Care: Constructing Social Responsibility Through Feminist Care Ethics."

118 Hathcock and Vinopal, "Feminist Praxis in Library Leadership."

119 Clements, "'Nothing More than a Gear in Your Car:' Neutrality and Feminist Reference in the Academic Library."

120 Olson, "How We Construct Subjects."

121 Hathcock and Vinopal, "Feminist Praxis in Library Leadership," 162.

122 Clements, "'Nothing More than a Gear in Your Car:' Neutrality and Feminist Reference in the Academic Library."

123 Accardi, *Feminist Pedagogy for Library Instruction*.

through a focus on mutuality and the recognition of interdependence, care can help people live a value of social responsibility.[124] For care ethics, the individual is not the primary unit of society, but rather the relational pair is the central epistemological entity.[125] In this way, the ethics of care also provides persuasive arguments for limiting market forces. Held advances the thesis that care ethics can provide a counterbalance to market forces in higher education.[126] Over the last few decades, universities have adopted the corporate language and thinking of efficiency and productivity, and subsequently workloads have increased while wages decreased. Market logic assumes that every actor operates with individualistic self-interest, but care ethics posits that cooperation and relationship-building can lead to a better world:

> The values of *shared* enjoyment or *social* responsibility, or *collective* caring may well be worth promoting in the realm of culture and in the activities or practices of communication, but these are values that cannot even be registered in calculations of maximizing individual preferences.[127]

Care ethics also provides space for conflicting values, and suggests approaches for resolving such conflicts based on prioritization: "It seems better to see education and the market as having different *priorities*, as *ordering* their values differently."[128] In the context of LIS values, Higgins suggests feminist ethics as a framework for resolving potential conflicts among values: "A feminist standpoint toward the 'Core Values' would center Social Responsibility and The Public Good as the values that drive and inform the ways in which access to collections, information, spaces, and services are provided."[129] As an expression of practical ethics, the ethics of care provides a guide for conduct, and can also serve as a constructive point of reference in developing the *Values Classification for Library Assessment*.

---

124 Held, *The Ethics of Care*.

125 Noddings, *Caring*.

126 Held, *The Ethics of Care*.

127 Held, 118.

128 Held, 123.

129 Higgins, "Embracing the Feminization of Librarianship," 82.

LIS professionals have a long history of performing care labor.[130] For library assessment, care ethics provides a practical apparatus for developing alternative approaches for understanding and measuring success. At the reference desk, Howard invokes the values of equality and justice in encouraging librarians to build co-experiential, relational interactions with students, and then to assess this work not only by quantitative measures that would produce a count of how many references interactions, but also by the quality of the collaboration and the shared experience between the librarian and the student.[131] In the context of digital libraries, Dohe marks out a care ethics assessment practice that balances quantitative measures with qualitative accounts of emotional labor—calling, for instance, for institutional repository managers to "de-emphasize and decouple quantity of submissions (especially faculty submissions) in repositories as a metric of performance" and to "emphasize demonstrable methods of emotional work."[132] Dohe presents care ethics as a framework for enhancing inclusivity, democracy, and participation in the design, governance, and assessment of digital library software.

Nowviskie further develops care ethics in LIS settings in the context of digital humanities.[133] Nowviskie describes care ethics as a set of practices that include collective acts of mutual care and maintenance for the world, each other, our devices, and our instruments. This practice reorients practitioners away from the dominant paradigm of objective evaluation and towards an understanding of LIS practice as contextual and interdependent. Moreover, Nowviskie outlines a care ethics that provides new space for measuring value: "A competitive capitalist marketplace depends upon but does not assign much value to things we create through networks of reciprocity, compassion, generosity, mending, and care."[134]

Maintenance is seen as a notable aspect of care work, and maintenance is also seen as a notable aspect of LIS work—Olson et al. assert

---

130 Słoniowski, "Affective Labor, Resistance, and the Academic Librarian."

131 Howard, "Purposeful and Productive Care: The Feminist Ethic of Care and the Reference Desk."

132 Dohe, "Care, Code, and Digital Libraries," para. 30.

133 Nowviskie, "On Capacity and Care."

134 Nowviskie, para. 27.

that information maintenance is care work.[135] Like Nowviskie, Olson et al. outline an ethics of care composed of contextual and interrelated responsibilities. A central aspect of these responsibilities is assessment via self-reflection rooted in humility and empathy. Olson et al. suggest the following self-reflective prompts that can help challenge the status quo of market capitalism and objectivity: "Who is allowed to care and in what spaces? Who orders, elevates, and acknowledges or rewards the labor?" Combined with justice-oriented goal setting, these and other care-oriented self-reflective assessments can help provide alternative, qualitative measures of success that counter or complement prevailing assessments that center numerical indicators.

We can look again to practitioners in the archives for examples of ethics in action. Punzalan and Marsh describe a process of building reciprocal relationships between archival institutions and Indigenous communities who are represented in the collections or who use the archives.[136] This community-based relationship-building is advanced in a wider context of feminist ethics of care and responsible stewardship of collections. Calling back to Caswell's notion of imagining otherwise, Punzalan and Marsh describe community-based archives as an *otherwising* practice, as it illuminates a transformative model of archival practice that challenges existing norms by working toward mutual benefit and trust with communities that have been historically exploited through traditional, extractive archival practice. Punzalan and Marsh also point to a model of reciprocity assessment, where the success of an archive is measured by the level of reciprocity with a community—has social justice or mutual trust been achieved? This presents a compelling alternative to a more capitalistic use-based assessment that would base success on, for example, the number of patrons who access a collection.

Care is a potent counterpoint to neoliberal capitalism, and "holds possibilities as a means toward equitable, inclusive, anti-neoliberal futures."[137] As a practical demonstration, care ethics has been applied in the archives as a way to shift LIS practice and assessment from market-based postures of objectivity and neutrality and toward social change and social justice, as described by Caswell and Cifor, who

---

135 Olson et al., "Information Maintenance as a Practice of Care."

136 Punzalan and Marsh, "Reciprocity."

137 Higgins, "Embracing the Feminization of Librarianship," 73.

investigate an ethics of care as a model for supporting social justice.[138] As Olson recognized a bibliographic record situated within an interconnected web of relationships, so Caswell and Cifor recognize archivists situated within a relational web of mutual responsibility involving records creators, subjects, users and communities. Within a context of care ethics, archivists become caregivers for archival records and researchers. A national review of assessment projects found that the practice of assessment can be most effective through collaborative, team-based assessment that places value on relationships, context, and connection—this highlights the applicability of care ethics for library assessment.[139]

Finally, Arellano Douglas has perhaps most directly linked care with assessment: Arellano Douglas seeks a "reframing of the conversation around assessment from one of demonstrating value to one of embodying a value of care and connection in learning for both students and librarians."[140] This reframing would happen through questioning the status quo, activating the participation of students and others who are assessed, building relationships with stakeholders, and working towards diversity and justice. Notably, care-as-assessment centers values and their realization as a measure of value: "To care through assessment, we will emphasize what we value, not that we have value."[141] In Arellano Douglas's inspiring vision, the values that matter are co-determined with students, and the relationships built and maintained through the learning experience that support those values become the objects of assessment and the statements of value.

For library assessment, care ethics is theoretically well suited for supporting an ethical assessment practice in alignment with LIS values, especially as it contains ready responses for the two key pressure points identified in Chapter 3, neutrality and market forces: first, care ethics recognizes and celebrates different and unique cultural identities of individuals and their interrelations, thus advancing anti-neutrality viewpoints; second, care ethics calls for reconfiguring

---

138 Caswell and Cifor, "From Human Rights to Feminist Ethics."

139 Malenfant and Brown, "Creating Sustainable Assessment through Collaboration: A National Program Reveals Effective Practices."

140 Arellano Douglas, "Moving from Critical Assessment to Assessment as Care," 46.

141 Arellano Douglas, 56.

the boundaries of market norms and influences, thus advancing market-critical viewpoints.

Analysis: Characteristics of Ethical Assessment

We've now taken a tour through five areas of assessment: critical assessment, co-design, strategic planning, norms and regulations, and care ethics. To build a cohesive sense of how these areas are connected, I completed an inductive analysis of the literature. For each reference, I assigned a code, and through a process of theming and sub-theming, I arrived at a group of characteristics. These characteristics offer a sense of commonality across the practice areas. This analysis can begin to show us the contours of a values-based, ethical assessment practice. More detail about the literature analysis is in the research dataset, available via the Qualitative Data Repository with the following title and URL: *Practitioner Perspectives on the Values and Ethics of Library Assessment*, https://doi.org/10.5064/F6ORSLQF.

Ultimately, the analysis produced eleven characteristics that were present in the literature across the five assessment practice areas discussed in this chapter. The eleven characteristics are listed below. Each characteristic includes a description and a self-reflective prompt. The self-reflective prompt serves as a practical marker or a diagnostic for evaluating an assessment practice. These characteristics are a step in answering the questions of this chapter—what assessment practices have been developed in response to ethical tensions? What does a values-based practice look like? The characteristics listed below are some indicators of an ethical assessment practice.

Community co-determination

Community co-determination happens when appropriate assessment questions and methods are determined in partnership with the subjects of assessment and other key stakeholders, whereby the assessor is not the sole source of decision-making. Co-determination equalizes power relations, with the goal of creating a shared dynamic through the assessment process that gives voice to those who have traditionally lacked.

Self-reflective prompt: Throughout the assessment lifecycle, do key stakeholders (such as students) have a meaningful voice in determining research questions, the selection of methods, interpretation of data, and the application of results?

Stated Values and Positions

An assessment practice demonstrates *stated values* when practitioners have articulated an explicit set of values that guide the practice, and have stated positions through an acknowledgement of one's subjective societal and organizational position, including cultural identity and related viewpoints, values, privileges, oppressions, and biases.

Self-reflective prompts: Does your practice explicitly articulate values? Does your practice assess the achievement of those values? Does your assessment practice explicitly acknowledge how your unique personal viewpoints and cultural identities affect your practice?

Imagining Otherwise

Imagining otherwise is marked first by questioning prevailing norms and the status quo (such as market forces and neutrality), and then by creating new approaches as counterpoints to those norms.

Self-reflective prompts: Does your practice engage critically with assessment norms? Does your practice envision and make possible different futures?

Lifelong Learning

Lifelong learning is achieved through ongoing professional development, training, and education.

Self-reflective prompts: Is your practice continually strengthened through professional development?

Privacy

Privacy is achieved when data collection procedures are sensitive to the privacy of the people who are represented in the data. Privacy also means that data is collected only in service to an explicit assessment question, and never collected indiscriminately "just in case."

Self-reflective prompts: Do your assessments collect only necessary data? Do you protect the privacy of the people represented in the assessment data?

Qualitative measures

Qualitative measures highlight the voices of the assessed through narrative storytelling, and can help achieve a methodological balance with quantitative measures. When quantitative approaches can tend to reduce or simplify, qualitative measures also serve to complete the assessment picture.

Self-reflective prompts: Does your practice give appropriate weight to qualitative measures?

Relational

Relational means attending to the relationship-building throughout the assessment process, including relationships with students, faculty, community members, tools and devices, and the natural environment. A relational practice recognizes the interconnectivity of stakeholders and ideas, with a sense of mutual learning, mutual responsibility, care, empathy, and humility.

Self-reflective prompts: Does your practice seek to build and sustain relationships of mutual benefit and trust with relevant stakeholders? Does your practice include the assessment of those relationships?

Self-reflection

Self-reflection is the act of pausing to consider the process, application, and impact of assessment.

Self-reflective prompt: Does your assessment practice contain dedicated time for self-reflection?

Social impacts and social justice

Social impacts and social justice recognize that assessment practice has a social history and a social impact, and that practitioners can work to address historical injustices, especially those related to race, gender, and class.

Self-reflective prompts: Does your practice account for social impacts? Does your practice work to achieve social justice through, for example, a framework of diversity, inclusion, and equity?

Sustainability

Sustainability means accounting for the longer-term impacts of assessment, including data collection and relationships.

Self-reflective prompts: Does your practice account for longer-term sustainability in project planning and community relationship-building?

Transparency

Transparency is realized through the open documentation of process, result, application, and decision-making, resulting in sustained trust with stakeholders and the public.

Self-reflective prompts: Does your assessment practice include regular documentation, including process, result, application, and decision-making?

Table 4.1 presents a distribution matrix of characteristics across practice areas.

	Critical Assessment	Co-Design	Strategic Planning	Norms and Regulations	Care Ethics
Community co-determination	x	x	x	x	x
Stated values and positions	x	x	x	x	x
Imagining otherwise	x	x	x	x	x
Lifelong Learning		x		x	
Privacy	x			x	
Qualitative measures	x		x		
Relationality	x	x	x	x	x
Self-reflection	x	x	x	x	x
Social impacts and social justice	x	x	x	x	x
Sustainability	x				x
Transparency	x	x	x	x	x

Table 4.1 Distribution Matrix of Ethical Characteristics across Practice Areas. The characteristics appear vertically, and the practice areas appear horizontally.

In demonstrating the concentration of characteristics across the practice areas, we can begin to see a scope and a perspective for ethical library assessment, as seven of the eleven characteristics are shared by all five practice areas examined in this chapter. It is these seven characteristics that provide a pathway toward an assessment practice that operationalizes a set of specific values and introduces a specific ethical viewpoint. These key characteristics include:

- Community co-determination
- Stated values and positions
- Imagining otherwise
- Self-reflection
- Social impacts and social justice
- Relationality
- Transparency

These seven characteristics point to an assessment practice that is deeply connected to wider communities, seeks to produce outcomes that are socially beneficial to traditionally under-resourced and under-represented groups, and committed to self-reflection, growth, and transparency through the process of conducting assessment. Notably, this analysis reveals a values-oriented point of view for an ethical assessment practice. The characteristic of "stated values and positions" is realized in the practitioner and the organization by questioning neutrality and taking an explicit stand by communicating their values and viewpoint.

Looking Back and Looking Ahead

This chapter presented five areas of ethical assessment practice, along with a set of characteristics shared across these practices. Up to this point in the book, the discussion of the LIS literature has focused on professional values, ethical dilemmas, and the practices for supporting values-based assessment: Chapter 2 provided a view of the historical development of professional values in LIS, Chapter 3 provided a discussion of the ethical decision-points or sites of tension that are present in LIS and that affect library assessment, and Chapter 4 has now provided a set of characteristics that begin to give shape to ethical assessment practice.

Thinking back to Chapter 1 of the book, the main question of this research is *how can library assessment be practiced ethically*? Our discussion of the literature so far has established the groundwork for further investigation into this main question: ethics, values, dilemmas, and practical resolutions. As a way of looking at all of this, I've introduced a lens of practical ethics. Practical ethics involves applying different values in different scenarios, so as to resolve tensions that may be present. Applying values helps us to know what the right thing to do is. At this stage of the book, we can formulate an answer to the main question: library assessment can be practiced ethically by identifying the right values and implementing them at the right times. But this is only a partial answer. To complete the answer, it is necessary to know which values are relevant to assessment practice. The characteristics of ethical practice described in the section above begin to show us what those assessment values look like. Now we need more data to complete the picture. And that is where we're headed next.

As a next step on this research project, we're going to look closer at the values that apply specifically to library assessment. We want to identify the values that operate in the context of assessment, so that we can apply those relevant values to the decisions that we make in our practice. To generate new data in support of this goal, I administered a survey that asked library assessment practitioners to discuss the values that are relevant to their practice. Chapter 5 presents the survey results and data analysis. Through this data analysis, I produced the *Values Classification for Library Assessment*, a set of values relevant for the practice of assessment. The new *Values Classification* reflects and integrates the characteristics developed in this chapter. Finally, Chapter 6 discusses the process of validating the *Values Classification* through interviews with assessment practitioners, and of developing the practical toolkit for ethical assessment, the *Values-Sensitive Library Assessment Toolkit*.

Bibliography

Accardi, Maria T. *Feminist Pedagogy for Library Instruction*. Sacramento, CA: Library Juice Press, 2013.

Agate, Nicky. "Humane Metrics and the Value of Values." Presented at the ARL Executive Seminar, Denver, CO, 2018. http://web.archive.org/web/20211011031213/http://nickyagate.com/humane-metrics-values/.

Agate, Nicky. "Walking the Talk: Toward a Values-Aligned Academy," February 17, 2022. https://hcommons.org/deposits/item/hc:44631/.

Agate, Nicky, Rebecca Kennison, Stacy Konkiel, Christopher P. Long, Jason Rhody, Simone Sacchi, and Penelope Weber. "The Transformative Power of Values-Enacted Scholarship." *Humanities and Social Sciences Communications* 7, no. 1 (December 7, 2020): 1–12. https://doi.org/10.1057/s41599-020-00647-z.

Albrecht, Jan Philipp. "How the GDPR Will Change the World." *European Data Protection Law Review* 2, no. 3 (2016): 287–89. https://doi.org/10.21552/EDPL/2016/3/4.

Almeida Teixeira, Gonçalo, Miguel Mira da Silva, and Ruben Pereira. "The Critical Success Factors of GDPR Implementation: A Systematic Literature Review." *Digital Policy, Regulation and Governance* 21, no. 4 (January 1, 2019): 402–18. https://doi.org/10.1108/DPRG-01-2019-0007.

Arellano Douglas, Veronica. "Moving from Critical Assessment to Assessment as Care." *Communications in Information Literacy* 14, no. 1 (June 2020): 46–65.

Arnold, Hillel. "Practicing Care: Constructing Social Responsibility Through Feminist Care Ethics." In *Archival Values: Essays in Honor of Mark A. Greene*, edited by Christine Weideman and Mary A. Caldera, 30–41. ALA Editions, 2020.

Badia, Giovanna. "Combining Critical Reflection and Action Research to Improve Pedagogy." *Portal: Libraries and the Academy* 17, no. 4 (October 10, 2017): 695–720. https://doi.org/10.1353/pla.2017.0042.

Baich, Tina. "Guided by Values: Creating an Open Values Statement." Presented at the CNI Spring 2020 Virtual Membership Meeting, 2020. https://www.cni.org/topics/information-access-retrieval/guided-by-values-creating-an-open-values-statement.

Bamberger, Kenneth A., and Deirdre K. Mulligan. "Privacy in Europe: Initial Data on Governance Choices and Corporate Practices." *George Washington Law Review* 81, no. 5 (2013): 1529–1664.

Bats, Raphaëlle. "Information Literacy, Participatory Projects and the Development of Political Roles for Librarians." In *Information Literacy: Key to an Inclusive Society*, edited by Serap Kurbanoğlu, Joumana Boustany, Sonja Špiranec, Esther Grassian, Diane Mizrachi, Loriene Roy, and Tolga Çakmak, 33–44. Communications in Computer and Information Science. Springer International Publishing, 2016.

Belanger, Jackie, Victoria Bryant, Derek Flora, Reed Garber-Pearson, Maryneth Jones, Charlotte McGrew, Cara Phillips, Angela Rosette-Tavares, Christine Tawatao, and Perry Yee. "We're All Online Students Now: Using Participatory Design to Meet the Needs of Students at the University of Washington Libraries," 330–40, 2021.

Bourg, Chris. "Beyond Measure: Valuing Libraries." *Feral Librarian* (blog), May 20, 2013. https://web.archive.org/web/20210427003926/https://chrisbourg.wordpress.com/2013/05/19/beyond-measure-valuing-libraries/.

Brown, Robin, and Scott Sheidlower. "Claiming Our Space: A Quantitative and Qualitative Picture of Disabled Librarians." *Library Trends* 67, no. 3 (May 8, 2019): 471–86. https://doi.org/10.1353/lib.2019.0007.

Caswell, Michelle, and Marika Cifor. "From Human Rights to Feminist Ethics: Radical Empathy in the Archives." *Archivaria* 81 (May 6, 2016): 23–43.

Caswell, Michelle, Alda Allina Migoni, Noah Geraci, and Marika Cifor. "'To Be Able to Imagine Otherwise': Community Archives and the Importance of Representation." *Archives and Records* 38, no. 1 (January 2, 2017): 5–26. https://doi.org/10.1080/23257962.2016.1260445.

Cifor, Marika, and Stacy Wood. "Critical Feminism in the Archives." *Journal of Critical Library and Information Studies* 1, no. 2 (2017). https://doi.org/10.24242/jclis.v1i2.27.

Clarke, Rachel Ivy. "From 'Library Science' to 'Library Design': Recasting the Narrative of Academic Librarianship." In *Recasting the Narrative: The Proceedings of the ACRL 2019 Conference*, 22–30. Cleveland, Ohio: Association of College and Research Libraries, 2019.

Clarke, Rachel Ivy. "How We Done It Good: Research through Design as a Legitimate Methodology for Librarianship." *Library & Information Science Research* 40, no. 3 (July 1, 2018): 255–61. https://doi.org/10.1016/j.lisr.2018.09.007.

Clarke, Rachel Ivy. "Toward a Design Epistemology for Librarianship." *The Library Quarterly* 88, no. 1 (December 11, 2017): 41–59. https://doi.org/10.1086/694872.

Clements, Nina. "'Nothing More than a Gear in Your Car:' Neutrality and Feminist Reference in the Academic Library." In *The Feminist Reference Desk: Concepts, Critiques, and Conversations*, edited by Maria T. Accardi, 47–60. Sacramento, CA: Library Juice Press, 2017.

Corrado, Edward M. "Libraries and Protecting Patron Privacy." *Technical Services Quarterly* 37, no. 1 (January 2, 2020): 44–54. https://doi.org/10.1080/07317131.2019.1691761.

Corrall, Sheila. "Seven Stories of Performativity and Advocacy: A Review of the Published Work of Stephen Town." Edited by Stephen Town. *Performance Measurement and Metrics* 17, no. 2 (January 1, 2016): 99–121. https://doi.org/10.1108/PMM-06-2016-0024.

Cox, Jenelys. "Understanding GDPR: Libraries, Repositories, & Privacy Policies." Presented at the Digital Commons – Heartland Users Group meeting, Hays, Kansas, October 15, 2018. https://scholars.fhsu.edu/dc-hug18/dchug18/information/11.

Cox, Krista L. "Legal Landscape of Consumer/ User Data Privacy and Current Policy Discussions." *Research Library Issues*, no. 297 (May 6, 2019): 15–37. https://doi.org/10.29242/rli.297.3.

Crowe, Kathryn M. "Strategic Library Assessment: Aligning with Your University's Strategic Plan." In *Proceedings of the 2018 Library Assessment Conference: Building Effective, Sustainable, Practical Assessment: December 5–7, 2018,*

Houston, TX, 447–56. Association of Research Libraries, 2019. https://doi.org/10.29242/lac.2018.40.

Davis, Meredith. "Design Futures Trend: Core Values Matter." AIGA: The Professional Association for Design, 2018.

Davis, Robin Camille. "Participatory Paper Prototyping: Revealing User Needs and Priorities." Presented at the Designing For Digital Conference, Austin, TX, 2020. https://docs.google.com/presentation/d/1tbAP6BT2RtDZ8NWd_frtNx5ZVTDi64WqUeBvVlWcAsE/edit?usp=sharing&usp=embed_facebook.

Deitering, Anne-Marie, Hannah Gascho Rempel, and Tim Jensen. "Reflective Information Literacy: Empowering Graduate Student Teachers." In *Transforming Libraries to Serve Graduate Students*, edited by Crystal Renfro and Cheryl Stiles. Chicago, Illinois: American Library Association, 2018.

Delaney, Geraldine, and Jessica Bates. "Envisioning the Academic Library: A Reflection on Roles, Relevancy and Relationships." *New Review of Academic Librarianship* 21, no. 1 (January 2, 2015): 30–51. https://doi.org/10.1080/13614533.2014.911194.

DeLuca Fernández, Sonia. "Critical Assessment." Presented at the Student Affairs Assessment Leaders (SAAL) Structured Conversations, 2015. http://studentaffairsassessment.org/files/documents/SAAL-SC-Critical-Assessment-sdf-9-dec-2015-FINAL.pdf.

Dohe, Kate. "Care, Code, and Digital Libraries: Embracing Critical Practice in Digital Library Communities." *In The Library With The Lead Pipe*, 2019. http://web.archive.org/web/20210619220625/https://www.inthelibrarywiththeleadpipe.org/2019/digital-libraries-critical-practice-in-communities/.

Dole, Wanda V. "Strategic Planning and Assessment: Pigs of the Same Sow?" *Journal of Library Administration* 53, no. 4 (May 1, 2013): 283–92. https://doi.org/10.1080/01930826.2013.865397.

Doucette, Lise. "Acknowledging the Political, Economic, and Values-Based Motivators of Assessment Work: An Analysis of Publications on Academic Library Assessment." In *Proceedings of the 2016 Library Assessment Conference*, edited by Sue Baughman, Steve Hiller, Katie Monroe, and Angela Pappalardo, 288–98. Arlington, VA: Association of Research Libraries, 2016.

Douglas, Veronica Arellano, Joanna Gadsby, Lalitha Nataraj, Anastasia Chiu, and Alana Kumbier. "A Practice of Connection: Applying Relational Cultural Theory to Librarianship." Presented at the Critical Librarianship & Pedagogy Symposium, University of Arizona, Tucson, AZ, 2018.

Drabinski, Emily. "What Is Critical about Critical Librarianship?" *Art Libraries Journal* 44, no. 2 (April 2019): 49–57. https://doi.org/10.1017/alj.2019.3.

Drake, Jarrett M. "Diversity's Discontents: In Search of an Archive of the Oppressed." *Archives and Manuscripts* 47, no. 2 (May 4, 2019): 270–79. https://doi.org/10.1080/01576895.2019.1570470.

Drew, Cat. "Design for Data Ethics: Using Service Design Approaches to Operationalize Ethical Principles on Four Projects." *Philosophical Transactions of the Royal Society A: Mathematical, Physical and Engineering Sciences* 376, no. 2128 (September 13, 2018): 20170353. https://doi.org/10.1098/rsta.2017.0353.

Ehn, Pelle. "Scandinavian Design: On Participation and Skill." In *Participatory Design: Principles and Practice*, edited by Douglas Schuler and Aki Namioka, 41–77. New York: CRC / Lawrence Erlbaum Associates, 1993.

Fisher, Zoe, Ebony Magnus, and Nicole Branch. "Critical Assessment Practices: A Discussion of When and How to Use Student Learning Data Without Doing Harm," 2019, 57.

Foos, Donald D., and Nancy C. Pack. *How Libraries Must Comply with the Americans with Disabilities Act (ADA)*. Oryx Press, 1992.

Galvan, Scarlet. "The Values Driven Library Resource License." Presented at the OpenCon Community Call, 2020. http://web.archive.org/web/20210509135236/https://speakerdeck.com/galvan/the-values-driven-library-resource-license.

Gamboni, Valentina. "Developing Academic Librarians' Skills in e-Book Services through Participatory Action Research." *Information and Learning Sciences* 118, no. 9/10 (October 10, 2017): 535–46. https://doi.org/10.1108/ILS-05-2017-0044.

Gaudry, Adam J. P. "Insurgent Research." *Wicazo Sa Review* 26, no. 1 (2011): 113–36. https://doi.org/10.5749/wicazosareview.26.1.0113.

Gilliland, Anne J, and Sue McKemmish. "The Role of Participatory Archives in Furthering Human Rights, Reconciliation and Recovery." *Atlanti* 24, no. 1 (2014): 79–88.

Graf, Anne Jumonville, and Benjamin R. Harris. "Reflective Assessment: Opportunities and Challenges." *Reference Services Review* 44, no. 1 (February 1, 2016): 38–47. https://doi.org/10.1108/RSR-06-2015-0027.

Hannay, Bill, Bruce Strauch, Bryan M. Carson, and Jack Montgomery. "Legally Speaking—U.S. Libraries and the GDPR." *Against the Grain* 30, no. 3 (January 1, 2018). https://doi.org/10.7771/2380-176X.8256.

Hanson, Cody. "Libraries Are Software." *Cody Hanson* (blog), September 2015. https://web.archive.org/web/20190414030741/https://www.codyh.com/writing/software.html.

Harland, Fiona, Glenn Stewart, and Christine Bruce. "Aligning Library and University Strategic Directions: A Constructivist Grounded Theory Study of Academic Library Leadership in Australia and the U.S.A." *New Review of Academic Librarianship* 24, no. 3–4 (October 2, 2018): 263–85. https://doi.org/10.1080/13614533.2018.1498797.

Hathcock, April, and Jennifer Vinopal. "Feminist Praxis in Library Leadership." In *Feminists Among Us: Resistance and Advocacy in Library Leadership*, edited by Shirley Lew and Baharark Yousefi, 147–71. Sacramento, CA: Library Juice Press, 2017. https://kb.osu.edu/handle/1811/81299.

Held, Virginia. *The Ethics of Care: Personal, Political, and Global*. Oxford; New York: Oxford University Press, 2006.

Heller, Margaret. "Keeping Up With… General Data Protection Regulation (GDPR)." *Association of College & Research Libraries (ACRL)* (blog), June 18, 2018. https://web.archive.org/web/20200609230307/http://www.ala.org/acrl/publications/keeping_up_with/gdpr.

Higgins, Shana. "Embracing the Feminization of Librarianship." In *Feminists Among Us: Resistance and Advocacy in Library Leadership*, edited by Shirley Lew and Yousefi Baharark, 67–90. Sacramento, CA: Library Juice Press, 2017.

Hill, Heather. "Disability and Accessibility in the Library and Information Science Literature: A Content Analysis." *Library & Information Science Research* 35, no. 2 (April 1, 2013): 137–42. https://doi.org/10.1016/j.lisr.2012.11.002.

Hodge, Twanna. "Integrating Cultural Humility into Public Services Librarianship." *International Information & Library Review* 51, no. 3 (July 3, 2019): 268–74. https://doi.org/10.1080/10572317.2019.1629070.

Hoel, Tore, and Weiqin Chen. "Privacy and Data Protection in Learning Analytics Should Be Motivated by an Educational Maxim—Towards a Proposal." *Research and Practice in Technology Enhanced Learning* 13, no. 1 (December 11, 2018): 20. https://doi.org/10.1186/s41039-018-0086-8.

Howard, Sara. "Purposeful and Productive Care: The Feminist Ethic of Care and the Reference Desk." In *The Feminist Reference Desk: Concepts, Critiques, and Conversations*, edited by Maria T. Accardi. Sacramento, CA: Library Juice Press, 2017.

"HuMetricsHSS," 2023. https://web.archive.org/web/20230330142220/https://humetricshss.org/.

Hustwit, Gary, director. *Rams*. 2018. 74 minutes. https://web.archive.org/web/20230316005838/https://www.hustwit.com/rams/

Iacovino, Livia. "Shaping and Reshaping Cultural Identity and Memory: Maximising Human Rights through a Participatory Archive." *Archives and Manuscripts* 43, no. 1 (January 2, 2015): 29–41. https://doi.org/10.1080/01576895.2014.961491.

International Federation of Library Associations. "What Data Privacy Means for Libraries in 2020." *Library Policy and Advocacy Blog* (blog), January 28, 2020. https://web.archive.org/web/20200218102251/http://blogs.ifla.org/lpa/2020/01/28/what-data-privacy-means-for-libraries-in-2020/.

Jaggar, Alison M. "Feminist Ethics." In *The Blackwell Guide to Ethical Theory*, 433–60. John Wiley & Sons, Ltd, 2017. https://doi.org/10.1111/b.9780631201199.1999.00022.x.

Jules, Bergis, Ed Summers, and Vernon Mitchell, Jr. "Ethical Considerations for Archiving Social Media Content Generated by Contemporary Social Movements: Challenges, Opportunities, and Recommendations." Documenting the Now, 2018. https://web.archive.org/web/20200407200136/https://www.docnow.io/docs/docnow-whitepaper-2018.pdf.

Kalbag, Laura. "This One Weird Trick Tells Us Everything About You." In *Smashing Print #1: Ethics & Privacy*, edited by Rachel Andrew, 35–43. Freiburg, Germany: Smashing Media AG, 2019.

Kensing, Finn, and Joan Greenbaum. "Heritage: Having a Say." In *Routledge International Handbook of Participatory Design*, 21–36. New York: Routledge, 2013.

Kimura, Amy Kazuye. "Defining, Evaluating, and Achieving Accessible Library Resources: A Review of Theories and Methods." *Reference Services Review* 46, no. 3 (January 1, 2018): 425–38. https://doi.org/10.1108/RSR-03-2018-0040.

Konkiel, Stacy, Rebecca Kennison, Nicky Agate, Christopher Long, Jason Rhody, and Simone Sacchi. "Exploring Values-Based (Alt)Metrics to Enhance Library Services." Warsaw, Poland, 2017. http://library.ifla.org/1778/.

Kumbier, Alana, and Julia Starkey. "Access Is Not Problem Solving: Disability Justice and Libraries." *Library Trends* 64, no. 3 (April 4, 2016): 468–91. https://doi.org/10.1353/lib.2016.0004.

Macaluso, Stephan J. "Incorporating Self-Assessment and Peer Assessment into Library Instructional Practice." In *Curriculum-Based Library Instruction: From Cultivating Faculty Relationships to Assessment*, edited by Amy Blevins and Megan Inman, 97–105. Lanham, Maryland: Rowman & Littlefield, 2014.

Macdonald, Sharon. "Otherwise: Rethinking Museums and Heritage." Berlin: Centre for Anthropological Research on Museums and Heritage, 2018. http://web.archive.org/web/20220531110831/https://www.carmah.berlin/wp-content/uploads/2018/07/CARMAH-2018-Otherwise-Rethinking-Museums-and-Heritage.pdf.

Magnus, Ebony, Jackie Belanger, and Maggie Faber. "Towards a Critical Assessment Practice." *In the Library With the Lead Pipe*, 2018. http://www.inthelibrarywiththeleadpipe.org/2018/towards-critical-assessment-practice/.

Malenfant, Kara J., and Karen Brown. "Creating Sustainable Assessment through Collaboration: A National Program Reveals Effective Practices." National Institute for Learning Outcomes Assessment, 2017.

Marquez, Joe, and Annie Downey. "Service Design: An Introduction to a Holistic Assessment Methodology of Library Services." *Weave: Journal of Library User Experience* 1, no. 2 (2015). http://dx.doi.org/10.3998/weave.12535642.0001.201.

Marsh, Diana E., Ricardo L. Punzalan, Robert Leopold, Brian Butler, and Massimo Petrozzi. "Stories of Impact: The Role of Narrative in Understanding the Value and Impact of Digital Collections." *Archival Science* 16, no. 4 (December 1, 2016): 327–72. https://doi.org/10.1007/s10502-015-9253-5.

McCartin, Lyda Fontes, and Rachel Dineen. *Toward a Critical-Inclusive Assessment Practice for Library Instruction*. Sacramento, CA: Library Juice Press, 2018. https://litwinbooks.com/books/toward-a-critical-inclusive-assessment-practice-for-library-instruction/.

Moeller, Christine M. "Disability, Identity, and Professionalism: Precarity in Librarianship." *Library Trends* 67, no. 3 (May 8, 2019): 455–70. https://doi.org/10.1353/lib.2019.0006.

Montenegro, Erick, and Natasha A Jankowski. "A New Decade for Assessment: Embedding Equity into Assessment Praxis." Urbana, IL: University of Illinois and Indiana University, National Institute for Learning Outcomes Assessment (NILOA), January 2020. https://web.archive.org/web/20200610162708/https://www.learningoutcomesassessment.org/wp-content/uploads/2020/01/A-New-Decade-for-Assessment.pdf.

Muglia, Caroline, Elizabeth J. Kelly, Genya O'Gara, Ayla Stein, Santi Thompson, and Liz Wolcott. "How We Talk about Assessment: A New Framework for Digital Libraries." *The Serials Librarian* 76, no. 1–4 (June 14, 2019): 208–12. https://doi.org/10.1080/0361526X.2019.1586050.

Neurohr, Karen A., and Lucy E. Bailey. "Using Photo-Elicitation with Native American Students to Explore Perceptions of the Physical Library." *Evidence Based Library and Information Practice* 11, no. 2 (June 20, 2016): 56–73. https://doi.org/10.18438/B8D629.

Ng, Cynthia. "A Practical Guide to Improving Web Accessibility." *Weave: Journal of Library User Experience* 1, no. 7 (2017). http://dx.doi.org/10.3998/weave.12535642.0001.701.

Nissenbaum, Helen Fay. *Privacy in Context: Technology, Policy, and the Integrity of Social Life*. Stanford, Calif: Stanford Law Books, 2010.

Noddings, Nel. *Caring: A Relational Approach to Ethics & Moral Education*. Berkeley, California; Los Angeles; Londres: University of California Press, 2013.

Nowviskie, Bethany. "On Capacity and Care." *Bethany Nowviskie* (blog), October 4, 2015. https://web.archive.org/web/20200513105534/http://nowviskie.org/2015/on-capacity-and-care/.

Oakleaf, Megan. "The Value of Academic Libraries: A Comprehensive Research Review and Report." Chicago, IL: Association of College and Research Libraries, American Library Association, 2010.

O'Gara, Genya Morgan, Liz Woolcott, Elizabeth Joan Kelly, Caroline Muglia, Ayla Stein, and Santi Thompson. "Barriers and Solutions to Assessing Digital Library Reuse: Preliminary Findings." *Performance Measurement and Metrics*, October 4, 2018. https://doi.org/10.1108/PMM-03-2018-0012.

Olson, Devon, Jessica Meyerson, Mark A. Parsons, Juliana Castro, Monique Lassere, Dawn J. Wright, Hillel Arnold, et al. "Information Maintenance as a Practice of Care." Educopia Institute, 2019. https://doi.org/10.5281/zenodo.3251131.

Olson, Hope A. "How We Construct Subjects: A Feminist Analysis." *Library Trends* 56, no. 2 (2007): 509–41. https://doi.org/10.1353/lib.2008.0007.

Orphanides, Andreas. "Architecture Is Politics: The Power and the Perils of Systems Design." Presented at the Code4Lib Annual Conference, Philadelphia, 2016. https://web.archive.org/web/20200521194937/https://2016.code4lib.org/slides/architecture_is_politics-dre-orphanides.pdf.

Penney, Jonathon. "Chilling Effects and Transatlantic Privacy." *European Law Journal* 25, no. 2 (2019): 122–39. https://doi.org/10.1111/eulj.12315.

Pereyaslavska, Katya. "Accessibility Librarian Competencies," 2015. https://web.archive.org/web/20190813023558/https://accessibility.arl.org/2015/08/accessibility-librarian-competencies/.

Peters, Cara, and David A. Bradbard. "Web Accessibility: An Introduction and Ethical Implications." Edited by Antonio Marturano and Alessandro D'Atri. *Journal of Information, Communication and Ethics in Society* 8, no. 2 (January 1, 2010): 206–32. https://doi.org/10.1108/14779961011041757.

Pionke, J. J. "Beyond ADA Compliance: The Library as a Place for All." *Urban Library Journal* 23, no. 1 (January 1, 2017): 1–17.

Pionke, J.J. "Library Employee Views of Disability and Accessibility." *Journal of Library Administration* 60, no. 2 (February 17, 2020): 120–45. https://doi.org/10.1080/01930826.2019.1704560.

Puckett-Rodgers, Emily, Denise Leyton, and Kat King. "Participatory Data-Gathering and Community Building." In *Proceedings of the 2018 Library Assessment Conference*, 235–44. Houston, TX: Association of Research Libraries, 2019. https://doi.org/10.29242/lac.2018.21.

Punzalan, Ricardo L., and Diana E. Marsh. "Reciprocity: Building a Discourse in Archives." *The American Archivist* 85, no. 1 (July 1, 2022): 30–59. https://doi.org/10.17723/2327-9702-85.1.30.

Punzalan, Ricardo L., Diana E. Marsh, and Kyla Cools. "Beyond Clicks, Likes, and Downloads: Identifying Meaningful Impacts for Digitized Ethnographic Archives." *Archivaria* 84, no. 1 (2017): 61–102.

Reale, Michelle. *Becoming a Reflective Librarian and Teacher: Strategies for Mindful Academic Practice*. Chicago, Illinois: American Library Association, 2017.

Reidsma, Matthew. "Keynote 1: Ethical UX." In *User Experience in Libraries Yearbook 2017: Stories, Techniques, Insights*, edited by Andy Priestner, 9–22. Cambridge: CreateSpace Independent Publishing Platform, 2017.

Rigling, Lillian, Courtney Waugh, and Emily Carlisle. "In Pursuit of Equity: Applying Design Thinking to Develop a Values-Based Open Access Statement." *In the Library with the Lead Pipe*, 2018. https://doi.org/10.31229/osf.io/qp4xz.

Robertson, Toni, and Ina Wagner. "Ethics: Engagement, Representation and Politics-in-Action." In *Routledge International Handbook of Participatory Design*, 64–85. New York: Routledge, 2013.

Robinson, Shannon Marie. "Critical Design in Librarianship: Visual and Narrative Exploration for Critical Praxis." *The Library Quarterly* 89, no. 4 (October 1, 2019): 348–61. https://doi.org/10.1086/704965.

Rolan, Gregory. "Agency in the Archive: A Model for Participatory Recordkeeping." *Archival Science* 17, no. 3 (September 1, 2017): 195–225. https://doi.org/10.1007/s10502-016-9267-7.

Rosen, Stephanie. "Accessibility for Justice: Accessibility as a Tool for Promoting Justice in Librarianship." *In The Library With The Lead Pipe*, 2017. /2017/accessibility-for-justice/.

Saunders, Laura. "Room for Improvement: Priorities in Academic Libraries' Strategic Plans." *Journal of Library Administration* 56, no. 1 (January 2, 2016): 1–16. https://doi.org/10.1080/01930826.2015.1105029.

Schomberg, Jessica. "Disability at Work: Libraries, Built to Exclude." In *The Politics of Theory and the Practice of Critical Librarianship*, edited by Karen P. Nicholson and Maura Seale, 111–23. Sacramento, CA: Library Juice Press, 2018. https://cornerstone.lib.mnsu.edu/lib_services_fac_pubs/149.

Schomberg, Jessica, and Wendy Highby. *Beyond Accommodation: Creating an Inclusive Workplace for Disabled Library Workers*. Sacramento, CA: Library Juice Press, 2020.

Sentance, Nathan. "Engaging with the Uncomfortable." *Archival Decolonist* (blog), April 8, 2018. https://archivaldecolonist.com/2018/04/08/engaging-with-the-uncomfortable/.

Shilton, Katie, and Ramesh Srinivasan. "Participatory Appraisal and Arrangement for Multicultural Archival Collections." *Archivaria* 63 (2007): 87–101.

Słoniowski, Lisa. "Affective Labor, Resistance, and the Academic Librarian." *Library Trends* 64, no. 4 (September 13, 2016): 645–66. https://doi.org/10.1353/lib.2016.0013.

Slote, Michael A. *The Ethics of Care and Empathy*. New York; London: Routledge, 2007.

Tewell, Eamon. "Reframing Reference for Marginalized Students: A Participatory Visual Study." *Reference & User Services Quarterly* 58, no. 3 (June 22, 2019): 162–76. https://doi.org/10.5860/rusq.58.3.7044.

Town, J. Stephen. "Value, Impact, and the Transcendent Library: Progress and Pressures in Performance Measurement and Evaluation." *The Library Quarterly* 81, no. 1 (January 1, 2011): 111–25. https://doi.org/10.1086/657445.

Town, J. Stephen, and Martha Kyrillidou. "Developing a Values Scorecard." *Performance Measurement and Metrics* 14, no. 1 (January 1, 2013): 7–16. https://doi.org/10.1108/14678041311316095.

Town, Stephen. "Implementing the Value Scorecard." *Performance Measurement and Metrics* 16, no. 3 (November 9, 2015): 234–51. https://doi.org/10.1108/PMM-10-2015-0033.

Town, Stephen. "The Value Scorecard." *Information and Learning Sciences* 119, no. 1/2 (January 5, 2018): 25–38. https://doi.org/10.1108/ILS-10-2017-0098.

Utz, Christine, Martin Degeling, Sascha Fahl, Florian Schaub, and Thorsten Holz. "(Un)Informed Consent: Studying GDPR Consent Notices in the Field." In *Proceedings of the 2019 ACM SIGSAC Conference on Computer and Communications Security*, 973–90. CCS '19. London, United Kingdom: Association for Computing Machinery, 2019. https://doi.org/10.1145/3319535.3354212.

Wade, Gretchen L. "Serving the Visually Impaired User." *Portal: Libraries and the Academy* 3, no. 2 (May 23, 2003): 307–13. https://doi.org/10.1353/pla.2003.0048.

Wall, Andrew F., David Hursh, and Joseph W. Rodgers III. "Assessment for Whom: Repositioning Higher Education Assessment as an Ethical and Value-Focused Social Practice." *Research & Practice in Assessment* 9 (Summer 2014): 5–17.

Whitver, Sara Maurice. "Accessible Library Instruction in Practice." *Portal: Libraries and the Academy* 20, no. 2 (April 9, 2020): 381–98. https://doi.org/10.1353/pla.2020.0019.

Yoon, Kyunghye, Laura Hulscher, and Rachel Dols. "Accessibility and Diversity in Library and Information Science: Inclusive Information Architecture for Library Websites." *The Library Quarterly* 86, no. 2 (April 1, 2016): 213–29. https://doi.org/10.1086/685399.

Zavala, Jimmy, Alda Allina Migoni, Michelle Caswell, Noah Geraci, and Marika Cifor. "'A Process Where We're All at the Table': Community Archives Challenging Dominant Modes of Archival Practice." *Archives and Manuscripts* 45, no. 3 (September 2, 2017): 202–15. https://doi.org/10.1080/01576895.2017.1377088.

Chapter 5
New Insights into Library Assessment: Surveying the Field

Overview

In this chapter, I present and discuss results from a national survey of North American library assessment practitioners. The survey produced data focusing on the values that are relevant for decision-making in library assessment, and the practices put into action by assessment librarians when confronted with ethical challenges. The survey design was informed by review of the literature related to library values and ethics (discussed in Chapter 2), as well as a literature review involving common ethical dilemmas or sites of tension that assessment practitioners confront in the course of their work (discussed in Chapter 3), and an analysis of the characteristics of ethical assessment (presented in Chapter 4). The survey was then designed around the common values, tensions, and characteristics of ethical assessment practice uncovered in the literature, with ethical vignettes forming the centerpiece of the survey.

This chapter is organized into two main parts: survey results and data analysis. The survey results contain several sections that report on the results, organized according to the order of the questionnaire. I followed a constructivist grounded theory approach to make sense of the survey data. In a grounded theory approach, the researcher develops a theory that is grounded in the data—for this book, I developed a theory of library assessment values, grounded in the research data. The research data represents the real viewpoints and experiences of practitioners working in our field of library assessment. The analysis that I produced from this rich dataset demonstrates one theoretical possibility for the values shared by library assessment practitioners. Throughout this chapter, in instances where I cite directly from the research data, I include a 6-digit alphanumeric code that corresponds to the response ID in the survey data.

Survey Design

To more fully understand the ethical dilemmas and ethical decision-making of library assessment practitioners, I conducted a survey of assessment practitioners that prompted ethical reflection and response. Following Peterson,[1] the survey was designed in three main parts: 1) questions relating to values that are relevant to ethical decision-making; 2) questions related to ethical dilemmas in practice; 3) respondent demographics. In this section, I provide an overview of the survey design. Further detail about the procedures, sampling, and analyses for the survey is in the research dataset, available via the Qualitative Data Repository with the following title and URL: *Practitioner Perspectives on the Values and Ethics of Library Assessment*, https://doi.org/10.5064/F6ORSLQF.

In Part 1, the survey design was based around the *ALA Core Values of Librarianship*. While not necessarily the primary document for ethical decision-making, this document is a point of reference for practitioners. In this section, participants were asked to evaluate the *importance* and *frequency of consideration* for each of the 12 ALA Core Values, followed by free-text responses for supplying further values that are relevant for the work of library assessment.

In Part 2, the survey focused on practitioner responses to ethical dilemmas. I chose vignettes as an approach for understanding decision-making in certain situations.[2] Vignettes are "short descriptions of real-life situations that are employed in a survey to assess attitudes and intentions."[3] A vignette approach "allows researchers to include factors that are relevant to the research question," and, importantly

---

1 Peterson, *Constructing Effective Questionnaires*.

2 Alexander and Becker, "The Use of Vignettes in Survey Research"; Evans et al., "Vignette Methodologies for Studying Clinicians' Decision-Making"; Magalhães-Sant'Ana and Hanlon, "Straight from the Horse's Mouth."

3 Eifler and Petzold, "Validity Aspects of Vignette Experiments," 393.

for ethics-related research, "provides researchers with the ability to create hypothetical scenarios that address sensitive topics."[4]

The development of the ethical scenarios followed guidelines indicating that scenarios should be brief and should reflect real-world situations as discussed in the relevant literature.[5] I developed vignettes that followed an "actual derived cases" approach so as to "represent concrete values found in actual settings."[6] Ultimately, 6 vignettes were developed and presented to research participants. This number was chosen as it allowed a full range of dilemmas to be represented across the vignettes; the vignettes were each crafted to reflect the main themes related to ethical dilemmas as found in the literature and discussed in Chapter 3:

- Value and Impact
- Information Technologies, Data, and Privacy
- Learning Analytics and Student Success
- Social Responsibility and Neutrality
- Information Literacy
- Cataloging and Classification

These ethical topics areas were distributed across the vignettes, with the aim of achieving a balance of topics that could represent a variety of real-world situations. The survey design then prompted participants to produce the values that are relevant to those ethical topics. The following sections present the vignettes as seen in the survey:

Scenario 1: Library Value and Impact

"There is a perceived need on campus for the library to demonstrate its value to university administration in order to receive continued financial support. The assessment librarian thinks about conducting a study that would produce a return-on-investment (ROI) measure for the library's e-resources. The librarian knows that this assessment would resonate with university administration. At the same time, the librarian thinks that dollars-and-cents calculations might not be

---

4 Aguinis and Bradley, "Best Practice Recommendations for Designing and Implementing Experimental Vignette Methodology Studies," 357.

5 Evans et al., "Vignette Methodologies for Studying Clinicians' Decision-Making."

6 Aguinis and Bradley, "Best Practice Recommendations for Designing and Implementing Experimental Vignette Methodology Studies," 362.

appropriate for measuring abstract educational outcomes of learning and research. The librarian decides not to conduct the study."

Scenario 2: Information Technologies, Data, and Privacy

"In order to assess the library website, the assessment librarian is considering implementing new analytics software that captures screen recordings of website visits. The analytics software is operated by a privately-owned e-commerce company, and the screen recordings would be stored on the company's cloud servers, which could affect the privacy of library users. But this company's software can provide advanced analytics that would be applied to improve library web services. The librarian decides to implement the software."

Scenario 3: Learning Analytics and Student Success

"The assessment librarian maintains anonymous student data related to library gate counts. University administration has requested that the library begin identifying this data using card swipe records, and then share the data into a centralized learning analytics data warehouse. University administration would analyze the data and develop interventions with students to improve retention. But the assessment librarian is concerned that this approach doesn't reflect library professional values, and considers raising an objection. Still, the librarian feels a sense of commitment to the institution, and ultimately decides to identify and share the data."

Scenario 4: Social Responsibility, Neutrality, and Cataloging

"The assessment librarian is working with the university's prison abolition student group to assess the library's usage of subject headings related to incarceration. At the same time, the librarian recognizes that this project would affect the library's position of neutrality, since the topic is politically charged, the library's affiliation with this group could be controversial, and the results might be viewed as biased. Despite these reservations, the librarian sees the benefit of this project, and decides to conduct the assessment."

Scenario 5: Instruction, Student Participation, and Social Responsibility

"The assessment librarian has formed a student working group to help inform a study of library instruction. The student group proposes a study that assesses how the library instruction program is experienced by students of different immigrant statuses. The librarian is hesitant because this assessment doesn't align with existing institutional priorities, and the results might not be received well by other librarians and administrators. But the assessment librarian feels that student voices should be meaningfully included in the assessment process, even if student viewpoints challenge existing perspectives and processes. The librarian ultimately decides to advocate for the student group, and to co-develop an immigration-focused assessment with the students."

Scenario 6: Archives and Community Participation

"The assessment librarian is assessing the accessibility of special collections finding aids. The librarian considers inviting disabled members of the university community to be participants in the assessment process, as they could provide relevant cultural perspectives. But the librarian doesn't have an existing relationship with this community, and isn't sure how to involve them or how much time it would take. The assessment librarian decides not to involve the community members."

Survey Results

This section presents a selection of the survey results, according to the three main parts of the survey:

1. Description of the sample, showing demographic responses
2. Values that are relevant for assessment decision-making
3. Analysis of Vignettes
   a. Presentation and analysis of results within each individual vignette
   b. Presentation and analysis of results aggregated across all vignettes
4. Interpretation of the data

Full research data and analysis is available via the Qualitative Data Repository: https://doi.org/10.5064/F6ORSLQF.

Description of the Sample

The survey recorded 239 responses; of those responses, 166 were partially complete and 73 were complete. The Qualtrics software used to administer the survey records a response when the survey link is clicked and the first page loads in a web browser. A few respondents exited the survey at various points following the first page, while most of the non-complete responses exited on the first page of the survey. The two subsections below describe the demographics of the sample. Respondents provided demographic information for themselves as individual practitioners, and also information about their respective institutions. See the associated dataset for supplemental demographic charts.

Individual Demographics

For years of experience (n=71), most of the sample (42.2%) have 1–4 years of experience. The next most common category (22.5%) was 5–9 years of experience, followed by 10–14 years (12.7%), less than 1 year (12.7%), 15–19 years (5.6%), and 20 years or more (1.4%). "Prefer not to answer" was selected by 2.8% of the sample. Table 5.1 shows years of experience of the sample.

Experience in the field	Frequency (n=71)
Less than 1 year	9
1–4 years	30
5–9 years	16
10–14 years	9
15–19 years	4
20 years or more	1
Prefer not to answer	2

Table 5.1. Years Experience in the Field

For highest degree earned (n=72), most of the sample (77.7%) have earned a Master's degree. Doctoral degrees have been earned by 15.2% of the sample, followed by Bachelor's degrees (4.2%). "None of the above" and "Prefer not to answer" were each selected by 1.4% of the sample. Table 5.2 shows highest degree earned of the sample.

Highest Degree Earned	Frequency (n=72)
Bachelor's	3
Master's	56
Doctoral	11
None of the above	1
Prefer not to answer	1

Table 5.2. Highest Degree Earned

For primary job classification (n=72), most of the sample (44.4%) selected Librarian, followed by Faculty (23.6%), Administration (16.6%), Professional Staff (11.1%). Classified Staff, Other: Fellow, and Other: Graduate Assistance were each selected by 1.3% of the sample. Table 5.3 shows primary job classification.

Primary job classification	Frequency (n=72)
Classified staff	1
Faculty	17
Administration	12
Professional Staff	8
Librarian	32
Other: Fellow	1
Other: Graduate Assistant	1

Table 5.3. Primary Job Classification

The survey asked, "How many assessment staff do you supervise?" Of these responses (n=72), 79.1% of the sample selected None, 11.1% selected 1, and 9.7% selected 2–3. Table 5.4 shows the number of direct reports.

Direct Reports	Frequency (n=72)
None	57
1	8
2–3	7

Table 5.4. Number of Direct Reports

For membership in the American Library Association (n=72), the sample is composed mostly of current members of ALA (47.2%), followed closely by those who are not currently a member but previously have been a member (40.2%). A smaller portion of the sample are not members and have never been a member (12.5%). Table 5.5 shows ALA membership of the sample.

Member of ALA	Frequency (n=72)
Yes, currently	34
No, never	9
No, but previously I have been a member	29

Table 5.5. Membership in American Library Association

The survey also asked about membership in other professional organizations; responses (n=72) were as follows: Association of College and Research Libraries (48.6%), ALA Core (13.9%), We Here (8.3%), Canadian Association of Professional Academic Libraries (4.2%), Society of American Archivists (4.2%), Association for the Assessment of Learning in Higher Education (2.8%), Association of Information Science and Technology (2.1%), American Educational Research Association (1.4%), Association of Computing Machinery (1.4%), International Federation of Library Associations and Institutions (1.4%), Progressive Librarians Guild (1.4%). State library associations were included by 4.1% of the sample in the category for "other." Further responses in the Other category include the following, each representing 1.4% of the sample: Digital Publishing Forum; Library and Information Association of New Zealand Aotearoa; Malawi Library Association; The National Association to Promote Library and Information Services to Latinos and the Spanish-Speaking; Reference and User Services Association; Special

Libraries Association; Oklahoma Chapter of the Association of College and Research Libraries, Potomac Technical Processing Librarians, Society of Southwest Archivists; The League of Awesome Librarians, Association of Christian Librarians.

In response to the statement, "I feel that I have job security," respondents (n=71) mostly selected Agree (57.7%), followed by Strongly Agree (36.6%), Disagree (2.8%), and Strongly Disagree (2.8%). The survey asked respondents to self-identify as a member of a historically oppressed group. Of the sample (n=70), 75.7% selected No, and 24.2% selected Yes. Table 5.6 shows job security.

I feel that I have job security	Frequency (n=71)
Strongly agree	26
Agree	41
Disagree	2
Strongly disagree	2

Table 5.6. Job Security of the Sample

The survey also asked if respondents felt that they were a member of a historically oppressed group. Of the respondents (n=70), 24% selected "yes" and 76% selected "no." Table 5.7 shows this demographic data.

Historically Oppressed Group	Frequency (n=70)
Yes	17
No	53

Table 5.7. Historically Oppressed Self-identification

Institutional Demographics

The survey asked how many library staff are assigned to assessment, including the respondent. The sample (n=72) mostly consists of institutions that have either 2–3 staff (40.2%) or 1 staff (33.3%). The remaining responses included None and 4–5 staff, each with 6.9% of the sample, and 6+ staff (12.5%). Table 5.8 shows how many staff are assigned to assessment.

Assessment Staff	72
None	5
1	24
2–3	29
4–5	5
6+	9

Table 5.8. Assessment Staff Assigned to Assessment

In terms of the extent of library assessment in practice, the sample (n=72) indicated that assessment is typically practiced "in most areas of operation" (32%) or "in some areas of operation" (32%). Assessment is practiced "in a few areas of operation" for 23.6% of the sample, while for 12.5% of the sample, assessment is practiced "in all areas of operation." Table 5.9 shows the extent of assessment practice.

Assessment Practice	72
In all areas of operation	9
In most areas of operation	23
In some areas of operation	23
In a few areas of operation	17

Table 5.9. Extent of Assessment Practice

The survey also inquired about budgetary support by asking respondents to agree or disagree with the statement, "I have sufficient funding to conduct assessment." Of those responses, (n=72), 48.6% agreed and 2.7% strongly agreed, while 30.5% disagreed and 18.1% strongly disagreed. Table 5.10 shows the funding situations for the sample.

I have sufficient funding for assessment	Frequency (n=72)
Strongly agree	2
Agree	35
Disagree	22
Strongly disagree	13

Table 5.10. Assessment Funding

Values Relevant for Assessment Decision-Making

ALA Core Values and Assessment Decision-Making

The survey first asked, "I refer to the ALA Core Values when making decisions about my assessment practice." This question points to the relevancy of the ALA Core Values as a set of values. This question does not yet ask the participant to respond to any individual value. Responses (n=92) included the following: always (n=3), most of the time (n=8), about half the time (n=4), sometimes (n=30), never (n=47). Only 12% of the sample refer to the ALA Core Values always or most of the time, while 84% either sometimes or never refer to the ALA Core Values. This result suggests that the ALA Core Values may not be a critical point of reference for decisions relating to the practice of library assessment. Table 5.11 shows how often assessment practitioners refer to the ALA Core Values.

I refer to the ALA Core Values when making decisions about my assessment practice	Frequency (n=92)
Always	3
Most of the time	8
About half the time	4
Sometimes	30
Never	47

Table 5.11. ALA Core Values and Assessment Practice

Importance of the ALA Core Values

The first substantive section of the survey focused on the function of values in library assessment decision-making. The first question asked respondents to rank the ALA Core Values by degree of importance: "Which of the ALA Core Values are most important to your assessment practice?" Respondents (n=92) selected up to four values. The most selected value was Confidentiality/Privacy, which was selected 63 times across the 92 respondents. Composing the top next five most-selected values were Access and Service, each with 37 selections, followed by Diversity with 34 selections, Social Responsibility with 31 selections, Education and Lifelong Learning with 25 selections, and The Public Good with 17 selections. The six least-commonly selected values included Intellectual Freedom with 14 selections, Professionalism with 12 selections, Sustainability with 11 selections, Democracy with 7 selections, and Preservation with 4 selections. None was selected 8 times.

Frequency of Consideration of the ALA Core Values

The survey then asked respondents to mark each value according to its frequency of consideration in their assessment practice, with choices that included "often considered," "sometimes considered," "rarely considered," and "not applicable." Each value received 89 responses, except for Sustainability, which received 90 responses. The value most selected as "often considered" was Confidentiality/Privacy (n=65), followed by Service, Access, Diversity, and Social Responsibility. Figure 5.1 shows how many times respondents marked "often considered" for each value. Additional charts showing the full responses to this question are available in the research dataset.

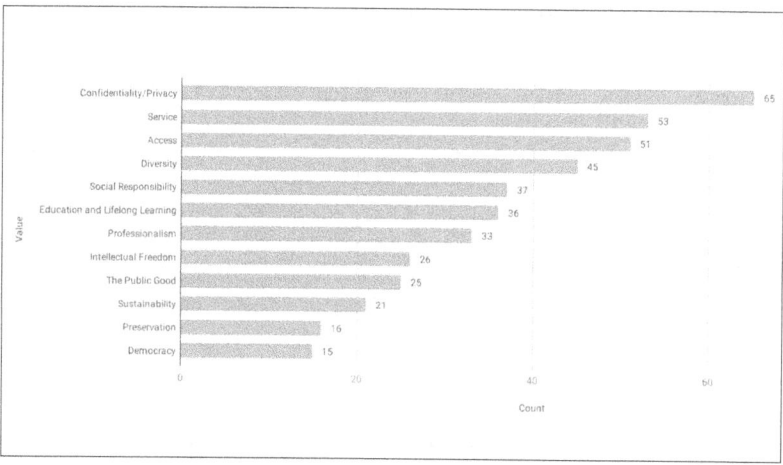

Figure 5.1. ALA Core Values "Often considered in your assessment practice."

Next, we turn to identifying values—not in the ALA Core Values—that were identified by participants as relevant to assessment.

Other Values Beyond the ALA Core Values

Beyond the ALA Core Values, the survey also asks respondents to share any other value not already included in the set of Core Values.

Results shown in Figure 5.2 were generated by coding the survey respondents' free-text response to the following question: "Which other values are relevant in your assessment practice? These can include personal, professional, institutional, or any other values not listed [in the ALA Core Values] above." These additional 12 non-ALA values were derived from 53 total responses: Validity (n=12), Justice (n=7), Alignment (n=7), Care (n=6), Human-centered (n=6), Collaboration (n=4), Transparency (n=3), Communication (n=2), None (n=2), Stewardship (n=2), Imagining Otherwise (n=1), and Positionality (n=1). Figure 5.2 shows the frequency of values across these responses.

> **Note**: as a reference for the discussion of the non-ALA values here and in further sections below, please refer to Chapter 1, which lists the value names and their descriptions (except for *human-centered*, which I talk more about in the next chapter).

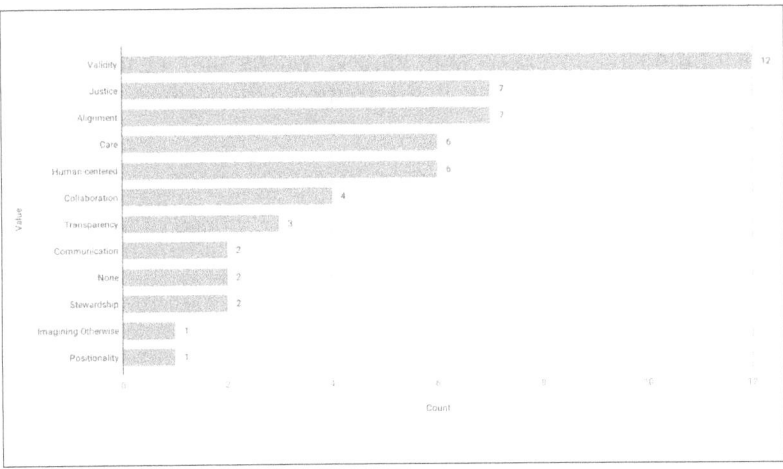

Figure 5.2. Frequency for Other (non-ALA) Values Relevant to Assessment Practice

The most common response to the question of other values was coded as *validity*. This code relates to finding the right fit between research question and research method. Responses from the *validity* code include:

- "In my view, if we can't act on some evidence that we gather, we generally should not ask about it, as that will undermine all stakeholders' perception of our ability to listen and be responsive" (R_1BYn).

- "Making decisions on sound evidence" (R_2QMx).
- "Accuracy, design, sample size, focus, actionable results" (R_3dMU).

The *justice* theme includes a range of topics related to equity and inclusion. Responses from the *justice* theme include:

- "I try to be as inclusive as possible in my assessment practice. I also try to treat participants in assessment as equal partners in the process as much as possible" (R_3MbA).
- "Inclusivity. That all our patrons feel the library is welcoming and for them" (R_cUZZ).

Also emerging as a leading value is *alignment*, a code that includes responses that focus on finding common ground among various stakeholders by aligning assessment activity with existing documentation such as mission statements and value statements. Responses within the alignment code included:

- "Institutional (university and library) values and goals that describe our library's values, in the context of ALA values among others" (R_1E6X).
- "Our university's values statement" (R_AFO0).
- "The mission, vision, and values of the library and institution" (R_1n2E).

Locally-developed Values Statement

On the topic of values, the survey also asked: "Do you have a locally-developed values statement that guides assessment practice at your library?" To this question, 26 respondents marked "yes" while 66 marked "no." As a follow-up for those who marked "yes", the survey asked, "Can you list the values that are included in your local values statement?" To this question, 20 respondents listed the values that are included in their local statement, with 95 unique values or value statements. Responses coded into the following: Justice (n=19), Validity (n=14), Collaboration (n=12), Imagining Otherwise (n=12), Human-centered (n=6), Communication (n=5), Alignment (n=3), Respect (n=3), Transparency (n=3), Positionality (n=2), Stewardship (n=1), Other: Faith (n=1), Other: Leadership (n=1), Other: Wisdom (n=1). Of the 95 values, 15 were restatements of ALA Core Values. These included: Service (n=7), Access (n=4), Lifelong Learning (n=1), Privacy (n=1), Sustainability (n=1), Intellectual Freedom (n=1). Figure 5.3 shows the codes produced from these responses.

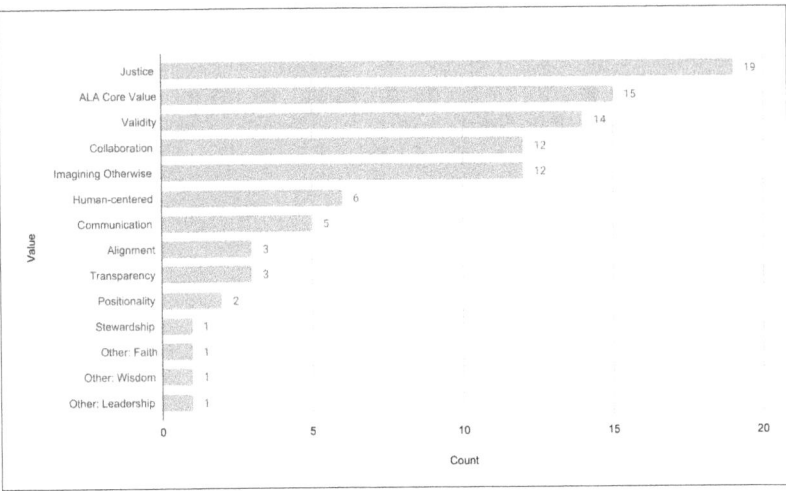

Figure 5.3. Frequency of values included in a local values statement

The subsections above presented results related to values; results included ALA Core Values, other values not in the ALA Core Values, and locally-developed value statements. Patterns from the responses in these three areas begin to bring into view a picture of relevant values for assessment librarians.

Next, we turn to the application of these values in practice, as seen through survey responses to the ethical vignettes.

Ethical Vignettes

The vignettes were designed to prompt ethical deliberation and decision-making from survey respondents. The vignettes were shaped around ethical topics present in the literature. Respondents were asked to read and review a series of six scenarios, and then to respond to four questions for each scenario:

1. What is the likelihood that you would take the same action as this librarian?

2. In your opinion, which values are relevant to the decision in this scenario?

3. Which other values are relevant to the decision in this scenario?

4. As an assessment practitioner, how else could you respond in this scenario?

In this results section, I will first present results that show patterns across all six vignettes, then I will present result summaries for each individual vignettes (for an even more detailed presentation of results, please see the supplemental results in the research dataset).

Results Across Vignettes

Likelihood

For each vignette, the survey first asked, "What is the likelihood that you would take the same action as this librarian?" Results to this question varied across vignettes. Scenario 1 (n=78) produced the most balanced response, with 51.3% of the sample unlikely to take the same action and 48.7% likely to take the same action. Scenario 2 saw 86.7 % of the sample unlikely to take the same action and 14.2% likely to take the same action. In response to Scenario 3, 69.7 % of the sample is unlikely to take the same action and 30.0% is likely to take the same action. Scenario 4 produced the strongest response in favor of the same action, with 10.8 % of the sample unlikely to take the same action and 89.2% likely to take the same action. In response to Scenario

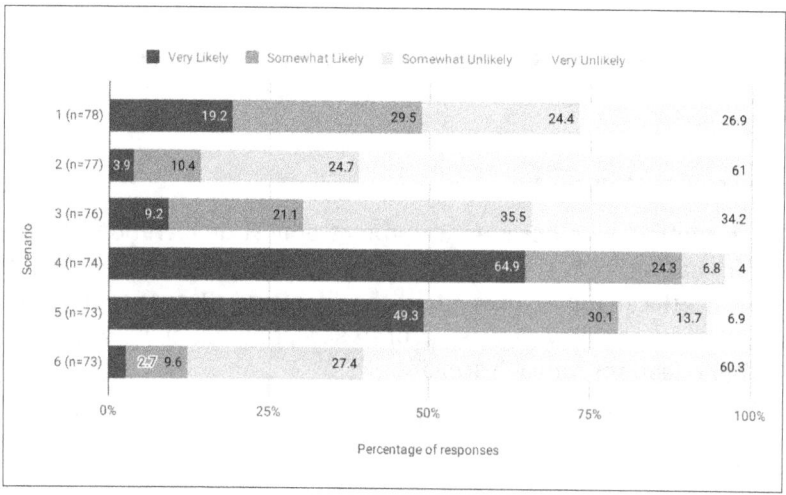

Figure 5.4. Likelihood of Respondents to Follow the Same Action as the Librarian Described in Each Scenario

5, 20.6 % of the sample is unlikely to take the same action and 79.4% is likely to take the same action. Scenario 6 produced the strongest response against the same action, with 87.7 % of the sample unlikely to take the same action and 12.3% likely to take the same action. Figure 5.4 below shows the likelihood of respondents to follow the same action as the librarian described in each scenario.

ALA Core Values

For each vignette, the survey then asked, "Which values are relevant to the decision in this scenario?" Participants were asked to select from among the ALA Core Values. Participants were allowed to select as many values as applied, or none. Each response selected an average of 4.6 values per vignette. The calculations for each scenario are shown in Table 5.12.

Scenario	Responses	Total ALA Core Values selected	Average number of ALA Core Values selected
1	77	309	4
2	77	275	3.6
3	76	316	4.2
4	73	384	5.3
5	73	383	5.2
6	73	407	5.6

Table 5.12. ALA Core Value Selections by Scenario

These calculations provide an insight into the ethical complexity of a scenario. Scenario 2, with only 3.6 values selected, is perhaps a more straightforward situation than Scenario 6, which received an average of 5.6 values. On the other hand, Scenarios 2 and 6 are similar in that participants most strongly disagreed with the action in these two situations. When viewed alongside Figure 5.4 (the likelihood results), further complexity comes into view: the scenarios that produced the widest variety of likelihood responses—Scenarios 1 and 3—were the fourth and fifth in terms of average number of Core Values selected. This suggests that the number of operating values is not indicative of complexity. Rather, the tension of a dilemma is perhaps better understood by examining which specific values are relevant and potentially in conflict.

In terms of which values were selected in and across the vignettes, the most selected values included social responsibility (283 selections), diversity (227 selections), access (225 selections), service (215 selections), and confidentiality/privacy (212 selections), and the public good (199 selections). The least commonly selected were none (5 selections), preservation (20 selections), sustainability (46 selections), professionalism (143 selections), intellectual freedom (156 selections), democracy (168 selections), and education and lifelong learning (175 selections). Figure 5.5 below shows the selection of ALA Core Values across vignettes.

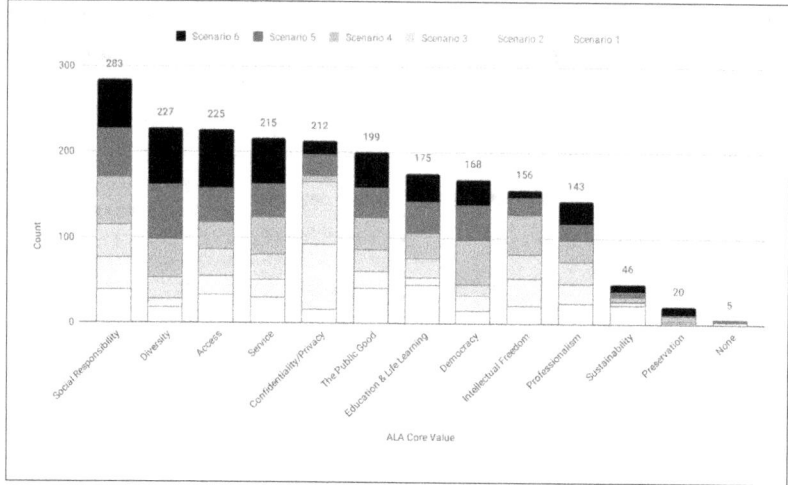

Figure 5.5. "Which Values Are Relevant to the Decision in This Scenario?" Responses across all scenarios.

In comparing 1) the ALA Core Values that were selected as important and considered, with 2) the ALA Core Values that were selected as relevant to the vignettes with, a view emerges of the most important values that are also most often considered and most relevant for the practitioners in this study population. Table 5.13 shows this comparison. This suggests that there is some coherence and consistency to the values that are relevant to library assessment practitioners, at least from within the bounds of the ALA Core Values. Table 5.13 shows a comparison of responses across these three questions.

Most important Core Values	Most often considered Core Values	Most relevant Core Values (across all vignettes)
1. Confidentiality/Privacy	1. Confidentiality/Privacy	1. Social Responsibility
2. Access	2. Service	2. Diversity
3. Service	3. Access	3. Access
4. Diversity	4. Diversity	4. Service
5. Social Responsibility	5. Social Responsibility	5. Confidentiality/Privacy

Table 5.13. Comparative View of Most Important Values, Most Often Considered Values, and Most Relevant Values

From these questions, five Core Values emerge as consistently applicable for library assessment practitioners: Access, Confidentiality/Privacy, Diversity, Service, Social Responsibility.

To expand our results and analysis, we turn next to values other than the ALA Core Values.

Other Values Across All Vignettes

The survey asked participants: "Which other values are relevant to the decision in this scenario? These can include personal, professional, institutional, or any other values not listed above." Participants were instructed to provide values not included in the ALA Core Values. These free-text responses (n=128) were coded according to grounded theory analysis, discussed in Chapter 1. Coded themes for values that appear across all vignettes include the following: validity (n=30), alignment (n=20), justice (n=19), positionality (n=11), collaboration (n=9), transparency (n=9), imagining otherwise (n=8), human-centered (n=7), stewardship (n=5), care (n=5), none (n=4), and communication (n=1).

Practices Across All Vignettes

Finally for each vignette, the survey asked: "As an assessment practitioner, how else could you respond in this scenario?" Responses to this question generated valuable data that provided insight into the practice of assessment librarians, with patterns emerging that reveal common responses in support of shared values.

> *A special note about "other values" and the practical responses to the ethical vignettes*
>
> For each vignette, the survey asked about "other values" that are relevant to the scenario. For these questions, survey respondents completed free-text responses to provide any values relevant to their practice and to the vignettes that are not already included in the ALA Core Values. These responses were crucial to the outcome of this research, as these questions prompted practitioners to share the unique values that apply to their practice of library assessment. This data represents the heart of the research—what are our assessment values? How do we prioritize them, and when do we apply them?
>
> The survey also asked practitioners to provide practical responses to the vignettes. Along with the non-ALA values, these responses were highly influential in shaping the final result of this research. For these questions, survey respondents offered rich descriptions of the practical actions that they would take in addressing the dilemmas. Together, responses to these two questions—"Which other values are relevant to the decision in this scenario?" and "How else could you respond in this scenario?"—form the basis for the development of the *Values Classification for Library Assessment*. In the *Values-Sensitive Library Assessment Toolkit*, the reflective prompts that accompany the values are directly informed by the practical actions described by survey respondents.
>
> For the sake of space, I don't offer here a detailed presentation and analysis of responses to the question, "How else could you respond in this scenario?" For further description of these responses, please see the supplemental analysis of results in the research dataset, available via the Qualitative Data Repository: https://doi.org/10.5064/F6ORSLQF.

In the following sections, I present results and discuss analysis for each of the six individual vignettes.

Scenario 1: Library Value and Impact

In this scenario, respondents were asked to evaluate an ethical dilemma involving the use of financial measures to tell a story of library value. In the scenario, the librarian considers conducting an ROI evaluation as a way to determine library value, knowing that an ROI measure would resonate with university administration. The librarian decides not to conduct the assessment, however, on the thinking that financial metrics don't speak well to the impact of the library. This scenario reflects the theme of library value and impact as found in the literature (discussed in Chapter 3).

Respondents evenly marked their likelihood of taking the same action as the librarian described in the Scenario 1, with 48.7% saying they are somewhat or very likely to take the same action. From the ALA Core Values, respondents (n=77) selected 309 values total, for an average of 4 values selected per response. The top three ALA Core Values included: Education and Lifelong Learning (n=45), The Public Good (n=41) Social Responsibility (n=39). For values other than the ALA Core Values, the top three from all responses (n=27) included: Validity (n=8), Imagining Otherwise (n=6), and Alignment (n=5).

Respondents discerned the ethical dilemma of Scenario 1 primarily to involve the limitations of applying a single measure for determining such a high-stakes result as library value. Many respondents recognized that the financial pressures of higher education compel library assessment practitioners to account for economic impacts. Whether going with or against this pressure, respondents understood that these pressures needed to be addressed. Thus the dilemma in this scenario revolves around how to measure and tell the story of library value in the face of financial expectations. Within the theme of *validity*, respondents posed questions that aimed to produce a completed and accurate project, especially focusing on finding the right match between research question and research method—if the method does not match the question, then that can provide grounds for re-examining and revising the assessment. Also relevant to this scenario was the theme of *imagining otherwise*, which includes values of thinking beyond the status quo. In this scenario, the status quo involves financial measures that are based on a premise of economic value and neoliberal capitalism. Several respondents took note of neoliberal associations with ROI measures and other financial views into library values, and expressed values of questioning the current paradigm and creating new counter-narratives as a way to open new pathways for assessment. In these responses was a call to not simply accept the status quo, but rather to question the existing economic paradigm, resist dominant narratives of assessment and value, and pose alternative storytelling. At the same time, other respondents spoke to the theme of *alignment*, where the values of the university drive the action of assessment, as one respondent said, "If dollars and cents communicates to administration, then that is better than a message that does not address their viewpoint at all" (R_SUxB). Interestingly, these two values themes—*imagining otherwise* and *alignment*—converged in one response: "I might see if I could realign the parameters of the inquiry to help it move forward" (R_1BYn). This response represents a practical and creative approach for resolving conflicts between these two values.

As a way of responding to the scenario, respondents overwhelmingly offered two paths forward for resolving these dilemmas: seeking alternative methods and providing context for the assessment. Alternative methods were seen as a way to introduce greater nuance into the conversation of library value. Respondents note that there is usually more than one tool that can be used to conduct an assessment; when one method presents an ethical dilemma, seek an alternative that achieves the same goal with less ethical complication. Respondents suggested that the financial measure could be completed, but alongside and as a complement to other measures that speak more accurately to the unique strengths of the library. In terms of context, practitioners could provide a view of the wider context surrounding the collection, analysis, and application of data. This can introduce a more complete and accurate representation of library value, as practitioners can mark the limitations of a single measure while also supplementing that measure with other appropriate assessments and contextual factors. A further consideration involves the theme of alignment—by understanding and addressing different perspectives on an assessment project, multiple stakeholder interests can be satisfied, including parent entities, other campus units, and personal values. Finally, within the theme of pragmatism, practitioners were motivated to follow guidelines provided by supervisors and to conduct the assessment, provided the project could be completed within the scope of professional standards such as accuracy and privacy.

Scenario 2: Information Technologies, Data, and Privacy

In this scenario, a librarian considers implementing a third-party tracking tool to assess website usage. The tracking tool is operated by a private company that would retain the data on their servers. The tool records screen captures, which is a powerful analytics capability, but user privacy could be compromised since the data is passed to the servers of the private company. The library in the scenario decides to implement the tracking tool. This scenario reflects the themes of information technologies, data, and privacy as found in the literature (discussed in Chapter 3).

Respondents were not likely to follow the same action as the librarian described in Scenario 2, with 85.7% saying that they are somewhat or very unlikely to take the same action. From the ALA Core Values, respondents (n=77) selected 275 values total, for an average of 3.6 values selected per response. Privacy (n=76) was overwhelmingly the most selected value from the ALA Core Values, followed by social responsibility (n=38) and intellectual freedom (n=32). For values other than the ALA Core Values, the top three of all responses (n=23) included: Validity (n=7), Transparency (n=7), and Alignment (n=4).

Respondents discerned the ethical dilemma to involve a tension between service assessment and data privacy. In the theme of *validity* are appeals to accepted standards, especially in this case involving data stewardship. Values related to *transparency* were also highly relevant to this scenario, with many respondents focusing on issues of disclosure and consent. If the library will record screen captures, then users should be made aware that such an assessment is occurring and, even more, be given the opportunity to opt in or out of participation.

As a way to resolve the tension, the most common response involved seeking alternative assessment approaches—rather than install a privacy-violating analytics tool, practitioners can identify another similar tool that accomplishes the assessment without compromising privacy. Furthermore, an assessment such as this should be made transparent with users, which should also include an opportunity for users to provide informed consent to participate. Since this scenario involved a third-party, respondents also suggested negotiating with the third-party for more desirable terms. If the vendor supplies a unique and desirable service but offers an undesirable contract, it's worth negotiating for a contract that reflects library values.

Scenario 3: Learning Analytics and Student Success

In this scenario, an assessment librarian is asked to share library card swipe data with a central data warehouse operated at the university level. Data would be used to develop student interventions. In the scenario, the librarian considers raising an objection on the grounds that the approach does not reflect library values, but ultimately agrees to participate in the assessment due to a commitment to the institution. This scenario reflects the themes of learning analytics and student success as found in the literature (discussed in Chapter 3).

Respondents were mostly in agreement that they would not follow this same action as the librarian in Scenario 3, with 69.7% marking that they were somewhat or very unlikely to take the same action. From the ALA Core Values, respondents (n=76) selected 316 values total, for an average of 4.2 values selected per response. Of the ALA Core Values relevant to the decision, Confidentiality/Privacy (n=74) was the most selected value, followed by social responsibility (n=38) and access (n=31). Of the values other than the ALA Core Values, the three most included of all responses (n=18) included Validity (n=7), Alignment (n=5), and Justice (n=4).

Overall, respondents discerned the dilemma to involve matters of data collection and data sharing, with potential risks to student confidentiality weighed against the potential insights produced by this assessment. Many respondents noted that this data collection was not suitable for the goal, therefore it may not be appropriate to conduct this assessment without revision to the data collection methods. If, however, the project were to move forward, special care should be paid to the procedures for data collection, storage, and sharing, with a view toward collecting the least amount of data necessary to conduct the assessment. Such data stewardship can help ensure that research participants are properly protected. In this way, data stewardship practices also relate to privacy, and, when seeking different approaches to data collection, this practice overlaps with alternative methods. Similarly, a practice of transparency should be followed, whereby users are made aware of the assessment. *Alignment* is also relevant here—the practice of communicating with and united key stakeholders of an assessment, including university administration, library administration, and the practitioner. As with Scenario 1, the pursuit of alternative methods is relevant here, as several respondents suggested that they could identify other assessments that can accomplish a similar result without compromising values.

Scenario 4: Social Responsibility and Neutrality

In this scenario, a librarian partners with a student group to assess the subject headings found in the library catalog. Specifically, the group is a prison abolition student organization, and the subject headings in question relate to incarceration. The librarian considers not conducting the assessment so as to achieve library neutrality, but ultimately decides to work with the students group to conduct the assessment. This scenario reflects the themes of neutrality and cataloging as found in the literature (discussed in Chapter 3).

Respondents tended to agree with the librarian in Scenario 4, with 89.2% marking that they are somewhat or very likely to take the same action. From the ALA Core Values, respondents (n=73) selected 384 values total, for an average of 5.3 values selected per response. Of the ALA Core Values, the three most relevant included: Social Responsibility (n=56), Democracy (n=52), and Intellectual Freedom (n=46). For values other than the ALA Core Values, the top three from all responses (n=23) included: Positionality (n=10), Justice (n=3), and Validity (n=3).

Respondents found that the ethical dilemma in the scenario turned on two axes: the first related to whether it was right to assess subject headings, and the second related to whether it was right to involve this student group in a politically-engaged project. On the first point, all respondents agreed that subject headings are an appropriate area of assessment. On the second point, responses were more varied, with a range of possibilities for how to move forward. As the most relevant value in this scenario, the principle of directly invoking values and positions—a value of *positionality*—was seen as especially useful for guiding action, as one respondent remarked: "I'm a prison abolitionist, so that would come into play in how I work with the program" (R_1n3f). In this instance, the practitioner clearly identifies their own operating principles, and then matches those principles with the actual practice of assessment.

In terms of how to respond to the scenario, respondents indicated that the main approach to resolving these dilemmas involved identifying and invoking values, as one respondent describes: "All choices are grounded in (a set of) values. Any choice we make is a choice between values. Prior to working on the project, create a values statement grounded in the institution's mission/vision as well as professional values as a way of guiding the project" (R_3LXr). More directly, another respondent noted, "Library neutrality is BS anyway, and working with the group actually upholds values of diversity and inclusion" (R_3MbA). Even when confronting neutrality, and politically-engaged work, previously agreed-upon values can resolve any ethical tensions: "My library recently responded to the Black Lives Matter movement with a public statement declaring that we are not neutral. If my library meant what they said, then we should accept that we will take active roles in social issues" (R_10UV). In terms of operational considerations, a few respondents also pointed to staffing and budgetary sustainability as relevant to the decision. In this way, longer-term library workload capacity can help clarify decision-making.

Scenario 5: Student Participation

In this scenario, a librarian convenes a student working group to assist in an assessment of library instruction. The students propose an assessment that involves the identification of immigrant status among library users, but the librarian is hesitant because an immigration-focused assessment does not align with institutional priorities. The librarian ultimately chooses to support the student group and advocate for this assessment. This scenario reflects the themes of student participation as found in the literature (discussed in Chapter 3).

In response to Scenario 5, 79.4% of respondents said that they are very or somewhat likely to take the same action as the librarian in the scenario. From the ALA Core Values, respondents (n=73) selected 383 total, for an average of 5.2 values selected per response. Of the ALA Core Values, the three most relevant included diversity (n=64) and social responsibility (n=56), and Democracy (n=41). For values other than the ALA Core Values, the top three from all responses (n=22) included Justice (n=6), Care (n=3), and Alignment (n=3).

Respondents discerned the ethical dilemmas to involve two aspects—first, how to conduct an assessment that does not match with institutional priorities; second, how to conduct an assessment that involves sensitive identities of participants. The most common response for resolving the ethical dilemmas involved *alignment*, which involves checking with and adhering to other stakeholder expectations, including those of the parent-entity, the library, and the practitioners themselves. In terms of library expectations, one respondent remarked, "Expending resources on non-strategic plan/priorities aligned projects is a non-starter for me" (R_1rON). Others noted that a stringent adherence to existing policy may not be necessary, but that communicating upward is useful: "I would consult with library leadership and those responsible for instruction to gain their input and support so they are aware of the assessment and are not blindsided, but informed by it" (R_1Op1). Another set of themes addressed the assessment participants, including the students themselves and other stakeholder groups that would be affected by the assessment. These themes include relationship-building, co-determination, and care. Together, these themes point to ethical resolution via a practice of collaboration and partnership in support of outcomes that support the wellbeing of participants.

Scenario 6: Community Participation

In this scenario, a librarian is conducting an assessment that involves accessibility of special collections finding aids. The librarian considers involving members of the disabled community, but doesn't have existing relationships to leverage. For the sake of ease and expediency, the librarian decides to move forward without involving the community members This scenario reflects the themes of community participation and archives as found in the literature (discussed in Chapter 3).

In response to Scenario 6, 87.7% of respondents said that they are very or somewhat unlikely to take the same action as the librarian in the scenario. From the ALA Core Values, respondents (n=73) selected 407 values total, for an average of 5.6 values selected per response. The three values from the ALA Core Values were Access (n=67), Diversity (n=65), and Social Responsibility (n=56). Of the values other than the ALA Core Values, the top three from all responses (n=17) included Collaboration (n=5), Justice (n=4), and Alignment (n=3).

In terms of how else to respond to this scenario, respondents discerned the ethical dilemma to involve a tension between community engagement and the time required to build relationships with the community. For this scenario, respondents were consistent in suggesting potential resolutions. On the theme of relationship-building, the practitioner can first engage the community to develop collaborative ties that can support the assessment. One respondent stated, "I would start with asking the department on campus that works with the disabled community and go from there" (R_RrkF). With that having been established, the assessment practitioner can go further to implement deeper partnerships through shared decision-making. On this theme of co-determination, one respondent said, "It would be essential to involve members from that community in the assessment. I would partner with university access services and other university entities along with members from this community to help design and implement this assessment" (R_10p1). These two themes—relationship-building and co-determination—can operate in concert as a response to ethical dilemmas involving questions of community participation.

Insights

In the sections below, I offer five areas of insight from the survey data: ethical complexity, locating library assessment values, ethical tensions, ethical resolutions, and idealism vs. pragmatism. In sum, the data shows that assessment practitioners are attuned to values and are equipped to act ethically, but are challenged by the complex array of values that may be relevant in any given situation.

Ethics is Complex and Multifaceted

A main takeaway from the data is that library assessment values and practices are complex and multifaceted. This aspect may be the precondition for all related tensions, as values-in-conflict form the basis of a dilemma in the context of practical ethics. And there are so many potential values. Survey respondents collectively reported hundreds of different values as relevant to their practice, with wide variation within any one scenario. This translates into a high degree of choice and possibility for practice, but it also means that unification or coherence across the field is more difficult to achieve. A high range of values also obscures, rather than clarifies, decision-making: if there are dozens of values in play, it can be difficult to know which value should take priority. Among the many values and practices identified by the sample, no single value or practice was predominant. This also leads to a lack of clarity as to which values are most relevant for practice ethical assessment. Librarians don't always know where to turn for values, especially since there are so many potential places to look: the ALA, personal values, library values, or university values. It's hard to know which values matter in a given situation.

A power dimension further complicates this landscape: do librarians have the power to implement their values? If a practitioner were to decide on the values relevant for a certain assessment project, are they able to implement and enact those values in a meaningful way? Even if values are known, practitioners don't always feel empowered within their organizations to apply them. An assessment librarian operates within an academic library that is often characterized by multi-stakeholder, hierarchical dynamics. The ability to identify and apply a value may be constrained in such an environment. As an example of this effect, one respondent remarked in response to Scenario 3 (contributing student data to a centralized data warehouse): "This situation is very difficult. I would rely on working with senior administration to advocate and educate institutional colleagues about the importance of privacy relative to libraries. I think that libraries have an important tradition of privacy and that this would be an instance where the larger profession of librarianship is greater than the academic objectives" (R_10UV). In this example, the practitioner is speaking to a privacy value, while acknowledging the wider context of operating within an environment that includes stakeholders who might not adhere to their practice the same value. The practitioner here recognizes that education and advocacy around values is necessary, but nevertheless may not be sufficient for enacting this value in practice.

On Locating Library Assessment Values

From this place of ethical complexity, how can a set of values relevant for library assessment be identified? This book began with an investigation into the stated values of library and information science as a profession (Chapter 2). The process of locating the profession's values yielded a wide-ranging collection of values, numbering in the dozens. My research inquiry then led me to delve into the values of library assessment per se, starting with the ALA Core Values as a key reference point. The role of the ALA Core Values was a question from the literature that I wanted to answer in the survey. In the search for a coherent system of values for library assessment, I hypothesized that the *ALA Core Values of Librarianship* was capable of providing a common point of reference for library assessment practice. When asked to respond to individual values within the scope of the ALA Core Values, the sample highlighted five ALA Core Values that are of particular relevance for library assessment: Confidentiality/Privacy, Access, Service, Diversity, Social Responsibility. But, when looking the ALA Core Values as a coherent set of values vis-à-vis assessment practice, nearly half the sample indicated that the ALA Core Values are never referenced, and only 12% of the sample refer to the ALA Core Values always or most of the time when practicing assessment. Though the ALA Core Values seeks to be the single, centralized, coherent set of values that guide library practice, library assessment practitioners do not appear to reference it meaningfully in their work. This points to a lack of a central, community-endorsed classification of values by and for assessment librarians.

This result also speaks to the diverse nature of library practice. The ALA Core Values are written from a very high level, and attempt to speak inclusively for the greatest extent of library practitioners. But the field of LIS is so broad that practitioners working within a specialty may not find much use for a values statement developed from a centralized body. Some values articulated by the ALA, such as service and privacy, are indeed relevant to many LIS specialties, including assessment. But there are assessment-specific values appearing in the dataset that have not risen to the level of the ALA, such as *validity* and *alignment*. These could be questions returned to the community for further reflection: why is the *ALA Core Values of Librarianship* document not a more important reference point for the assessment community? What would be required to motivate the community to build, maintain, and apply a set of values relevant for library assessment?

Insofar as the research here can answer the question of library assessment values, we can look closer at the data to find insight into the practice of assessment as a specific specialty of LIS. Grounded theory coding revealed themes of special importance to the assessment community, namely those related to research. Many of the responses connected library assessment to research methods, with practitioners mentioning the validity of a study, identifying different approaches for different projects, and ensuring an appropriate degree of methodological soundness for any assessment. Survey respondents spoke about the primary importance of research design, research methods, and the validity of results derived from assessment. These factors are crucial in making decisions about assessment, suggesting that many assessment practitioners see themselves as researchers who operate in a library setting. This is perhaps a unique characteristic of the assessment practitioner community within the wider field of LIS, in that the practice of assessment can often take the form of research. When factoring in the identifying characteristics of library assessment, we can begin to see a set of values that are likewise particularly to assessment, especially those related to research as a central practice of assessment, and to research validity as a central value.

This landscape of values reflects local idiosyncrasy: the ALA Core Values have been shown not to be a central point of reference for assessment practitioners, and no comparative professional organization for library assessment exists that could craft a statement of values relevant for the assessment specialty. When making ethical decisions, it appears that the local context is more immediately influential than the ALA, which is comparatively abstract and far away. This environment produces a "values vacuum," whereby practitioners create their own core values that are relevant to their own particular setting. In this environment, values are highly contextual and idiosyncratic. Indeed, for many practitioners, a known set of values was available from which to choose: many respondents appealed to their library or university mission statement or value statement, if not a values statement developed within their own assessment department or program. And most respondents produced values beyond the ALA Core Values for the specific scenarios and for their practice.

The sample was diverse in terms of the type of library in which a respondent worked. The variety of local settings and employment contexts amplified the heterogeneity of responses. With thousands of universities in the US, the potential for different values in play is exponential. In short, the landscape of values is wide-ranging, with a diverse and multifaceted array of values and practices available to librarians working in idiosyncratic local contexts. This points to a practitioner community that wants to practice values-based assessment and is equipped to apply values, but is left to identify and enact values from a position of isolation or idiosyncrasy. Library assessment values are created in hybrid way—partly drawing on a centralized values system (as with privacy from the ALA Core Values) but ultimately completing the assessment values system with values developed to suit the needs of assessment per se (as with validity) or in response to local conditions (as with alignment).

With this in mind, a toolkit for values-based assessment should aim to find a balance of rigidity and flexibility. The main outcome of this book project is a toolkit to aid values-based practice, so this insight is especially relevant. In terms of rigidity, the toolkit should be recognizable as a set of values relevant to assessment practitioners *as a group*, yet also be flexible enough to accommodate other values relevant to an assessment practitioner *as an individual* in order to meet idiosyncratic needs at the local level. Given the many different local contexts—with each context carrying its own set of pressures and priorities—an ethical tool would need to be flexible or adaptable so as to accommodate many different possible needs and outcomes.

Values-in-Conflict: Ethical Tensions

With such a high range of values available to assessment practitioners, there's also a potential for values to be in conflict in a given situation. I note three values-in-conflict.

The first involves *positionality* and *justice*. On the one hand, many survey respondents spoke in favor of values such as equity, inclusion, and other values that support social justice outcomes. These values depend on the rejection of neutrality, as they take a strong political point of view. Yet other respondents spoke in favor of neutrality. This tension was surfaced in the literature review, and it appeared again in the survey results. In Scenario 4, for example, which involved a librarian partnering with a student group to assess the subject headings found in the library catalog, the topic of neutrality was directly addressed in the scenario description. As a response, one respondent remarked: "Educate my colleagues about why library neutrality is a dangerous myth" (R_sL6p). Yet another respondent said: "Neutrality may be more valuable than is currently thought" (R_1ou9). In assessments that involve social factors and values related to justice, what if the librarian's position is one of neutrality? Such a tension must be addressed and resolved.

The second tension involves *positionality* and *alignment*, which can be summarized with the question: what if your personal position is at odds with library or university administration? To illustrate this, Scenario 1 involved the application of financial measures to tell a story of value for the library. In this instance, the assessment practitioner recognizes equally that economic measures don't speak to the strength or purpose of a library, but that economic measures do speak to the interests of university administrators. Responses from the sample demonstrate this tension. One respondent commented that this assessment should not be completed as currently designed, as "ROI is a neoliberal metric" (R_2WMg). This is a strong expression of positionality, in that the librarian is staking out a stance on the assessment. In this case, however, that stance is in opposition to the perceived desires of university administration. *Alignment* would suggest integrating parent-entity values, or even prioritizing those values in the assessment, as another respondent suggested: "It's politics. Create the report that administration wants" (R_u3xg). When a practitioner's personal views (*positionality*) may conflict with those of administration (*alignment*), how is such a tension resolved?

The third tension also relates to external pressures, namely *alignment* in conflict with *validity*, as when administration requests an assessment that—rather than going against the personal values of a practitioners—goes against professional best practice. In Scenario 3, for example, an assessment librarian is asked to share library card swipe data with a central data warehouse operated at the university level. This data would be used by the university to develop student interventions in support of student success. The scenario reflects discussion found in the literature related to learning analytics. The assessment community is divided on this topic, with some holding that the library should contribute data whenever possible to help university learning analytics efforts, while others object to such assessments based on privacy concerns or on the grounds that library data cannot be meaningfully integrated into complex learning analytics software. Survey responses were similarly divided. Nearly all respondents discerned the dilemmas to involve either privacy or validity in conflict with university alignment. With respect to validity, one respondent shared: "I'd add that from a methodological point of view retention is very unlikely to be a sensitive enough variable to observe the effect of visiting the library. This is a classic spurious correlation and is generally bad social science" (R_sL6p). Despite serious reservations about this assessment, respondents were unsure about how to ultimately resolve the tension. Some advised to share concerns with the library director, or to make the assessment transparent to students, or to ensure that data is properly collected and managed. The idea of tension with administration was present in many responses, such as:

- "I feel that some libraries may be forced into collecting the data by university administration" (R_3rPc).

- "I would want more information on how administration planning on operationalizing library use data. I would likely push back, but can't say I would hold my ground if I felt my job was threatened (for this level of data)" (R_VQil).

- "If administration refused to budge on this approach to assessment, I would resign in protest" (R_3qKg).

- "I have my fingers crossed that we are not put into this position, because it is difficult for library to push back. If we lost the fight, I would push for transparency around the data collection and advocate that data be deleted as soon as possible as a condition for library participation" (R_2Cx1).

The responses to this scenario highlight values-in-conflict and professional responsibility. Who and what are assessment librarians ultimately responsible to: a professional statement of values, personal values, professional standards of best practice, parent entity administrators? The answer to this question shifts according to the context from which it originates. This underscores the need for a reliable approach to identifying and prioritizing values, such that tensions among them may be identified and resolved.

Values-in-Conflict: Practical Resolutions

The sample demonstrated a sensitivity to ethical dilemmas and an interest in engaging a key question of practical ethics: "what is the right thing to do?" A takeaway from that data is that assessment librarians have a high capacity for discerning dilemmas and identifying resolutions. The scenarios were designed to include an ethical dilemma in the form of values-in-conflict. Respondents generally recognized one or more dilemmas in each scenario, and also offered paths forward for resolving the dilemmas. The paths offered were also multifaceted. Importantly, many respondents appealed to local conditions as a factor in their responses, resulting in a similarly high degree of complexity and diversity of responses in terms of ethical resolutions. One possible interpretation of this result is that practitioners could benefit from additional support in evaluating dilemmas and decisions, so that tensions shared across the profession, such as learning analytics, do not become overwhelmingly idiosyncratic. A closer look at the results helps illustrate this point.

The likelihood responses in particular illuminate ethical sensitivity. Scenarios 1 and 3 resulted in a balance of responses across the 4-point likelihood scale (very likely, somewhat likely, somewhat unlikely, very unlikely). Scenarios 2, 4, 5, and 6 were more strongly weighted in one direction. Starting with the strongly weighted scenarios, Scenario 2 featured a tension involving third-party tracking software to assess web services. The librarian in Scenario 2 decides to implement the third-party tracking software, despite concerns about privacy. Only

14.3% of the sample was likely to take this same action, with several responses indicating that the assessment should be outright rejected, and with many others offering revisions to the assessment such as alternative tracking software or greater transparency and opt-in/opt-out choices about the tool. Scenarios 4 and 6 also produced likelihood results that were heavily balanced in one direction. In Scenario 4, the assessment librarian partners with a prison abolition student group to evaluate subject headings involving incarceration. The librarian considers not conducting the assessment in light of the project's politically-charged social aspects and the library's position on neutrality, but ultimately decides to move forward.

The sample agreed, with only 10.8% saying that they were unlikely to take the same action. This scenario was developed in response to the presence of neutrality in the literature. The sample overwhelmingly rejected neutrality as a barrier to this assessment, and did not discern a dilemma in this case. In Scenario 5, the assessment librarian convenes a group of students to co-lead an assessment project. The students suggest assessing library instruction vis-à-vis student immigration status. The librarian decides to conduct the assessment. This was a polarizing scenario, with only 20.6% of the sample indicating that they were unlikely to take the same action. This was the most complicated scenario, involving issues of both student participation and social responsibility. Despite some reservations about how to proceed with an assessment that included sensitive identities, responses overall indicated a desire to work with students and to engage on social issues.

In Scenario 6, the assessment would impact members of a particular community, but developing community partnerships would extend the timeline of the project. To complete the project faster, the assessment librarian decides to conduct the assessment without the involvement of the community. Only 12.3% of the sample was likely to take this same action. In each of these cases, the scenario offers an ethical point of reflection. Responses from the sample are invaluable for marking the territory of that ethical reflection: Scenario 2 indicates that privacy is a vitally important value to put into practice; Scenario 4 indicates that neutrality is a less relevant value; Scenario 5 indicates that participation and social responsibility are relevant values; Scenario 6 further indicates that community participation is essential, especially when the assessment impacts members of that community. The sample understood that the librarian in each of these scenarios was making a decision that was clearly aligned or misaligned with the community-accepted values of privacy, social responsibility, and participation.

Scenarios 1 and 3 were more balanced in the likelihood responses. Scenarios 1 and 3 involved negotiating the library administrator and parent-entity expectations. Unlike Scenarios 2, 4, 5, and 6—in which the assessment librarian was working autonomously and primarily interfacing with students and the community—Scenarios 1 and 3 feature a librarian working in response to parent-entity requests and interfacing primarily with university administration. Such scenarios place different pressures on assessment practice that affect values-in-conflict. In these cases, a dilemma is understood to be present, but the resolution is less clear. In Scenario 1, the librarian considers an ROI assessment to satisfy parent-entity expectations, but reservations about ROI as a valid measure for library value lead the librarian not to conduct the assessment. This scenario produced the most balanced likelihood result, with 51.3% of the sample unlikely to take the same action and 48.7% likely to take the same action, indicating a deeper division within the field as to resolution of this ethical dilemma. Scenario 3 involved a similar assessment, in which university administration requests that the library share library building card swipe data to assess student success. The librarian decides to conduct the assessment. In response, 69.7 % of the sample was unlikely to take the same action and 30.0% likely to take the same action. Even though this scenario also involved matters of privacy similar to Scenario 2, the sample was half as likely to make a decision that upheld privacy. In contrast to Scenario 2, which featured an assessment that was contained within the library and self-directed by the librarian, the assessment of Scenario 3 involved responding to a direct parent-entity request. Scenarios 1 and 3 suggest that when assessment involves parent entity pressures, commonly-held values such as privacy or validity are under greater pressure as well. The *Values Classification for Library Assessment* that is the ultimate product of this book should be able to accommodate local contexts such as the parent-entity pressures present in Scenarios 1 and 3.

Idealism vs. Pragmatism

Viewing the two main data sources of the book at this point—the literature and the survey—we can see intriguing differences. In the literature review, I focused on publications that spoke to a more radical practice, with many articles presenting a new theory of practice or otherwise specifically calling for a new approach to assessment. Overall, the literature carried a sense of idealism and a vision for a different future of library assessment. On the other hand, survey data emphasized a more pragmatic approach. In response to Scenario 1 (using financial measures to tell a story of library value), for example, the most common survey responses articulated a desire to find a way to complete the assessment, if not exactly as requested. The following response illustrates this pragmatic approach:

- "As an administration, I can sympathize with this position, but as an assessment practitioner – I can see more uses for gathering such data than a simple ROI report to higher administration. I might see if I could realign the parameters of the inquiry to help it move forward" (R_1BYn).

- "Perform an assessment that includes more than just the financial perspective. Use the assessment to both communicate with the university administration along their axis of interest as well as to enhance their understanding of your work and different measurements of value" (R_1OUV).

- "Use the ROI as one point in a multi-point report or program" (R_1n2E).

- "The assessment would proceed as outlined, but parallel assessments would seek to address the intangible importance of the library resources. This triangulation would create a better view of what is involved and impacted by cuts. It shows them we can speak their language while teaching them some of our language" (R_1Op1).

Such pragmatism was more present in the survey, suggesting that library assessment faces external pressures that affect internal values. If a practitioner holds an anti-capitalist ideal that is critical of financial measures, the decision of this scenario might be to reject it outright. At the same time, assessment practitioners value collaboration, and possess a keen sensitivity to ethical tensions. The survey responses indicated a strong interest in acknowledging different perspectives and accommodating multiple values. Rather than reject an assessment, practitioners are interested in revising an assessment. In this instance, the revised assessment might still include economic indicators, but produced and contextualized through the particular knowledge, skills, and values held by assessment practitioners.

Summary

This chapter presented results from a nationwide survey of assessment practitioners. The survey produced data related to the values and the practices that are relevant for decision-making in library assessment. Grounded theory analysis produced a set of codes or themes for values that apply to the practice of library assessment. This chapter starts to complete the response to this book's main question: how can library assessment be practiced ethically? An ethical practice is based on knowing our values, and then applying the right values at the right times. As a result of this survey data and analysis, we are beginning to see what those assessment values are, and how they can be applied in different scenarios. The search for values in LIS, the ethical challenges of library assessment, and new insights into ethical practice: the next chapter will bring these pieces together and present the *Values Classification for Library Assessment*—a set of 10 values relevant for library assessment—along with the *Values-Sensitive Library Assessment Toolkit,* practical toolkit for putting the values into action.

Bibliography

Aguinis, Herman, and Kyle J. Bradley. "Best Practice Recommendations for Designing and Implementing Experimental Vignette Methodology Studies." *Organizational Research Methods* 17, no. 4 (October 1, 2014): 351–71. https://doi.org/10.1177/1094428114547952.

Alexander, Cheryl S., and Henry Jay Becker. "The Use of Vignettes in Survey Research." *Public Opinion Quarterly* 42, no. 1 (January 1, 1978): 93–104. https://doi.org/10.1086/268432.

Eifler, Stefanie, and Knut Petzold. "Validity Aspects of Vignette Experiments: Expected 'What-If' Differences Between Reports of Behavioral Intentions and Actual Behavior." In *Experimental Methods in Survey Research*, 393–416. John Wiley & Sons, Ltd, 2019. https://doi.org/10.1002/9781119083771.ch20.

Evans, Spencer C., Michael C. Roberts, Jared W. Keeley, Jennifer B. Blossom, Christina M. Amaro, Andrea M. Garcia, Cathleen Odar Stough, Kimberly S. Canter, Rebeca Robles, and Geoffrey M. Reed. "Vignette Methodologies for Studying Clinicians' Decision-Making: Validity, Utility, and Application in ICD-11 Field Studies." *International Journal of Clinical and Health Psychology* 15, no. 2 (May 1, 2015): 160–70. https://doi.org/10.1016/j.ijchp.2014.12.001.

Magalhães-Sant'Ana, Manuel, and Alison J. Hanlon. "Straight from the Horse's Mouth: Using Vignettes to Support Student Learning in Veterinary Ethics." *Journal of Veterinary Medical Education* 43, no. 3 (January 1, 2016): 321–30. https://doi.org/10.3138/jvme.0815-137R1.

Peterson, Robert A. *Constructing Effective Questionnaires*. Thousand Oaks, CA: Sage, 2000.

Chapter 6
A Classification of Values and a Practical Toolkit for Ethical Library Assessment

Overview

This chapter introduces the *Values Classification for Library Assessment* and a new toolkit for implementing the values, the *Values-Sensitive Library Assessment Toolkit*. The *Values Classification for Library Assessment* provides an overview of values that are relevant for library assessment, along with reflective prompts for practical action. This new classification of library assessment values is developed from a review of relevant literature, a survey with practitioners, and follow-up interview research that is original to this book project. Ultimately, the *Values Classification* represents one "value model" for assessment in LIS, as described by Rubin: "the professional foundation of LIS is not its knowledge or techniques, but its fundamental values. The significance of LIS lies not in mastery of sources, organizational skills, or technological competence, but in why LIS professionals perform the functions they do."[1] In articulating a value model for library assessment, the *Values Classification* establishes a piece of a foundation for the ethical practice of library assessment.

The toolkit then serves to operationalize the values. The toolkit is called the *Values-Sensitive Library Assessment Toolkit*. The toolkit takes the form of a deck of cards, consisting of 10 values that are relevant to library assessment, along with 3 exercises for working with the

---

1 Rubin, "Library and Information Science: An Evolving Profession," 283–284.

values. The values are based on the survey research presented in the previous chapter. The values and the toolkit together have been further developed and tested through interviews with assessment practitioners working in our field. In this chapter, I discuss the *Values Classification*, the interviews, and the toolkit.

The Values Classification for Library Assessment

The *Values Classification for Library Assessment* presents a set of values relevant to the practice of library assessment. The *Values Classification* includes 10 values. Each entry in the classification includes two parts: a name and description of the value, and reflective prompts for enacting the value in practice. In this section, I first describe the process for developing the final set of values and the accompanying toolkit, and then I present the values.

Developing the Values Classification

The classification was developed from the research data presented in Chapter 5. Following a constructivist grounded theory approach for analyzing the survey data (described in Chapter 1), I generated coded themes for the values and practices described by the survey respondents. From that coding process, I constructed a theory of library assessment values. From the research data, ten values emerged, along with reflective prompts for enacting the values. These values give shape to what an ethical library assessment practice can look like. I then developed the toolkit as a visual and operational expression of the values. First, I developed an initial version of the toolkit. To test the *Values Classification* and the toolkit prototype, I conducted follow-up interviews with library assessment practitioners. The interviews focused on the values and the operational aspects of the toolkit, with the goal of producing a functional tool that accurately reflects the values of library assessment practitioners.

This last step—the interviews—helped inform revisions and improvements to the values and the toolkit. Following the interviews, I made improvements to the values by clarifying some of the definitions and revising the reflective prompts. For the toolkit, I was primarily concerned with two operational questions related to values and assessment decision-making: as presented in the toolkit, 1) do the values work? 2) does the toolkit work? Importantly, the interview population represented a subset of the survey population. In conducting the interviews, I was able to talk with some of the same practitioners who provided responses to the survey. In this way, the interview stage of the research was designed so that I could check back with the research participants to make sure that I had in fact developed values relevant to assessment, that those values were described accurately, and that the toolkit exercises effectively allowed practitioners to interact meaningfully with the values. I presented the toolkit to interview participants, asking them to comment on the accuracy of the values and the functionality of the toolkit in terms of the exercises included. The ultimate goal is a working toolkit that assessment librarians can integrate into their practice. More detail about the interview method is in the research dataset, available via the Qualitative Data Repository with the following title and URL: *Practitioner Perspectives on the Values and Ethics of Library Assessment*, https://doi.org/10.5064/F6ORSLQF.

In the subsections below, I enumerate the values, including their corresponding descriptions and prompts. I also include a brief discussion of this value, drawing on the insights from the practitioner interviews. In instances where I cite directly from the research data, I include a 3-digit alphanumeric code that corresponds to the Interview Participant code in the interview data.

Alignment

Description

- Connecting assessment work to existing plans or statements, including organizational mission statements, strategic priorities, or professional values.

Reflective Prompts

- How can shared values help bring together collaborators and stakeholders?
- How can an assessment project advance strategic priorities of the library, or how does the project enact relevant values?

Discussion

Many interview participants spoke to the importance of *alignment*—connecting assessment activity to library strategic planning and priorities. Participants indicated that the priorities of their library organization took precedence over the statements of professional societies, other campus units, and the university. One participant's feedback illustrates this point: "This is my starting point. I always align with library goals and mission. This could be mentioned more explicitly" (IP6).

Care

Description

- Maximizing well-being, while minimizing harm.

Reflective Prompts

- How would you describe your responsibility to the different stakeholders of the assessment, especially the participants? How will you know that you've fulfilled your responsibility?
- How does the assessment account for the well-being of participants and collaborators?
- What kind of harms could result from this work? How could those harms be mitigated?

Discussion

The idea of well-being for assessment participants was identified as a key value for interview participants. In addition to the aspect of well-being, participants also focused on harm as an important complementary aspect of care. Participants spoke of maximizing well-being while minimizing harm. The reflective prompts for this value therefore focus on the well-being and harm considerations of individual participants and collaborators in an assessment. I have also included an additional reflective prompt to underscore the feminist ethic of care (discussed in Chapter 5) that understands care to be an interconnectivity, where people and communities are linked together through shared responsibilities.

The *care* value also integrates aspects of human-centeredness. From the survey, my data analysis produced a code for a *human-centered* value, encompassing user experience design, human-centered design, usability, and accessibility. But through the interviews, assessment practitioners told me that—while human-centeredness was related to assessment—it wasn't necessarily a central part of an assessment practice, and that it didn't rise to the importance of a stand-alone value. According to interview participants, human-centered design applications could appear within a larger assessment practice, but that UX and human-centered design are practice areas unto themselves—practice areas that include domain-specific knowledge and skills that assessment practitioners may not possess. Human-centered aspects such as user experience, usability, and accessibility are typically located in other departments or programs within the library. For interview participants, components such as usability and accessibility are more relevant to assessment not as values, but rather as practical outcomes that result from the application of other values, such as *care*. In fact, multiple participants connected human-centered approaches with the value of *care* for library users. In this way, library assessment and human-centered design share a key similarity: carefully considering the needs and desires of participants and stakeholders. As one participant expressed: "Keeping participants at the center of the research is important" (IP8). In response to the interviewer data, the *care* value incorporates a people-oriented aspect of the human-centered design tradition.

Collaboration

Description

- Building and sustaining mutually beneficial relationships.

Reflective Prompts

- How does the project involve collaborators and partnerships?
- How does your approach to collaboration and relationship-building support mutual benefit and trust among stakeholders? Stakeholders can include students, campus collaborators, community members, or other assessment participants.

Discussion

Participants indicated that *collaboration* was one of the most relevant values to their practice, and also one of the most complex and contextual. A key aspect of this value is who may be involved in the collaboration, such as students or community members. From there, it's important to determine the particular needs of the collaborators to ensure a successful partnership. Through the interviews, practitioners emphasized the importance of mutually-beneficial relationships: assessment collaborations should be more than the assessment librarian talking to students. To ensure mutual benefit, assessment procedures and outcomes can be co-determined with participants and collaborators. This aspect of collaboration reflects the practice of community co-determination, identified as an ethical assessment characteristic in Chapter 4. Such deep collaborations are not typical, however, as one participant remarked: "I've never seen a fully collaborative assessment... usually the people that are doing the assessing need something, and it's been extracted from the people being assessed" (IP10). To help support meaningful collaborations, interview participants encouraged an attunement to power relationships so that assessments don't always follow historical paths of one-way data extraction. In this way, the *collaboration* value has a strong connection with the *positionality* value.

Communication

Description

- "Closing the loop" of assessment by communicating an assessment and its results to relevant audiences.

Reflective Prompts

- How will project results be shared out to others, such as administrators, collaborators, and the wider professional community?
- Are you communicating the assessment in a way that your different audiences can each understand?
- What story are you telling with the data? What is the most readily-available reading of the assessment, or the most dominant narrative driving interpretation? What other readings are available?
- Would the project report benefit from including a fuller landscape of measures, activities, and impacts, including a risk/benefit analysis, social impacts, or any other contextual factor that helps explain or situate the assessment?

Discussion

Communication was an important value for the interview participants. Participants agreed that talking about assessment and sharing the work of assessment is highly relevant to their practice. Practitioners distilled the main point of this value to be about communicating an assessment and its results to relevant audiences. Participants wanted to know—who are we communicating to, what are we communicating, and how are we communicating it? For the interview participants, *communication* is ultimately about "closing the loop" of assessment, which involves sharing results back to participants and out to other stakeholders. As one participant summarized: "Don't do research without a plan to communicate your research" (IP8).

Imagining otherwise

Description

- Imagining and embracing different approaches to assessment, and ensuring that results support change.

Reflective Prompts

- How will the assessment project generate improvement or change? Who is responsible for leading that change, and who benefits from that change?
- Can the assessment project be made stronger by introducing alternative or complementary methods?
- If a third-party vendor is involved, can you work with the vendor for terms more reflective of library values, or can you change vendors?

Discussion

Imagining otherwise was a value that resonated with participants, who welcomed this value as a prompt for considering the methods employed in their assessment practice and the capacity for their assessment results to act as a vehicle for change. One participant interpreted this value as: "I'm always questioning, 'why do we do things this way?'…That undergird[s] everything I do in the assessment, because my ultimate mental end game is that these assessments are going to change things" (IP6). The connection between assessment and change was very strong, as participants expressed a clear desire that their assessment work will be applied toward improvement or change in their library.

Conversations around this value were helpful for illuminating the kinds of negotiation that assessment practitioners do in support of imagining other futures. With respect to third-party vendors, some participants noted that their practice doesn't typically involve third party negotiation; on the other hand, other participants viewed third-party negotiation as integral, and remarked that practitioners should regularly challenge third-party vendors to adhere to library values. But participants spoke mainly to negotiation happening with their direct collaborators and other stakeholders such as library administration. Here, the subject of negotiation focused on deciding the methods and interpreting the results of an assessment. Participants discussed a nuanced and multi-perspective approach to the selection of method, as expressed by one participant: "I always like to break down the quantitative/qualitative divide" (IP8). Rather than reinforcing this divide and putting methods into conflict with each other, this participant and others spoke to finding a balance of methods and embracing new forms of assessment. The act of imagination is thus expressed as imagining different approaches into and throughout the assessment lifecycle. The narrative component of this card operates in support of this intended change. Here, participants spoke of framing the assessment data and analysis through narrative storytelling in such a way as to guide interpretation and application of assessment results.

Justice

Description

- Diversity, inclusion, equity, and allyship.

Reflective Prompts

- Do stakeholders and participants have a voice in determining research questions, methods, interpretation of data, and the application of results?
- Does the project result in social or material benefits for participants and collaborators?
- How does the project engage with structural social inequalities?
- Does the project support social justice outcomes?

Discussion

Every participant considered *justice* to be a relevant value to their practice. Through the interviews, participants marked out an important categorical distinction between *justice* and *care*: *care* is a value concerned with individuals, and *justice* is concerned with groups. This points to an important relationship between these two values and the concepts that they each represent. Crucially, participants spoke of a power element specific to values in assessment, namely: what power do assessment practitioners have to enact values? When confronting structural or systemic issues, how can an assessment practitioner or program meaningfully confront such large issues? In this way, the *justice* value intersects with the *positionality* value.

Positionality

Description

- Acknowledging perspectives, positions, and power.

Reflective Prompts

- Is the project guided or supported by explicit values? Does the project assess the achievement of those values?
- In the context of this assessment, over whom do you have power? Who has power over you? How do those power dynamics affect your ability to articulate and enact values?
- Based on your relative positions, what assumptions are you and others bringing to the project?
- Does the assessment project include dedicated time for self-reflection?

Discussion

Positionality was viewed as a relevant value by participants. Participants recognized the function of this value as foundation-setting for establishing other values, with one participant describing positionality as "implicit" or as a "precursor" to other values (IP10). Another participant connected this value to the ongoing act of positioning and re-positioning oneself: "This is a really crucial one...a good reminder for people to constantly remind themselves of" (IP12).

Two main points emerged through the interviews. First, practitioners viewed issues of power as directly connected to those of positionality, especially through the practice of marking the relative power of different stakeholders involved in the assessment. The following excerpts capture this point:

- "It's really hard to get a group of people, even within the same profession—who ostensibly share professional values—to talk about their own values or their own perspectives and the idea of positionality. How much relative power do the various members of a group have? That's going to change the conversations about how they might articulate their values" (IP3).

- "Positionality isn't about whether or not you're a good or bad person, it's being where you are in the system, so that you can move the system" (IP7).

- "Understanding your position as a researcher relative to what you're researching" (IP8).

Beyond relative power dynamics, participants also spoke of understanding the different assumptions that may be generated from relative positions. As expressed by one participant: "I feel like our positionality is based on what assumptions we're bringing to the project, and making sure that those are explicit and not just unsaid is an important part of positionality" (IP2).

Stewardship

Description

- Ensuring that an assessment reflects organizational capacities—including staffing models, budgetary considerations, and data management and retention.

Reflective Prompts

- Does the project account for longer-term impacts in budget, staffing needs, and community relationship-building?
- If there are resource constraints, how can the project be scoped so that the assessment is completable?
- What policies or practices govern the collection, retention, usage, and sharing of assessment-related data?

Discussion

The *stewardship* value is focused on resource sustainability and management, and it generated extensive discussion with interview participants. This value is seen as a necessary point of reference for decision-making in assessment. Thinking pragmatically, practitioners demonstrated a carefully considered approach to the *stewardship* value in a way that acknowledged the constraints that it exerts on the practice of assessment. But ultimately, at the heart of the *stewardship* value is the idea of professional responsibility for resource sustainability. In terms of resources constraints, one participant shared: "This resonates with me. This is my lived experience…But it's something that I'm reluctantly stuck with having to deal with. And I think that's good. And it's good to address these things" (IP12). The pressure of limited resources is essential to consider when conducting assessment, as expressed by other participants:

- "Ahh—the realism…you can have the best intentions and design in the world, but if you don't have the people, the money, other resources to make it happen, then don't back yourself into a corner and end up doing it poorly as a result" (IP9).
- "Got to make sure you can do the thing you want to do" (IP8).
- "We need to be realistic about resources" (IP2).

These comments tell us that practitioners see the consideration of available resources as crucial for assessment. But in order to operate as a guiding principle, the orientation toward this concept needs to be positioned so that the concept is expressed as an outcome to be achieved or as a value to be enacted, rather than as a limitation that must be accounted for. With a view toward possibility, participants in the interviews spoke to a practice of creatively designing assessments that responsibly apply and manage resources:

- "If there's a way to look at it a little bit more possibly, than just getting the job done. The more important question is, 'how can we bring this so that it's completable?…How do we frame this or scale this project, so that it's completable?'" (IP5).
- "What's possible, given the right resources?" (IP3).
- "This part about being a good data steward…is something that needs to be addressed" (IP1)

For interview participants, the *stewardship* value is about institutional support and capacity, and also about an ethical and sustainable assessment practice. Interview participants took this value very seriously, viewing it as essential to the decision-making in their practice. Two participants spoke directly to the ethical aspects of resource consideration:

- "It is unethical to propose a bunch of stuff and not be able to actually see it through" (IP11).
- "If we're collecting this data, we have an ethical obligation to act on it" (IP12).

The interview participants offered a carefully framed understanding of resources in the context of assessment: instead of a constraining element focused on the limitation of resources, practitioners see themselves as responsible stewards of resources, working to ensure that an assessment is first possible and then sustainable, and that assessment data will be managed according to professional standards.

Transparency

Description

- Clear communication to participants about how data is collected, analyzed, and applied, with choices for participation.

Reflective Prompts

- Does your assessment practice include documentation, including process, result, application, and decision-making?
- How will project documentation and results be shared back with participants?
- Are participants able to opt in or out, and are they able to provide informed consent?

Discussion

Participants indicated that *transparency* is a relevant value for their assessment practice. Participants recognized that *transparency* is important for building and maintaining trust among stakeholders and collaborators. Practitioners noted a key question for this value—who is included as a stakeholder for transparency? Most participants answered that question by focusing on the population being assessed. Participants underscored the key aspects of achieving *transparency*: sharing procedural details with participants, securing informed consent, and sharing results of the assessment back with the study population. The *transparency* value operates as a pair with the *communication* value: the two values can function together to capture a full range of potential audiences or populations related to communication and transparency. The *communication* value specifically references administrators, collaborators, and the professional community, while *transparency* references participants in assessment.

Validity

Description

- Ensuring that an assessment is valid, especially focusing on a right fit between research question and research method.

Reflective Prompts

- Is there a strong match among the research question, the assessment method, the assessment population or service, and the intended result?
- Can the research question be answered by the method(s) that you are applying? Could a different method answer the question in a better way?

Discussion

Validity is an especially relevant value for library assessment. As a specialty within LIS that so tightly integrates research as a part of our practice, *validity* is perhaps the most defining value for library assessment. For the interview participants, *validity* means selecting the right method for an assessment project so that the right outcome can be achieved. One participant captured this: "I think of validity as, 'Am I measuring the thing I'm intending to measure?'" (IP8). Similarly, another participant described this value: "To me, validity is if the method and your answers to your questions really relate to what you want to know" (IP1). Along these lines, the *validity* value generated responses that focused on method selection, with related comments involving mixed-methods and triangulation as a way to support valid results. For example, one participant said of *validity*: "This is something I think about…The template I'm using [for my assessments] is built using multiple methods of assessment, and then combining the findings for a built-in triangulation" (IP6).

In terms of method selection, the *validity* value finds consonance with the *imagining otherwise* value. When faced with an assessment project that didn't appear to be valid (as with the case of Scenario 3 from the survey, which involved learning analytics and student success), interview participants showed less interest in rejecting the assessment, and more interest in revising the assessment. One participant related that there has not been a "single time" when an assessment has been rejected, rather, "A lot more conversations are around, 'Well, what if we tweak this? Make sure we talk to this participant group? Look at this methodology instead? Come at it from a different angle?'" (IP9). Another participant responded similarly: "My initial response wouldn't be to necessarily say a rejection. It would be, 'Okay, here's what we did wrong. Here's why this isn't as helpful to us as it could be. What can we either salvage or what can we redo? How can we rethink this project?...How do we know what this isn't telling us? And how can we get there?'" (IP5). For the interview participants, achieving *validity* is not about rejecting an assessment as invalid, but rather working to find the right assessment method for the research question so that a valid and meaningful assessment can be completed.

The Toolkit

The *Values-Sensitive Library Assessment Toolkit* is available at the following URL: **doi.org/10.17605/OSF.IO/ZS5C8**

Overview

We now have a class of values specific to the practice of library assessment. How then can these values be operationalized for actual practice? We now turn to the next major outcome of this research project—the *Values-Sensitive Library Assessment Toolkit*. To develop the toolkit, I drew inspiration from the tradition of participatory design, with its focus on creativity, tools and techniques, and collaborative meaning-making. First, let's define the goals of this toolkit.

Toolkit Goals

The toolkit is designed to generate thought and action in support of valued-based decision-making in the practice of library assessment. As a result of using the toolkit, practitioners will be able to accomplish the following:

1. Articulate the values that matter to an assessment practice.

2. Prioritize different values for different contexts, and understand how values can complement or conflict with each other.

3. Identify and remove barriers to implementing values; identify and amplify supporting factors for implementing values.

These outcomes are crafted in response to key questions related to values-based assessment, including:

1. Which values are relevant for a given assessment project?
2. Once values have been identified, how are those values prioritized?
3. With the relevant values having been identified, how can those values be put into practice?

The basic goal of the toolkit is to reveal relevant values and priorities for different assessment projects, and to aid practitioners in understanding how those values can be applied in practice. Let's look closer at how we can design a tool to accomplish these goals.

Designing the Toolkit

As the practical contribution of this book, the toolkit functions to operationalize the *Values Classification*. Through its visual and structural design and its instructional aspects, the toolkit provides approaches for achieving an ethical practice. The toolkit takes the shape of a card deck. The toolkit is composed of 15 cards: 1 instruction card, 10 cards that feature the values and reflective prompts from the *Values Classification*, 1 blank value card for expanding the set, and 3 exercise cards for working with the values. The toolkit aims to transform the *Values Classification* into a usable tool for assessment professionals. In the sections below, I detail the development process of the toolkit.

Relevant Design Traditions

The main question of this book is: "How can library assessment be practiced ethically?" As a researcher-practitioner, my approach to this question involves both research inquiries and practical considerations, with a strong focus on the *how* of the question. Through this book project, I aim to produce a research contribution that adds to the field's understanding of this topic, while also developing a real product that can be used by everyday practitioners. As a contribution to the theory of library assessment, this book presents new research related to ethics and values, culminating in the *Values Classification for Library Assessment*. And as a contribution to the practice of library assessment, this book presents a new tool for identifying and applying values, the *Values-Sensitive Library Assessment Toolkit*, a card deck that features values relevant for library assessment. These two parts operate together—the deck of cards is a way to give form and function to the research insights.

There are certain justifications for moving in this direction. From the survey data, it was evident that many different values could be in play at different times, and that not every value was relevant in every situation. Yet it was also evident that for many practitioners, a known set of values was available from which to choose, such as from a local values statement or a professional ethical code. In this way, values contain a balance of stability and flexibility. Stability may be found in a pre-defined set of values. This pre-defined set can form a reliable ethical foundation of values. From there, flexibility is achieved in that the practitioner can choose which values to apply for a given situation. This key characteristic—a mix of stability and flexibility—is expressed in the structural design of the toolkit as a card deck. Each card in the deck contains a value. The deck is a controlled set of values, and thereby establishes a sense of stability. At the same time, the cards may be shuffled and selected in different ways. A given card can be selected from the deck as relevant for a given assessment project, affording a degree of flexibility. A card deck offers affordances that suit both stability and flexibility. Finally, a card deck can be "played" individually or in small groups or teams. This also reflects the real-world decision-making of the survey participants, as practitioners may work alone to identify personal values, or more often collaborate with others to identify shared values.

The main feature of the card set is the enumeration of values, with the values each appearing on their own card. The card deck additionally includes three exercises to guide practitioners through a process of working with the value cards. When the exercises are completed in sequence, the final result of the toolkit is a ranked set of values relevant for a given assessment project. These exercises draw from the tradition of participatory design and co-design, whereby structured activities prompt creative thinking and collaborative work in group settings. Participatory design offers a rich disciplinary tradition of creative collaboration, with a history of applying tools and techniques—such as card deck with exercises—to generate new ideas.[2] And participa-

---

2 Kensing and Greenbaum, "Heritage: Having a Say"; Robertson and Simonsen, "Participatory Design: An Introduction."

tory design explicitly seeks to name and enact values in its practice. Through the design process, practitioners are prompted to attune themselves to values, and then to consider which values are applied in different situations to produce mutually-beneficial outcomes for professionals and participants. For this reason, applying participatory design at this stage is especially apt, as we are trying to activate the new assessment values in actual practice, to support an ethical practice that produces mutually-beneficial outcomes.

Related to participatory design is "research through design."[3] This paradigm is also useful in the context of this book. The toolkit prompts practitioners to research, in a sense, their own values vis-à-vis their own contexts. By "playing cards," a process of "research-through-design" is applied, whereby the practitioner researches their own ethical context and designs their own set of ranked values as appropriate to their particular context. Clarke advances a research-through-design approach as viable for LIS practice and suitable for LIS professional values, specifically highlighting how a design artifact can be applied to solve a problem in a specific library context.[4] To translate Clarke's formulation for this book: the toolkit is a design artifact that is being applied to solve the problem of professional values and ethical decision-making in the context of academic library assessment.

In the wider design world, a deck of cards as a design tool has numerous parallels.[5] In the context of LIS values, an example of a card deck used for creative investigation is the *Envisioning Cards*.[6] The Envisioning Cards are designed to evoke consideration and discussion about ethical technology development. Each card in the deck presents a different point of concern for long-term technology design and development. The values are organized into five suits: Stakeholders, Time, Values, Pervasiveness, and Multi-lifespan. *The Library Workers' Field Guide to Designing and Discovering Restorative Environments* is another example of participatory design used in LIS.[7] The field guide

---

3   Gaver, "What Should We Expect from Research through Design?"; Godin and Zahedi, "Aspects of Research through Design"; Isley and Rider, "Research-Through-Design."

4   Clarke, "How We Done It Good."

5   Hazenberg, *75 Tools for Creative Thinking*; Pascale, "Intùiti Creative Cards"; Urquhart and Craigon, "The Moral-IT Deck"; Climer, "Climer Cards."

6   Friedman et al., "Envisioning Cards."

7   Tench, "The Library Workers' Field Guide to Designing and Discovering Restorative Environments."

is a socially-engaged tool for improving the working conditions of library staff. The field guide provides a series of card-based activities that support creative, values-driven outcomes. As discussed in Chapter 3, co-design and participatory design as examples of ethical assessment practice. The toolkit then builds on findings from the literature. In looking back across the chapters, we can see continuity from the literature analysis that began in Chapter 2 through to the research output that concludes here in Chapter 6. With the toolkit, I am transforming the research findings into a useful design tool.

Structuring the card deck

This first card—numbered with a zero—outlines the step-by-step process for achieving an ethical assessment practice: identify the values that matter, then—for a given situation—prioritize the most relevant values and develop approaches for implementing the values within the context of that particular situation. The next 12 cards feature the 11 named values plus a blank card for expanding the set. The final 3 cards feature the exercises. The cards are accessed two ways, physically and digitally. The toolkit can function as a physical object, with the intention of interacting with the cards in physical space. The toolkit may also function as a digital object, with interaction taking place in a virtual space. In this way, the toolkit is designed with a view toward accessibility. The toolkit is available as a printable document, and can also be made available for digital access. Finally, as minor a visual note, to indicate that the instruction card and the exercise cards are a different category from the value cards, I have inverted the foreground and background colors so that the instruction cards and the exercise cards feature a dark-color background, while the value cards feature a light-color background.

Giving the Cards a Visual Layout

The toolkit takes the shape of a card set that contains values relevant for library assessment. To impart a sense of creativity while expressing the serious content of the cards, I created a visual layout for each card that deploys a balance of graphics, colors, and text. Figure 6.1 shows the layout of the value cards.

Figure 6.1 shows one complete value card, with the layout on the left representing the front of the card and the layout on the right representing the back of the card.

A Classification of Values and a Practical Toolkit for Ethical Library Assessment

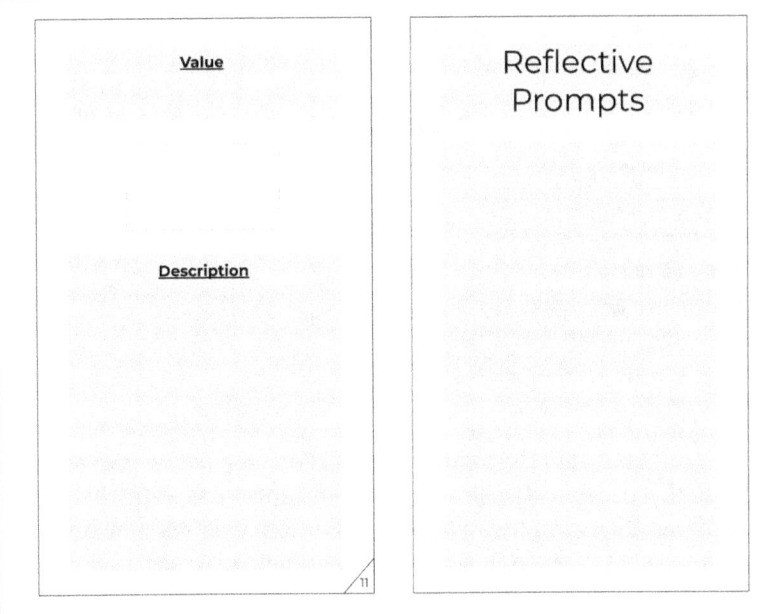

Figure 6.1 Visual Layout of the Value Card

Naming the Toolkit and Providing Instructions

The toolkit is given a name: the *Values-Sensitive Library Assessment Toolkit*. This title indicates that the toolkit is focused on library assessment values, with a process for centering those values in the practice of assessment. Cards are assembled and numbered into an order aimed at facilitating a first-time way through the cards. The first card, numbered with a zero, contains a set of instructions for the toolkit, explaining the background and purpose for the tool along with its constitutive parts and guidelines for use. Cards 1–10 provide the 10 values in alphabetical order. Card 11 is a blank value card for expansion of the values. Cards 12–14 present the exercises. Next, let's turn to the exercise cards.

The Toolkit Exercises

To provide a structure and a guide for working with the cards, I adapted three exercises from the design world, each to serve a different purpose. Table 6.1 provides an overview of the exercise included in the toolkit along with their respective antecedents.

Exercise Name	Purpose	Source Material
Connect Two	To define and interrelate values	"Show Me Your Values"[1]
Must-Haves	To prioritize values	"MoSCoW"[2]
Anchors and Sails	To implement values	"Speedboat"[3]

Table 6.1 Toolkit Exercises

1 Gray, Brown, and Macanufo, Gamestorming: A Playbook for Innovators, Rulebreakers, and Changemakers.
2 Digital Society School, Amsterdam University, "MoSCoW."
3 Hohmann, Innovation Games.

These exercises operate together. First, *Connect Two* works as a defining activity, where the practitioner first interacts with the values and creates their own meaning and definition. This initial exercise allows the practitioner to find their relevant values, make connections among the values, and create definitions that suit their local setting. Once the practitioner has established an understanding of the values, *Must-Haves* works as a sorting exercise, prompting the practitioner to consider a specific assessment project and prioritize the values in the context of that assessment. Finally, with the values having been prioritized, *Anchors and Sails* applies the metaphor of a boat to generate dialogue around the constraints and opportunities in implementing values. The exercises are intended to be completed either individually or in groups. Each exercise can be completed on its own, or the exercises can be sequenced together to form a cycle of values-sensitive library assessment: understanding, prioritizing, and implementing values.

Exercise Demonstration: Anchors and Sails

As an example of an exercise is use, I will briefly discuss the Anchors and Sails activity that was completed during the interviews. In the Anchors and Sails exercise, participants apply the metaphor of a boat to discuss constraints and opportunities in implementing values. Of the four participants to complete this exercise, all indicated that the goal of this card was achieved through the instruction. Figure 6.2 shows a representation of one participant's visual elicitation produced through this exercise (IP11).

In this example, the participant chose the value card for *care*. The Anchors on the boat—the constraints in implementing the value—are

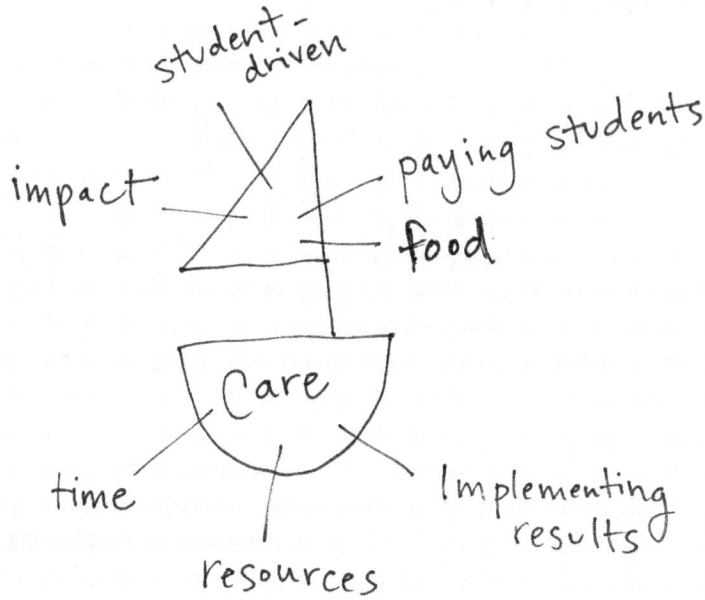

Figure 6.2 Anchors and Sails Exercise for the Care Value

time, resources, and implementing results. The sails—the supporting factors for the value—are impact, student-driven culture, and funds available to pay and to provide food for student participants. Figure 6.2 demonstrates how a simple drawing can elicit ideas and insights into the subject of inquiry. Of this exercise, one participant said, "It did do the piece of identifying ways that the project does and does not support the value, or things to be aware of, that—if we're saying this is really important—things to be aware of that we need to actually make sure that we're addressing, or this is not going to be achieved" (IP11). The exercises in the toolkit can be completed individually or in groups to spark new ideas and provide clarity about understanding relevant values (Connect Two), prioritizing values (Must-Haves), and implementing values in practice (Anchors and Sails).

The *Values-Sensitive Library Assessment Toolkit* is available at the following URL: **doi.org/10.17605/OSF.IO/ZS5C8**

The Toolkit in Use: Discussion

The aim of the toolkit is to center values in library assessment, in support of an ethical practice. During this interview stage of the research, I tested the toolkit with practitioners to see if the toolkit worked as intended. Through the interviews, I saw that the toolkit can work to generate thought and discussion regarding values, and that the exercises achieve their goal of aiding practitioners in working with values. This testing portion of the interviews also produced useful insight into the functionality of the toolkit. I discuss these insights in the subsections below: interrelation among values, the potential use-cases for the toolkit, and the limitations and constraints of the toolkit.

Interconnectivity of Values

Participants in the interview were keen to make connections among values. Even though the toolkit gives each value its own card, participants readily noted consonance and interrelation among the values. Participants paired cards, discussing how some values were complementary or conflicting. The interconnectivity of values reinforces an insight discussed in Chapter 5—that ethics are complex, multifaceted, and highly contextual. Multiple values are in play for any given situation, and the meaning of those values can shift across different situations and different value configurations. In the sections below, I discuss the value connections that produced the most dialogue in the interviews.

Imagining Otherwise, Validity, and Stewardship

These three values share a concern with the possibilities available to the practitioner. Each value applies a distinct lens to this concern. *Imagining otherwise* is about opening possibility in terms of the approach to assessment, and in interpreting the results of assessment. *Imagining otherwise* is about creativity in assessment. *Validity* seeks to ensure that the research question and the research method are in tune with one another. *Validity* is about the possibilities available to the practitioner for designing a valid study. *Stewardship* introduces a resource perspective and focuses on scope and sustainability in the context of organizational capacity. *Imagining otherwise* asks, "What is possible?" *Validity* asks, "Does it work?" And *stewardship* asks, "What are the available resources?" Altogether, the values ask, "What's possible for this assessment, does it work as a valid study, and is it achievable given the resources?" Participants in the interviews noted that these values take on different valences when configured together as a group of three, or in pairs. *Imagining otherwise* on its own might lead to big sky thinking, which could be desirable in some situations. But then *validity* provides a check to ensure that the creativity of *imagining otherwise* is grounded in professional standards of assessment. Likewise, *stewardship* provides its own grounding element to *imagining otherwise,* in that it can guide thinking within the bounds of organizational capacities.

Care and Justice

These two values demonstrate an interplay between individual and group aspects related to social issues. *Care* focuses on maximizing well-being and minimizing harm for individual participants in an assessment, while *justice* focuses on larger-scale, structural social inequalities. Interview participants recognized that these two aspects are important to account for when conducting assessment, and together they provide a fuller view of potential social benefits or harms of assessment.

Positionality and Alignment

Positionality and *alignment* both deal directly with values, though their respective orientations are inverted. *Positionality* prompts the practitioner to look inward so as to identify relevant personal values, and *alignment* prompts the practitioner to look outward so as to identify relevant institutional or professional values. Interview participants viewed these two cards functioning together as a complementary pair for identifying all possible values relevant to an assessment.

Transparency and Communication

Transparency and *Communication* function together to demonstrate the full scope of assessment communication. These values share similarities in seeking to talk with others about assessment, but they each provide finer points that help give more precise shape and direction this activity. *Transparency* focuses on "sharing back" the process and results of assessment with participants of the assessment. That alone was identified as a key value. Separate but related is *communication*, which focuses on "sharing out" the results and the impact of the assessment with other stakeholders such as administrators, collaborators, and the wider professional community.

Use-cases of the Toolkit

Participants articulated three potential use-cases for the toolkit: as a planning tool when designing a new assessment, as an evaluation tool when in the middle of an assessment or when looking back on a completed assessment, and as a teaching tool when educating about the practice of assessment. The final question of the interview produced data that illuminated these potential applications of the toolkit. I concluded each interview by asking participants to complete the following sentence: "After practicing with this toolkit, I will be able to..."

To this question, one participant responded: "I will be able to articulate the values that are involved in the decisions I make around assessment and how to conduct assessment, and what assessment I want to do. I thought that was really helpful...I hadn't thought about [values] in such a clear term. There's something about being able to see them that really is helpful" (IP11). Along these lines, another participant remarked, "I will be able to articulate my own values related to library assessment and apply them to my work more consciously" (IP1). The structure of the toolkit was notable to another participant, who said, "I will be able to approach planning a project more intentionally. I don't think there's anything in the toolkit that I've never thought about before, but having it in a structured way as you're going through it—helps make sure things don't get overlooked—is extremely valuable" (IP9).

A team-building and organizational development aspect was also expressed by the participants, as illustrated in this response: "I will be able to engage library administration in assessment efforts in a more meaningful way. I would like to do this with [our leadership group]. I think that would be really illuminating because I have a really solid handle on what my values as they relate to assessment are, but I actually don't for those folks. That would be crucial. I think this might be a good tool to get at that" (IP12). Another participant shared: "I will be able to initiate and enjoy discussions with my colleagues about assessment values, and I will be able to use the toolkit to plan future assessment work" (IP2). Similarly, another participant said of the toolkit: "Over time, if a group were to use the toolkit often, to keep returning to it, it could really have the potential to build a shared vocabulary...I have a relatively young team in our unit, and we've been talking about assessment and people's desire to learn more about assessment. I could see something like this being really useful" (IP3). On the topic of the toolkit as a teaching resource, another participant remarked, "Being able to clarify and classify the values of a particular project is something I'd be able to do, which I think is very useful. And also to be able to take this tool to people with less research design experience, and use it as a teaching tool. I think that's also quite useful" (IP8).

This feedback is evidence that the toolkit and its underlying research data reflects relevant values that can be made useful for practitioners. The use cases offered by participants demonstrate the potential applications of the toolkit, and indicate the toolkit is capable of achieving its goal of aiding an ethical assessment practice.

Limitations of the Toolkit

The interviews also revealed constraints and limitations. In the interviews, I also asked participants to complete the following sentence: "After practicing with this toolkit, I still felt that I needed…" Responses to this question in particular helped illuminate the boundaries of the toolkit's applicability. Three main areas of constraint emerged: internal communication and collaboration, practitioner empowerment, and ethical resolution.

Internal Communication and Collaboration

Reflecting the collaborative nature of assessment, the reach and impact of the toolkit will be enhanced when multiple practitioners or stakeholders are involved in the work of articulating and applying values. Participants discussed the many stakeholder interests connected to assessment, and the collaborative relationships on which assessment depends. An organizational culture of trust and communication may be a necessary precondition for the toolkit. Without collaborative relationships, the operation of the toolkit will be constrained. As participants recognized the potential for the toolkit to bring stakeholders together around shared values, there was a recognition that barriers can stand in the way in terms of interpersonal dynamics or organizational culture that prevent those stakeholders from communicating and collaborating. The toolkit may not operate well in an environment that is not supportive of discussion, reflection, and team building. The toolkit assumes that the practitioner and their organization have a built-in motivation to investigate values, enact values, and achieve an ethical practice from this perspective of applied values and practical ethics. As one participant said of using the toolkit: "A lot of these prompts [in the toolkit] are going to be things that you need to discuss with stakeholders...The development of those conversations is another kind of skill set that needs to be acknowledged...Conversations can be tough, especially if you're telling someone, 'Hey, I need you to challenge your beliefs or potential biases you might have.' They might not be as open to doing that. The art of giving and receiving feedback can be difficult...this is something the toolkit doesn't necessarily address" (IP4). This comment is crucial in understanding the functions and the constraints of the toolkit. The toolkit is designed to elicit dialogue about values. And the toolkit, via the exercises, provides a structure for facilitating that dialogue. But the toolkit assumes that dialogue is possible in the first place. The toolkit is not equipped to solve culture issues or interpersonal tensions within the workplace. Some practitioners may find themselves in a library setting where there is resistance to ethical reflection and ethical action. Such a setting will limit the applicability of the toolkit.

Practitioner Empowerment

This leads to a related limitation that was revealed in conversation with interview participants. The toolkit assumes that a practitioner has the power within their organization to enact values. But participants pointed out that this is not granted. There may be circumstances where values are imposed upon a project or a practitioner, or where a practitioner is not able to introduce values into an assessment environment. Observed one participant: "We have more or less power, depending on who is in relationship to whom. Librarians aren't the most powerful individuals. We have a lot of power over our users bureaucratically, but we're not able to just do whatever we want" (IP3). This factor of empowerment warrants special attention, as it directly affects the practitioner and their ability to practice ethical assessment. One participant captured this with the following: "A lot of assessment librarians...don't feel empowered to say, 'This isn't going to work...this isn't going to meet the values that we want to get to'" (IP5). The concept of power and empowerment is inherent to the functionality of the toolkit, in that the assessment practitioner needs to be able to activate a value in practice. The toolkit may be able to help foster such an environment, but a degree of openness to it would have to exist in the first place. A workplace that values neutrality, for instance, may present barriers to the toolkit. As one participant asserted: "[The toolkit] itself can't be a neutral tool" (IP7). This participant spoke to the neutralizing effect of neutrality as value: that the toolkit would be rendered ineffective if collaborators—especially those with greater power or authority—were to assert neutrality over any or all of the other values. Indeed, the toolkit is designed to counteract neutrality, and to provide an approach for taking a stand by articulating values. But it is not a given that the practitioner has the power to draw a principled line.

Resolving Dilemmas

The final limitation surfaced in the interviews involves the toolkit's ability to resolve ethical dilemmas. As designed, the cards don't seek to provide answers on their own. The values in the toolkit are not positioned as the authoritative set of values for library assessment, nor do the descriptions of those values seek to be comprehensive or definitive. Rather, the toolkit serves to orient practitioners toward values, and to model for practitioners one possible universe of values that can be relevant for their work. The toolkit then prompts the participants to find the definitions and resolutions that are suitable for their own local context. One participant discerned this aspect of the toolkit, saying, "the discussion and the reflection is part of the point. You may understand some of these values differently, but part of that discussion is what we're trying to do with this toolkit" (IP8). The toolkit doesn't contain resolutions to ethical dilemmas, but the toolkit will help enhance a practitioner's sensitivity to dilemmas, which the practitioner then resolves based on the values that are relevant in that particular situation, as identified by working with the toolkit.

The toolkit's best purpose is in providing a structure to ask the right questions. Chapter 2 and Chapter 3 of this book set the groundwork for the toolkit, by applying a lens of practical ethics to LIS practice and posing the question, "What is the right thing to do?" The toolkit orients the practitioner toward this question and provides a direction for their ethical inquiry. But the real-life resolutions are far from clear or straight-forward. One participant described this challenge when discussing the *care* value: "These are really big, complicated, thorny issues around this value...It's one thing to identify these issues, and a whole other thing to actually solve them" (IP11). Values-in-conflict are difficult to resolve, but discerning those values and those conflicts is an essential first condition toward resolution. If the toolkit prompts assessment practitioners to consider values in their practice, to confront thorny issues related to implementing those values, and to ask the question, "what is the right thing to do?"—then it will have been successful.

Summary

This chapter presented the *Values Classification for Library Assessment* and the accompanying *Values-Sensitive Toolkit for Library Assessment*. The classification is rooted in the grounded theory approach of coding and model-making as derived from research data. The classification shows a universe of values relevant to library assessment, along with reflective prompts for enacting the values. The toolkit then serves as an operational aid to support an ethical practice of values-based assessment. The toolkit is designed to guide the practitioner in naming the values that are relevant to their practice, building an understanding of those values, prioritizing the values, and ultimately putting the values into practice. More broadly, the toolkit can be considered as a decision-making guide when planning, conducting, or evaluating an assessment program or project. The toolkit is flexible and extendible according to contextual factors and local conditions. Together, the *Values Classification* and the toolkit represent an answer to the book's main question: "How can library assessment be practiced ethically?" In the next chapter, I offer concluding thoughts and future directions for this work.

Bibliography

Clarke, Rachel Ivy. "How We Done It Good: Research through Design as a Legitimate Methodology for Librarianship." *Library & Information Science Research* 40, no. 3 (July 1, 2018): 255–61. https://doi.org/10.1016/j.lisr.2018.09.007.

Climer, Amy. "Climer Cards," 2022. https://climercards.com/.

Digital Society School, Amsterdam University. "MoSCoW." In *Design Method Toolkit*, 2020. https://web.archive.org/web/20220331021202/https://toolkits.dss.cloud/design/method-card/moscow/.

Friedman, Batya, Lisa Nathan, Shaun Kane, and John Lin. "Envisioning Cards," 2011. http://www.envisioningcards.com/.

Gaver, William. "What Should We Expect from Research through Design?" In *Proceedings of the SIGCHI Conference on Human Factors in Computing Systems*, 937–46. CHI '12. New York, NY, USA: Association for Computing Machinery, 2012. https://doi.org/10.1145/2207676.2208538.

Godin, Danny, and Mithra Zahedi. "Aspects of Research through Design: A Literature Review." In *Design's Big Debates – DRS International Conference 2014*, edited by Y Lim, K Niedderer, J Redström, E Stolterman, and A Valtonen. Umeå, Sweden, 2014. https://dl.designresearchsociety.org/drs-conference-papers/drs2014/researchpapers/85.

Gray, Dave, Sunni Brown, and James Macanufo. *Gamestorming: A Playbook for Innovators, Rulebreakers, and Changemakers*. Sebastopol, CA: O'Reilly Media, 2010.

Hazenberg, Wimer. *75 Tools for Creative Thinking: A Fun Card Deck for Creative Inspiration*. Crds edition. Amsterdam: Laurence King Publishing, 2013.

Hohmann, Luke. *Innovation Games: Creating Breakthrough Products Through Collaborative Play*. Upper Saddle River, NJ: Addison-Wesley Professional, 2006.

Isley, C. Grey, and Traci Rider. "Research-Through-Design: Exploring a Design-Based Research Paradigm through Its Ontology, Epistemology, and Methodology." In *Design as a Catalyst for Change – DRS International Conference*, 359–68. Limerick, Ireland, 2018. https://doi.org/10.21606/drs.2018.263.

Kensing, Finn, and Joan Greenbaum. "Heritage: Having a Say." In *Routledge International Handbook of Participatory Design*, 21–36. New York: Routledge, 2013.

Pascale, Matteo di. "Intùiti Creative Cards," 2013. https://intuiti.it/.

Robertson, Toni, and Jesper Simonsen. "Participatory Design: An Introduction." In *Routledge International Handbook of Participatory Design*, edited by Jesper Simonsen and Toni Robertson, 1–17. New York: Routledge, 2013.

Rubin, Richard. "Library and Information Science: An Evolving Profession." In *Foundations of Library and Information Science*, 239–304. Chicago: Neal-Schuman Publishers, 2016.

Tench, Beck. "The Library Workers' Field Guide to Designing and Discovering Restorative Environments," June 2022. https://web.archive.org/web/20221223234800/https://static1.squarespace.com/static/62b5ac1f5e52db0ff863b3da/t/62d73290a77cb95ad-54cd5f3/1658270377237/Library+Workers+Field+Guide.pdf.

Urquhart, Lachlan D., and Peter J. Craigon. "The Moral-IT Deck: A Tool for Ethics by Design." *Journal of Responsible Innovation* 8, no. 1 (January 2, 2021): 94–126. https://doi.org/10.1080/23299460.2021.1880112.

Chapter 7
Contributions and Future Directions

This book centered around a research question and a research goal. The main research question is *how can library assessment be practiced ethically*? And the main research goal is *to produce a practical tool to support ethical library assessment practice*. To produce these outcomes, I applied a three-part research design: a literature review, a survey, and interviews. My research process culminated in two main outcomes: 1) the articulation of the *Values Classification for Library Assessment*, a set of values relevant for the practice of library assessment, and 2) the development of the *Values-Sensitive Library Assessment Toolkit*, a participatory design tool for applying the *Values Classification* in library settings. In this final chapter, I present a recap of the research that supported these outcomes, and I offer reflections on the contributions and future directions of this work.

Recap of the Book

This book provides an answer to its research question, "How can library assessment be practiced ethically?" As an answer, this book advances the theory that practitioners can practice ethical assessment by articulating and enacting the values that are relevant in their local contexts. To make this theory work in the real world of assessment practice, I introduce a set of values and a toolkit: the *Values Classification for Library Assessment* offers one set of relevant values for assessment, and the *Values-Sensitive Library Assessment Toolkit* is an ethical aid to support practitioners in naming and applying the values that matter in their situations. Let's recap how we arrived at this endpoint.

In Chapter 1, I described the methodological approach—constructivist grounded theory—for answering my research question. In Chapter 2, I traced the development of ethics and values within the field of Library and Information Science. I found that practical ethics was the predominate ethical perspective in the LIS literature. Practical ethics asks of a given situation, "What is the right thing to do?" Through a lens of practical ethics, practitioners can apply relevant values at the right time to know what is the right thing to do. This led me to look closer at the values of the LIS profession, and I found that over the last several decades LIS practitioners have named dozens of different values as relevant to their practice. I next sought to better understand the situations in which those values were applied. In Chapter 3, I investigated the ethical dilemmas that library assessment practitioners confront in their work. This examination revealed sites of tension where values or value systems may be in conflict. I then wanted to know how practitioners have responded to these tensions with a view toward ethics and values. And so, in Chapter 4, I analyzed literature that described ethical assessment approaches, deriving a set of characteristics for describing ethical assessment practice. Chapters 2, 3, and 4 together set the groundwork for a new survey that investigated ethics and values in library assessment.

The survey was designed to gather data that can further explicate the values and practices of ethical library assessment. This survey presented six ethical vignettes to practitioners. The vignettes reflected themes and situations found in the literature. For each vignette, I asked practitioners to share the values that are relevant, and to share practical responses suitable for their local setting. In this way, I essentially asked of each situation, "What is the right thing to do?" In Chapter 5, I presented the survey data and analyzed responses using constructivist grounded theory, deriving a set of codes that capture the values and practices relevant for ethical assessment. I then configured the values into the *Values Classification for Library Assessment*. In Chapter 6, I presented the *Values Classification* and its corresponding operational toolkit, the *Value-Sensitive Library Assessment Toolkit*. Finally, to make sure that the values were relevant for assessment and that the toolkit could work for practitioners, I tested and validated the values and the toolkit through interviews with library assessment practitioners.

Contributions to Library Assessment

I would like to highlight four main contributions that this research makes to the practice and scholarship of library assessment: 1) ethics in library assessment is highly complex and contextual, 2) an ethical practice can be achieved by articulating and applying values, 3), the *Values Classification for Library Assessment* is one potential set of values that our field can apply, and 4) the *Value-Sensitive Library Assessment Toolkit* is a viable tool for supporting an ethical practice of library assessment. In the subsections below, I provide an overview for each main contribution, as well as thoughts on limitations, constraints, and positionality.

Ethics as Complex and Contextual

The literature analysis and the survey data demonstrate that ethical decisions in assessment are complex and contextual. As a result of competing values and multiple right choices, ethical paths forward are ambiguous. Library assessment practitioners have a desire to apply values and achieve an ethical practice, but practitioners are challenged in that the landscape of values is wide-ranging and highly contextual. Furthermore, the library assessment community does not have a centralized professional body that can develop a statement of values that speaks to the specific skills and challenges of library assessment. In some ways, the lack of a central statement of values is suitable for library assessment practitioners, who operate in varied settings that call for varied sets of values that can be tuned according to local needs. The survey data and analysis presented in Chapter 5 shows that many different possible values are indeed available to practitioners, and those values shift and change according to the contextual factors present in different assessment situations.

The Importance of Articulating and Applying Values

From this place of contextual complexity, the act of choosing which values to apply in different situations is a central component of an ethical assessment practice. Preer lays it out clearly: "Ethics is about choices. As a system of principles determining right or wrong conduct; ethics defines the parameters of those choices."[1] This book and its

---

1   Preer, *Library Ethics*, 1.

toolkit aim to illuminate ethical choices by prompting ethical reflection and guiding ethical decision-making, so that practitioners in our field of library assessment can have clarity in the choice of values that are applied in our different professional settings. The research demonstrates that assessment practitioners do seek an ethical practice. One path toward an ethical practice can be found through the applied values approach of practical ethics: to achieve an ethical practice, practitioners can articulate and enact values that are meaningful to their practice. Applying values helps us to know the right thing to do. With this approach, practitioners have flexibility in identifying and implementing the values that are most appropriate in their local settings. In this way, an applied-values approach to ethical reflection and decision-making recognizes the complex and contextual nature of ethical practice. This approach helps in discerning and resolving tensions among competing viewpoints and values. Importantly for library assessment, this approach helps to untie the knot of values and value—we can apply values, as we pursue value. And to apply values, we must first know which values are relevant to our practice and to the situation. This leads to the next main contribution.

The Values Classification for Library Assessment

This book presents the *Values Classification for Library Assessment*, a set of ten values that are relevant to the practice of library assessment. The *Values Classification* is the culmination of the research design. The *Values Classification* integrates insights from the literature, the survey, and the interviews. The classification reflects the values and viewpoints of the library assessment professionals who comprise the study sample, as well as my own point of view as a researcher. In developing the *Values Classification*, I wanted to expand my own professional understanding of ethics in assessment, and then to share the results with the wider community of library assessment practitioners. The *Values Classification* seeks to answer a question about values in assessment: What are our assessment values? This question recognizes that there are many values and value sets from which to choose, yet absent from those choices is a statement of values tuned specifically to the practice of library assessment. Such a statement could unify the values perspective of assessment practitioners. But, as we've seen, values are complex and multifaceted, with practitioners choosing from a multitude of available values and value sets. To operate successfully, I think that the *Values Classification* would need to fit alongside or within other values systems already in place, such as the *ALA Core Values of Librarianship*, university value statements, local value statements, or the values of our user communities. The *Values Classification* should be viewed as complementing or extending these existing statements.

As a product of a subjective research process, the *Values Classification* is just one possible set of values, and one potential approach for practicing ethical assessment. Recalling Drabinski's argument that values are "continually produced and reproduced in the library discourse," and that values are "ideas to be struggled over in both discourse and practice,"[2] the *Values Classification* is one contribution to the discussion around values. Unlike Gorman and others working at the turn of millennium to find enduring values for the library (see back to Chapter 2), I don't position the assessment values as timeless to our specialty, but rather as a reflection of our contemporary views. The values, their definitions, and their applications will evolve over time as library assessment practice develops and our wider cultural contexts shift in new directions. In recognizing that values change over time, we can also counteract the pull of a vocational awe that wants our values to be steadfast and uncritically accepted as correct. The *Values Classification* is not an endpoint, but rather a contribution to our ongoing community effort toward understanding professional values and ethical practice. The values can be seen as a response to Preer, who argues that "a measure of a profession's development is its understanding of the values that govern its practice."[3] This is ultimately what the *Values Classification* represents—a model for what a values-based practice can be, in support of the continuing professional development of library assessment.

The Values-Sensitive Library Assessment Toolkit

Finally, as a practical contribution to library assessment, this book offers the *Value-Sensitive Library Assessment Toolkit*.

The *Values-Sensitive Library Assessment Toolkit* is available at the following URL: **doi.org/10.17605/OSF.IO/ZS5C8**

---

2 Drabinski, "Valuing Professionalism," 606.

3 Preer, *Library Ethics*, xiv.

The toolkit is the practical expression of the book's research into values and ethics in library assessment. If the *Values Classification* represents a response to the question *what are our assessment values*, then the toolkit extends that line of inquiry into practice—*how do we prioritize values, and how do we apply values in different situations*? Drawing on the tradition of participatory design, the toolkit operationalizes the theory that ethical assessment can be practiced by articulating and applying relevant values. The toolkit activates the research data by providing a visual representation of the *Values Classification*, with graphics, layout, and colors. The toolkit aids practitioners in identifying and choosing which values to apply in different situations. The toolkit features the ten values relevant to assessment practitioners that are included in the *Values Classification*, along with exercises for naming values, prioritizing values, and implementing values. Practitioners can apply the toolkit in their own settings to support a values-based assessment practice. The toolkit recognizes that each local setting offers special factors to consider, and so the toolkit is flexible and adaptable, and can expand to accommodate values that emerge contextually or are otherwise unique to a particular site of assessment. The exercises are structured to produce reliable outcomes, but also open-ended and interpretive so that the values can be applied in different ways to suit different assessment projects and programs. The toolkit can be considered as a decision-making guide when planning, conducting, or evaluating an assessment program or project. The toolkit can also be a teaching tool when educating about the practice of assessment.

The toolkit is a product of the research data and analysis, and it also reflects the LIS literature in this area, which prompts information professionals to increase awareness of professional situations and to become more sensitive to ethical decision-making.[4] In thinking back to the discussion of the definition of a value from Chapter 2, the new classification of assessment values and the toolkit combine elements of *aspirational* and *educational* understandings of a value. The *Values Classification* presents aspirational values in the sense of representing guiding principles or points of reference in decision-making for an ethical practice, and then the toolkit introduces an educational aspect by providing instructional components for enacting the values in

---

4   Hauptman, "Technological Implementations and Ethical Failures."

practice. As a tool to support ethical practice, the toolkit works to orient the practitioner toward values, and provides a direction for ethical reflection and action. The toolkit functions a practical response to Yousefi (discussed in Chapter 3), who observed that decision-making in libraries can be at odds with declared values.[5] With the toolkit as an ethical aid, we can be better positioned to make decisions that promote our values.

The toolkit also incorporates aspects of the ethical practice areas discussed in Chapter 4: norm development, strategic planning, participatory design and co-design, care, and critical assessment. The toolkit can be used to surface values in strategic planning, and to connect assessment efforts directly to values. By working regularly with the toolkit, values-based discussion and practice can be normalized within a workplace. The toolkit is itself a participatory design tool, stemming from the justice-oriented and values-forward tradition of co-design. Participatory design seeks to generate a sense of connectedness and purpose among participants. Likewise, the toolkit aims to achieve similar outcomes for assessment practitioners, participants, and stakeholders. In helping to name and prioritize values, the toolkit contains elements of care ethics, in that care ethics provides space for conflicting values, and suggests approaches for resolving such conflicts based on prioritization. And in cultivating ethical reflection and questioning existing values and practices, the toolkit can cultivate a critical assessment approach.

The toolkit also comes with certain constraints and limitations. The card-based form of the toolkit may limit its adoption in the professional community. The toolkit is based on design games that are well established in the traditions of co-design and participatory design, but such approaches are not yet common in library assessment. Some practitioners or library administrators may not be accustomed to "playing" a card game in a professional setting and may not initially be enthusiastic about a tool that could be perceived as unserious. The toolkit's operation also presupposes an environment that is conducive to trust, communication, inquiry, and reflection. Practitioners who are already oriented toward values will benefit from the toolkit's ability to further sensitize their practice to values. And organizational settings that already have a culture of communication will be more

---

5   Yousefi, "On the Disparity Between What We Say and What We Do in Libraries," 92.

able to integrate the toolkit into their processes. Conversely, the toolkit will not thrive in an environment of poor communication or low trust. Furthermore, the toolkit relies on a practitioner who is empowered in their organization to articulate and apply values. Some practitioners will be able to adopt this tool and implement their values. For example, assessment directors or librarians who have tenure status in their organization. Others, however, could struggle to implement values if they have relatively low levels of empowerment and authority, and lack the ability or comfort to assert the values that matter to them and their particular situations. Finally, the toolkit is limited in that the toolkit itself cannot resolve an ethical tension. The toolkit functions to sensitize practitioners to values, and provides prompts that invite the practitioner to identify the tensions and produce the resolutions that fit their local setting. As a tool of collaboration and creativity, the toolkit requires the sincere, active contribution of assessment practitioners and stakeholders to reach its potential of supporting an ethical practice of library assessment.

Researcher Positionality

The findings indicate that positionality is a relevant value for library assessment. Positionality means naming one's particular viewpoint and perspective relative to one's research. Positionality is an important aspect of my research method of constructive grounded theory. Through constructivist grounded theory, the researcher constructs a theory that is grounded in the data. In transforming the research data into a model of ethics, I am constructing one interpretive expression of a complex dataset, as seen from my unique viewpoint and imbued with my own values. As Charmaz describes: "Because constructivists see facts and values as linked, they acknowledge that what they see—and don't see—rests on values."[6] The positionality value is thus also highly relevant to this book. My unique position affords me a viewpoint that is particular to me. What I see and don't see rests on my values. My approach to this book comes from my position first as a researcher-practitioner. I apply a value of inquiry as a researcher, and as a practitioner I apply a value of pragmatism. In completing this book, I sought to build new knowledge about library assessment ethics, and also to produce a new practical contribution that my fellow

---

6   Charmaz, *Constructing Grounded Theory*, 131.

assessment practitioners can apply in real-world settings. As a User Experience & Assessment Librarian, I bring a background of participatory design and co-design, and this informed the development of the toolkit into its form as a card deck. In my own personal life and professional pursuits, I also seek to better understand histories of oppression and exploitation, and to work towards a more just world that centers accountability and redress. My justice-oriented views have guided my grounded theory analysis that produced values such as care, positionality, and justice. I am especially influenced by Caswell et al.'s ideas of imagining otherwise,[7] and Punzalan et al.'s practices of community-based assessment.[8] I want libraries to work better for more people, and my approach to this book reflects these values of inclusion and justice. In researching and designing a tool to support ethical assessment, I aim to help myself and other practitioners become more in tune with values. I hope to meet other practitioners as colleagues in a shared practice of ethical assessment that is mutually beneficial for practitioners, participants, and institutions.

Future Directions

The work of this book can continue in several directions. I would like to highlight six potential areas of future development: 1) refining the values of assessment and of other LIS specialties, 2) professional values and professional identity, 3) ethical priorities, 4) ethics and morale, 5) further analysis of the interview data, and 6) continued development of the toolkit, and 7) a values-as-value approach to library assessment. In the subsections below, I provide an overview for each direction of future work.

Values of LIS and of Assessment

To the question of values in LIS practice, there can be more work in establishing the values that are relevant to LIS practitioners within different specialties. The ALA Core Values are currently the primary point of reference for professional values in LIS, but the findings of Chapter 2 suggest that LIS professional values have a greater history and

---

[7] Caswell et al., "'To Be Able to Imagine Otherwise.'"

[8] Punzalan, Marsh, and Cools, "Beyond Clicks, Likes, and Downloads"; Punzalan and Marsh, "Reciprocity."

complexity than the ALA Core Values. In a similar vein, the survey results from Chapter 5 indicate that the ALA Core Values are well known but not commonly referenced as a source for applied values. From the survey we saw that certain values may be more suited for particular specialties, and that a general, profession-wide statement of values may not be that useful in practice. In our case, some values speak more to the specific needs and practices of assessment, notably the *validity* value and the *alignment* value, that are not present in the ALA Core Values.

In thinking about future directions, follow-up work could expand the scope of the research to include other LIS specialties, and to determine similarities and differences in relevant values across different specialties, such as reference, collections, circulation, scholarly communication, and data management. A similar scenario-based survey could be administered to alternative study populations. The question of values could also be approached with a different research design. A set of qualitative interviews, for instance, could be conducted that ask practitioners to describe real-life ethical dilemmas or scenarios of values-in-conflict that they have encountered. Such interview data could be analyzed to even better understand the tensions that practitioners encounter in the day-to-day operations of library assessment, and the values that practitioners apply in their work. Follow-up questions could be returned to the library assessment community for further development: why is *ALA Core Values of Librarianship* document not a more important reference point for the assessment community? What would be required to motivate the community to build, maintain, and apply a set of values relevant for library assessment?

Values and Identity

In my conversations with practitioners during the interview state of my research, important questions were raised about the relative power and authority of practitioners in implementing values. This specific aspect could be developed further, especially related to practitioner demographics. The survey collected some data in this regard, such as the size of the institution and the employment status of respondents. I did not analyze the data vis-à-vis this demographic data, but further analysis in this direction could reveal differences in values across different demographic or identity characteristics. Practitioners of different cultural backgrounds or age groups may have different values, for example. From the perspective of power and authority, values-orientation appears to change depending on one's position within an organizational structure. Administration, for example, could have different values than faculty, staff, or students. Once those value differences have been identified, there's a related question about the power to implement values. Organizational position again influences the ability to enact a value. When there are tensions among values and stakeholders, whose values take priority in different situations? Who gets to decide which values or what evidence matters? Work from Magnus, Faber, and Belanger point these questions in interesting directions.[9]

The population sample of the study should also be noted as a limiting aspect of the research, but also as a future direction. The values presented as relevant for library assessment apply primarily in the context of North American colleges and universities. Other national or geographical settings may produce additional values or exclude values that were generated here. Other settings of assessment practice may also produce varying results, such as public libraries, special libraries, school libraries, or private libraries. And within the context of North American higher education, the sample itself is not representative of all assessment practitioners. My survey sample was comprised of those who subscribe to certain email listservs, and my interview sample was comprised of a subset of the survey sample who opted into further conversation with me. The survey sample is thus biased in that it contains the views only of those who subscribe to a limited set of list servs. And the interview sample is biased in that it over-represents practitioners who have a stake or an interest in values-based, ethical assessment practice. With this limitation to the sample, I cannot claim that the values produced in my data analysis are representative of the full assessment community. Nor can I claim that the toolkit will function effectively for all assessment practitioners. Within the scope of my research design, I have verified that my data analysis, the values, and the toolkit are correct for my study population, which represents a cross-section of the assessment community.

To address this limitation and expand the landscape of values, future work could involve re-administering the survey using a nation-wide register of assessment practitioners, with a randomized sample of

---

9   Magnus, Faber, and Belanger, "A Consideration of Power Structures (and the Tensions They Create) in Library Assessment Activities"; Magnus, Faber, and Belanger, "So, What Now? Moving through Tensions to Practice in Critical Library Assessment."

respondents, or testing the toolkit with wider populations or more varied types of practitioners. A researcher could, for example, build a register of assessment practitioners working in an academic library setting. To my knowledge, such a list does not presently exist. But it could be constructed manually by visiting staff directories of universities and colleges in North America, and documenting the names and email contacts of personnel who carry assessment-related titles, such as Assessment Librarian or Director of Library Assessment. A randomized sample could then be generated from that list, with the resulting dataset serving as a representative sample of library assessment practitioners.

Ethical Priorities and Perceptions

The research also generated an intriguing and unanswered question about ethical priorities and perceptions, relating to the competing interests of different stakeholders. The toolkit, for its part, aims to help practitioners identify and implement the values that are relevant for a particular situation. But how are those value choices perceived by others? We have seen that an assessment practitioner can be influenced by the values of their university, library, profession, or their own personal values. These different entities present competing interests that call for resolution—how then does that resolution affect perceptions across stakeholder groups? My thinking here is influenced here by Hurst, who cites research indicating that "people who are highly identified with their employer are more likely to engage in unethical actions that benefit the organization."[10] In light of this, what of assessment librarians who identify with their library or university more than with their profession? If employer values are in conflict with professional values, and a practitioner chooses to resolve that tension by enacting employer values, to what extent would other members of the assessment community view those actions as unethical in light of professional values?

Ethics, Morale, and Wellness

A potentially fruitful line of inquiry can be found at the intersection of ethics, morale, and wellness. Kendrick et al. have advanced research

---

10 Hurst, "The 'Not Here' Syndrome."

into library employee wellness and morale.[11] A factor that potentially affects employee experience is perceived ethics, and whether an employee's values are applied in the workplace. This leads to questions about how applied values influence worker-related matters, such as employment duration, engagement in the workplace, and mental and physical health. Building on the work of Kendrick and others, further research in this area of ethics and wellness can reveal the mental and physical stakes of an ethical practice and a values-aligned workplace.

Interview Data

Another area of expansion is the interview dataset produced in the book. Within the scope of this research design, I applied the interview data analysis toward validating and revising the toolkit. But the interviews produced a rich dataset that can be analyzed with a view toward producing broader insights on the factors that influence practitioners' abilities to enact values and ethical practices in their daily work. In particular, interview participants described the constraints and opportunities they encounter in their organizations that help or hinder ethical assessment practice. The interview data could undergo a similar grounded theory analysis or other qualitative analysis to develop insights about values and ethics in assessment. The research data supporting this book project is available in the Qualitative Data Repository with the following title and URL: *Practitioner Perspectives on the Values and Ethics of Library Assessment*, https://doi.org/10.5064/F6ORSLQF.

Toolkit Development

The toolkit itself can also be expanded and further tested. With a view toward further testing, the toolkit as it is currently constructed can be studied in real-life situations to better understand its feasibility as a useful tool for practitioners. The toolkit comes packaged with three exercises, but the number and type of exercises can be expanded to create more pathways into the values. Additional exercises could

---

11 Kendrick and Leaver, "Impact of the Code of Ethics on Workplace Behavior in Academic Libraries"; Kendrick and Leaver, "The Code of Ethics and Workplace Behaviors: Implications for Leadership and Cultivating Ethical Leaders for Tomorrow's Academic Libraries"; Kendrick, "The Low Morale Experience of Academic Librarians"; Kendrick and Damasco, "Low Morale in Ethnic and Racial Minority Academic Librarians"; Kendrick, "Report: Low Morale at Unionized Library Workplaces – Part 1 (August 2022)."

produce new insights for enhancing the toolkit's goal of supporting values-based assessment. Different exercises could help support different dimensions that reflect practitioners' work environments. For example, assessment practitioners collaborate with a variety of stakeholders, from students to deans. Specific exercises could be developed that are optimized to work best when completed in collaboration with certain types of stakeholders. Different exercises could also enhance the inclusivity of the toolkit. The three current exercises involve writing and drawing, and one exercise applies the metaphor of a boat to generate dialogue and insight. Other exercises could be added to the toolkit that ask participants to share thoughts through different modalities, and different metaphors can be applied that allow participants to have greater choice in how to engage with the values and generate ideas in support of ethical assessment practice.

The physical nature of the toolkit is a key limitation and pathway of future development. The toolkit functions first as a table-top tool for in-person use. Accessibility of the toolkit is thus limited in its current design, as it privileges users who are sighted and do not have mobility impairments. Further toolkit development and testing can look toward accessibility and Universal Design for Learning so that more people of different abilities can use and interact with the tool. The toolkit can currently be accessed and used in a digital environment, but the cards could be further developed as a web application or as an app for mobile operating systems. This would provide broader accessibility for the toolkit and expand the use to include more people.

Inclusivity can also be understood in terms of assessment stakeholders. From this perspective, further toolkit development would also benefit from expanding its field of view to include different stakeholders in its planning and design. The validation step of my research design focused on assessment practitioners working as librarians. For the toolkit to reach its full potential, it needs to be able to bring together diverse stakeholders including librarians, but also library staff and library administrators. Further development could validate and test the toolkit with different audiences.

Finally, in looking further into the future of ethical assessment, this toolkit could form the basis of a professional development training series or a certification process for values-sensitive practice. The toolkit could constitute a day-long or even multi-day workshop, where practitioners learn how to work with the toolkit, and how to develop a facility with articulating and applying values. More formally, established professional conferences such as the *Library Assessment Conference* or the *Conference on Performance Measurement in Libraries* could be places from which to develop a workshop, training, or certification series. Or, looking to the American Library Association, existing interests around Core Values could be a launching point for developing an ethical training series based around values in assessment. The assessment community is extensive, with many practitioners working in library settings with library values. When looking widely across the field, a view comes into focus of the toolkit's applicability expanding in such a way as to bring those many others into the practice of value-sensitive assessment.

A Values-as-value Approach for Library Assessment

In looking back at the work of this book and looking ahead to the work beyond, we can see an important relationship between library value and library values. Over the last decade, libraries have been called to show value, typically according to economic or financial understandings of value. In response, library assessment practice has developed to include the measurement and demonstration of library value. As ethical practitioners, we seek to understand and demonstrate value while also enacting professional values in our practice. This dual aim reveals a connection between value and values, and suggests fruitful pathways for bringing together these two components: by practicing an assessment that intertwines values and value, we can advance an understanding of value that is rooted in values. When we lead with values, we assert a potent interpretation of value.

This is a promising future direction for values-based assessment, and it has already a firm foundation in the literature. Rubin posits a "value model" for LIS work, in which our identity and significance derives from articulating and enacting values.[12] In the context of library assessment, Town speaks of library value as achieved through values, concisely summarizing: "value reflects values."[13] Seminelli similarly argues that LIS values themselves represent the value that libraries can bring to our communities.[14] And Drabinski and Walter appeal to

---

12   Rubin, "Library and Information Science: An Evolving Profession."

13   Town, "Value, Impact, and the Transcendent Library," 122.

14   Seminelli, "Librarian as Professional."

a practice of investigating value and values in equal measure.[15] The Humane Metrics Initiative provides an instructive example: this framework of assessment in humanities scholarship presents values as the demonstration of value.[16] Along similar lines, I have collaborated on a collections assessment project that foregrounds the library's access value in a conversation with university administration regarding the library's collections budget.[17] In values-oriented approaches such as these, the central practice of library assessment is the measurement and demonstration of how a library enacts its values. We can take the call to show value, and turn it toward values. We can speak to the unique purpose, strengths, and values of libraries in a way that also resonates with and meets the expectations of external or parent entities. By showing our values, we speak to our value.

In signaling toward a values-as-value approach to assessment, I am looking beyond the book's research question toward a wider horizon of possibility for a library assessment practice that even more deeply integrates values. A values-as-value assessment thesis might say: in libraries, our values are our value. Libraries can be made manifestly valuable by demonstrating values in action. A values-as-value assessment practice would recognize that value and values are not opposites, but rather correlated elements of an effective, ethical assessment practice. Professional values and evidence of library value can operate symbiotically to support an inclusive, socially-engaged practice of library assessment.[18] Following Magnus, Belanger, and Faber, we can more closely examine the pressures we face as assessment practitioners and look with a critical eye at the status quo, "in order to imagine what a more critical assessment practice might look like."[19]

This path forward is exciting, but needs more work in the practical aspects. Which values, for instance, are most appropriate for this model? How can we present our values as our value in a way that effectively and consistently meets the expectations of our stakeholders?

---

15   Drabinski and Walter, "Asking Questions That Matter."

16   Agate et al., "The Transformative Power of Values-Enacted Scholarship"; Agate, "Walking the Talk"; "HuMetricsHSS."

17   Young and McKelvey, "Using Return-on-Investment to Tell a Story of Library Value and Library Values."

18   Bell, "Values-Based Practice in EBLIP."

19   Magnus, Belanger, and Faber, "Towards a Critical Assessment Practice," para. 40.

How can we shape the expectations of our stakeholder groups so that values resonate as value? How can we also integrate university values and user values? How can our wider practitioner community more fully operationalize a values-as-value approach to library assessment?

Closing Thoughts

This book began with a question about ethics in library assessment. My research process led me to conclude that we can practice ethical assessment by knowing and applying our values. The book ends with two main contributions that support a practice of knowing and applying values: the *Values Classification for Library Assessment* and the *Values-Sensitive Library Assessment Toolkit*. In presenting the classification and the toolkit to the assessment community, I am building on our field's shared work around the questions of professional values and practical assessment. I am responding to Bourg's call to "re-inject the core values of libraries and of our parent institutions into our work and our decision-making."[20] And I am following Arellano Douglas, who encourages us to "emphasize what we value, not that we have value."[21] The *Values Classification* provides a set of relevant values to consider when making decisions about library assessment, and the toolkit supports a practice that emphasizes what we value. I hope that the research insights presented in this book can add to our field's shared understanding of ethics, and I hope that the *Values Classification for Library Assessment* and the *Values-Sensitive Library Assessment Toolkit* can contribute to our community's practice of values-based library assessment.

Bibliography

Agate, Nicky. "Walking the Talk: Toward a Values-Aligned Academy," February 17, 2022. https://hcommons.org/deposits/item/hc:44631/.

Agate, Nicky, Rebecca Kennison, Stacy Konkiel, Christopher P. Long, Jason Rhody, Simone Sacchi, and Penelope Weber. "The Transformative Power of Values-Enacted Scholarship." *Humanities and Social Sciences Communications* 7, no. 1 (December 7, 2020): 1–12. https://doi.org/10.1057/s41599-020-00647-z.

---

20 Bourg, "Beyond Measure: Valuing Libraries," para. 11.
21 Arellano Douglas, "Moving from Critical Assessment to Assessment as Care," 46.

Arellano Douglas, Veronica. "Moving from Critical Assessment to Assessment as Care." *Communications in Information Literacy* 14, no. 1 (June 2020): 46–65.

Bell, Emilia C. "Values-Based Practice in EBLIP: A Review." *Evidence Based Library and Information Practice* 17, no. 3 (September 19, 2022): 119–34. https://doi.org/10.18438/eblip30176.

Bourg, Chris. "Beyond Measure: Valuing Libraries." Presented at the Acquisition Institute, 2013.

Caswell, Michelle, Alda Allina Migoni, Noah Geraci, and Marika Cifor. "'To Be Able to Imagine Otherwise': Community Archives and the Importance of Representation." *Archives and Records* 38, no. 1 (January 2, 2017): 5–26. https://doi.org/10.1080/23257962.2016.1260445.

Charmaz, Kathy. *Constructing Grounded Theory*. London: Sage, 2006.

Drabinski, Emily. "Valuing Professionalism: Discourse as Professional Practice." *Library Trends* 64, no. 3 (April 4, 2016): 604–14. https://doi.org/10.1353/lib.2016.0005.

Drabinski, Emily, and Scott Walter. "Asking Questions That Matter." *College & Research Libraries* 77, no. 3 (2016). https://crl.acrl.org/index.php/crl/article/view/16508/17954.

Hauptman, Robert. "Technological Implementations and Ethical Failures." *Library Trends* 49, no. 3 (2001): 433–40.

"HuMetricsHSS," 2023. https://web.archive.org/web/20230330142220/https://humetricshss.org/.

Hurst, Charlice. "The 'Not Here' Syndrome." *Stanford Social Innovation Review*, May 3, 2021. https://doi.org/10.48558/djgd-9p08.

Kendrick, Kaetrena Davis. "Report: Low Morale at Unionized Library Workplaces – Part 1 (August 2022)." Renewals, August 9, 2022. https://renewalslis.com/2022/08/09/report-low-morale-at-unionized-library-workplaces-part-1-august-2022/.

Kendrick, Kaetrena Davis. "The Low Morale Experience of Academic Librarians: A Phenomenological Study." *Journal of Library Administration* 57, no. 8 (November 17, 2017): 846–78. https://doi.org/10.1080/01930826.2017.1368325.

Kendrick, Kaetrena Davis, and Ione T. Damasco. "Low Morale in Ethnic and Racial Minority Academic Librarians: An Experiential Study." *Library Trends* 68, no. 2 (2019): 174–212. https://doi.org/10.1353/lib.2019.0036.

Kendrick, Kaetrena Davis, and Echo Leaver. "Impact of the Code of Ethics on Workplace Behavior in Academic Libraries." *Journal of Information Ethics* 20, no. 1 (Spring 2011): 86–112. http://dx.doi.org/10.3172/JIE.20.1.86.

Kendrick, Kaetrena Davis, and Echo Leaver. "The Code of Ethics and Workplace Behaviors: Implications for Leadership and Cultivating Ethical Leaders for Tomorrow's Academic Libraries." In *Human Rights and Ethics: Concepts, Methodologies, Tools, and Applications*, edited by Mehdi Khosrow-Pour. IGI Global, 2015. https://doi.org/10.4018/978-1-4666-6433-3.

Magnus, Ebony, Jackie Belanger, and Maggie Faber. "Towards a Critical Assessment Practice." *In the Library With the Lead Pipe*, 2018. http://www.inthelibrary-withtheleadpipe.org/2018/towards-critical-assessment-practice/.

Magnus, Ebony, Maggie Faber, and Jackie Belanger. "A Consideration of Power Structures (and the Tensions They Create) in Library Assessment Activities." In *Proceedings of the 2018 Library Assessment Conference: Building Effective, Sustainable, Practical Assessment: December 5–7, 2018, Houston, TX*, 600–606. Association of Research Libraries, 2019. https://doi.org/10.29242/lac.2018.55.

Magnus, Ebony, Maggie Faber, and Jackie Belanger. "So, What Now? Moving through Tensions to Practice in Critical Library Assessment." Presented at the Library Assessment Conference, 2020. https://web.archive.org/web/20230313180330/https://www.libraryassessment.org/wp-content/uploads/2021/01/209-Magnus-Faber-So-what-now.pdf.

Preer, Jean L. *Library Ethics*. Westport, Conn: Libraries Unlimited, 2008.

Punzalan, Ricardo L., and Diana E. Marsh. "Reciprocity: Building a Discourse in Archives." *The American Archivist* 85, no. 1 (July 1, 2022): 30–59. https://doi.org/10.17723/2327-9702-85.1.30.

Punzalan, Ricardo L., Diana E. Marsh, and Kyla Cools. "Beyond Clicks, Likes, and Downloads: Identifying Meaningful Impacts for Digitized Ethnographic Archives." *Archivaria* 84, no. 1 (2017): 61–102.

Rubin, Richard. "Library and Information Science: An Evolving Profession." In *Foundations of Library and Information Science*, 239–304. Chicago: Neal-Schuman Publishers, 2016.

Seminelli, Heather. "Librarian as Professional." *The Serials Librarian* 71, no. 1 (July 3, 2016): 63–69. https://doi.org/10.1080/0361526X.2016.1168667.

Town, J. Stephen. "Value, Impact, and the Transcendent Library: Progress and Pressures in Performance Measurement and Evaluation." *The Library Quarterly* 81, no. 1 (January 1, 2011): 111–25. https://doi.org/10.1086/657445.

Young, Scott W. H., and Hannah McKelvey. "Using Return-on-Investment to Tell a Story of Library Value and Library Values." In *Proceedings of the 14th International Conference on Performance Measurement in Libraries*, 312–16, 2021. https://libraryperformance.files.wordpress.com/2021/12/libpmc14_2021_proceedings.pdf#page=317.

Yousefi, Baharak. "On the Disparity Between What We Say and What We Do in Libraries," 2017. http://summit.sfu.ca/item/17387.

Index

ACRL. *See* Association of College and Research Libraries
ADA. *See* Americans with Disabilities Act
ALA. *See* American Library Association
ALA Code of Ethics. *See* American Library Association Code of Ethics
ALA Core Values of Librarianship. *See* American Library Association Core Values of Librarianship
ALA Glossary of Library and Information Science. *See* American Library Association Glossary of Library and Information Science
American Library Association, 69, 81
American Library Association Code of Ethics, 3, 39
American Library Association Core Values of Librarianship, 2, 19, 38, 39, 41–44, 50, 75, 158, 167–68, 173–76
American Library Association Core Values Task Force, 38–41
American Library Association Glossary of Library and Information Science, 19–20
American Library Association Second Core Values Task Force, 38–41
Americans with Disabilities Act, 129, 132–35
applied values, 19, 221, 230
assessment librarians. *See* librarians, assessment
Association of College and Research Libraries, 71

care ethics, 14, 135–41, 233, 236, 239
cataloging, 92–96
classification, 92–96
co-design, 121–25, 141, 212
community participation, 161, 183–84, 191
constructivist grounded theory, 9–10, 13, 157, 228
critical assessment, 116–21
critical information literacy, 89–92
critical librarianship. *See* librarianship, critical
CVTF1. *See* American Library Association Core Values Task Force
CVTF2. *See* American Library Association Second Core Values Task Force

DDS. *See* Dewey Decimal System
DEI. *See* Diversity, Equity and Inclusion

Dewey Decimal System, 94–95
Dewey, Melvil, 69, 81
Diversity Equity and Inclusion, 85–87

ethical decision-making, 1–2, 5, 158
ethical dilemmas, 3, 13, 61–63, 158, 228
ethical reflection, 158
ethical resolutions, 3
ethical tensions, 3, 128, 141, 182, 184, 188–90

feminist ethics, 135–36

GDPR. *See* General Data Protection Regulation
General Data Protection Regulation, 129–32, 134–35

HuMetricsHSS, 126
idealism, 192–93
IFLA Statement on Privacy in the Library Environment. *See* International Federation of Library Associations and Institutions Statement on Privacy on the Library Environment
information technologies, 179
International Federation of Library Associations and Institutions Statement on Privacy on the Library Environment, 3
interviews, 13, 15, 227

LCSH. *See* Library of Congress Subject Headings
learning analytics, 2, 77–81, 180
legislative regulations, 129–135
LibQUAL+, 73–74
librarians, assessment, 1, 157, 190
librarianship
  attributes of, 20
  definition of, 19–20
  duties of, 1, 61
  ethical codes in, 20
  lack of professional attributes in, 21–22
  professionalism in, 21–23
  universal values for, 20–21, 40
librarianship, critical, 90–91, 116, 121
Libraries: An American Value Statement, 39
library and information science

core values of, 3, 32–38, 41–47
ethics in, 19, 50, 228
history of, 14
impact assessment in, 71–74
literature about, 3–4, 20
market forces on, 3, 68–71, 98–99, 115
problems in, 2–3
professional ethics of, 22–23, 24–27
professional identity in, 19, 21
professional neutrality in, 81–84, 98–99, 115
values of, 13, 14, 19, 23–31, 74, 228, 235–36
library assessment
classification of values for, 14–15
data analysis in, 15
data warehousing in, 1, 2
decisions about, 1, 167–71
definition of, 1
ethical practice in, 1–2, 5, 15, 115–16, 141–45, 228, 229
ethics in, 229
future directions for, 14, 235–43
learning analytics in, 1, 2
new insights into, 14
professional values in, 15
protection of user privacy during, 1, 3–4
sites of tension for, 96–98
surveying the field of, 13–14
tools in, 2, 73–74, 126, 127–29, 230–34
values in, 1–2, 3, 13, 71–74, 229–230
Library Assessment Conference (2020-2021), 19
Library Bill of Rights, 39
library impact, 177–78
library neutrality, 181–82
library norms, 132
Library of Congress Subject Headings, 94–95
library spaces, 86–89
library value statements, 2, 170–71
LIS. *See* library and information science
literature reviews, 13, 15, 227, 228

national survey
design of, 157, 158–61, 228
insights from, 184–93
purpose of, 228
results of, 161–84, 228
vignette approach in, 158–61, 171–84, 228
website for, 158, 161, 176
normative behaviors, 129–35

Patriot Act, 76–77
positionality, 10–12, 234–35
practical ethics, 8–9, 15, 19, 49, 146, 228
pragmatism, 192–93
privacy, 74–77

Ranganathan's Five Laws of Library Science, 32
RDA. *See* Resource Description and Access
Resource Description and Access, 94–95

SACO. *See* Subject Authority Cooperative Organization
site of tension 1, 71–74, 228
site of tension 2, 74–77, 228
site of tension 3, 77–81, 228
site of tension 4, 84–89, 228
site of tension 5, 89–92, 228
site of tension 6, 92–96, 228
social responsibility, 84–89, 181–82
strategic planning, 125–129
student participation, 182–83
student success, 77–81, 180
Subject Authority Cooperative Organization, 94–95
surveys, 13, 14, 15, 227

value systems in conflict, 63–68, 188–92, 228
values-as-value approach, 241–43
Values Classification for Library Assessment
description of, 2, 5, 6–7, 194, 197, 227, 229, 230–31, 243
development of, 197, 228
values in, 197, 199–210
Values Scorecard, 127–29
Values-Sensitive Library Assessment Toolkit
description of, 5, 6, 7–8, 15, 194, 197–98, 227, 229, 231–34, 243
design of, 197–98, 211–17
development of, 2, 14, 198–99, 210, 228
goals, 210–11
limitations of, 221–23, 233–34
use cases for, 220–21
use of, 218–19
website for, 7, 210, 217, 231
vocational awe, 47–49, 50